Psychology
and Consumer Affairs

Psychology and Consumer Affairs

Milton L. Blum

Consumer Affairs Institute
of the University of Miami
and Florida International University

Harper & Row, Publishers
New York   Hagerstown   San Francisco   London

Sponsoring Editor: George A. Middendorf
Project Editor: Renee E. Beach
Designer: Andrea C. Goodman
Production Supervisor: Kewal K. Sharma
Compositor: Ruttle, Shaw & Wetherill, Inc.
Printer and Binder: The Murray Printing Company
Art Studio: Vantage Art Inc.

Psychology and Consumer Affairs

Library of Congress Cataloging in Publication Data

Blum, Milton L.
    Psychology and consumer affairs.

    Includes index.
    1. Consumers. 2. Consumer protection. I. Title.
HF5415.2.B54   381'.3   76-25449
ISBN 0-06-040782-4

Contents

1

Psychology and Consumer Affairs   1

2

Research as a Tool   65

3

Socialization—The Process of Becoming a Consumer 111

4

The Participants in Consumer Affairs 161

Is There a Better Way? 301

Preface

There are a number of motives behind the writing of this book. One is the belief that it can fill a void, or knowledge gap, since little has been written on the subject of consumer psychology. Another is an attempt to encourage a change in textbook writing style. A third is based on the need for colleges and the community to have more in common, especially by sharing the same books. The fourth motive is to offer a specific version of the psychology of consumer affairs.

This book interprets and applies some of the things we know about psychology so that the consumer's role in the buyer-seller-maker-transaction can be improved. It recognizes that the consumer is generally disadvantaged in such transactions. Too often the consumer either does not know he/she is disadvantaged or will not admit to being disadvantaged and, to make matters worse, cannot effectively handle the typical marketplace transaction.

Consumer psychology as presented here is quite different from the material presented in recently published books on "consumer behavior." It would appear to this author that little has been written from the consumer psychology point of view and that there may even be an overload from the consumer behavior point of view.

Another point of emphasis in this book is that it favors conflict reduction in consumer affairs as business, consumers, government, and labor interact. It recognizes that all four segments have incongruent goals. It further recognizes that the adversary-advocate system often tends to intensify conflicts. The system solves some problems, but it leaves scars.

The book draws heavily on the information and insights of psychologists. These include "listening" as well as applying the knowledge from such topical areas as perception, attitude, motivation, learning, and personality. Such knowledge application can help achieve the goal of making the consumer less disadvantaged wherever buying and selling of goods and services takes place, be it in the supermarket or anywhere else.

Another purpose of this book is to encourage thinking about textbook writing and, it is hoped, to reverse a trend. It appears that textbooks are quoting more and more from other authors and researchers and offering less and less in terms of the personal views of the authors themselves. An author, it seems to this writer, should have a point of view and express it. A book should be thought provoking and generate ideas. A textbook should not be a compendium of assorted facts that encourages rote learning so that the student can pass a multiple-choice exam.

Another matter in need of change is the view that headings and subheadings are necessary attributes of textbooks. The chapters in this book are not broken up by headings. The readers should read the material as a unit and select points of importance and interest with personal appeal. The reading of a chapter should not be divided into bits and pieces. The chapter should be a Gestalt, not a series of elements.

Still another reason for this book is that the chasm between introductory texts and books for the general public needs to be bridged. A book intended as an introduction to consumer psychology should be readable and understood equally by college and junior college students. Further, this book overlaps in subject matter with many consumer courses in business, home economics, and the social sciences, among others. It may also appeal to adults in the community. Readers should benefit personally from the information offered.

The book is intended to be equally critical of all four of the major groups involved in consumer affairs. If those favoring business accuse it of bias and those favoring government also accuse it of bias, then the book will have achieved its purpose. If labor feels that it has not been given enough attention, this will be a reflection of the fact that labor has not given consumer affairs enough attention. As for consumers and consumer leaders, change must take place if the consumer is to become less disadvantaged.

Last but not least, it is hoped that the book's provocations will encourage others to present additional views.

The book is divided into four parts: (1) "Psychology and Consumer Affairs," (2) "Research as a Tool," (3) "Socialization —The Process of Becoming a Consumer," and (4) " The Participants in Consumer Affairs." It also has a "fun chapter" called "Utopia—Next Stop." The reader may read the book in the order that seems logical to the author or in any order based on personal interest and background. "Utopia—Next Stop" should be read last, but some may want to peek ahead.

As for the chapters themselves, a very brief description follows.

Part 1 consists of six chapters and emphasizes five primary areas in psychology as they relate to consumer affairs.

Chapter 1 defines and describes the roles of business, consumer, government, and labor as they are related to consumer affairs, and how consumer psychology can lead to conflict reduction and less of a mismatch between product preference and expectations—a major source of dissatisfaction.

Chapter 2 considers perception and emphasizes that not all perception is real. Some is illusionary and the cause of many consumer problems.

Chapter 3 describes how attitudes reflect feelings and are measurable. It is important for the consumer to become more aware that attitudes can be irrational, preventing one from becoming a better consumer.

Chapter 4 demonstrates that Maslow's theory of motivation is most appropriate and applicable to the consumer. Most important, the consumer should become better informed and more mature. Clearer understanding of motives is helpful in this respect.

Chapter 5 considers learning as a modification of behavior resulting in better performance. To become a better shopper one must learn, and that means having the ability to modify one's behavior. Experience may or may not result in learning.

Chapter 6 offers the view that attempting to relate personality characteristics to the use of specific products or brands has led nowhere. Products can do very little to change an individual's personality to any appreciable degree or over any meaningful period. In other words, there's more to sex than toothpaste despite what some ads imply. More important, the consumer should be aware of anxiety symptoms in buyer-seller-maker transactions and should know how to cope with them.

The objective of Part 2 is to refer to different research

methodologies applicable in consumer psychology. It indicates why research in the field is necessary and controversial. It is not intended to prepare the reader to become a research technician.

Chapter 7 emphasizes the contribution that valid research can make to the field of consumer affairs and discusses two sins of research—stupidity and dishonesty.

Chapter 8 suggests that consumers, by developing observation forms, can be aided in their purchases and can enhance their satisfaction with products and services.

Chapter 9 describes and illustrates a specific technique for conducting interactional workshops as a form of qualitative research.

Chapter 10 considers quantitative research, recognizes the bias in its favor, but also points to many severe limitations. It cites three very different types of studies to illustrate the good and the bad in quantitative research.

Part 3 shows how the socialization process, as one becomes a consumer, invokes some fundamental social and societal issues. This section attempts to integrate the concepts of freedom and change into the socialization process.

Chapter 11 discusses four books: *The Jungle, Unsafe at any Speed, The Chemical Feast,* and *The Greening of America.* All four refer to perilous conditions, recognize the conflict between the powerful and the powerless, and are vivid vignettes of consumer affairs.

Chapter 12 emphasizes that freedom is finite and that the more of it one has, the less someone else has. The present trend is for consumers to get a larger share of the freedom in consumer affairs.

Chapter 13 stresses that the phenomenon of change is basic to an understanding of consumer affairs. Experience is often the antithesis of change, since it prepares one for the past to a greater extent than for the future. Coping with change is necessary. This chapter also considers Toffler's *Future Shock.*

Chapter 14 describes socialization as an evolving process and a result of subtle changes from day to day. Ten stages or phases of family life are briefly reviewed in relation to the changing preferences and needs of consumers.

Chapter 15 discusses ghetto dwellers and describes their common denominator of poverty and powerlessness. "Do-gooders" mean well, but ghetto dwellers must be motivated to climb out of the ghetto and not just sit there.

Chapter 16 compares the young and the old as consumers.

Part 4 emphasizes the conflicts, incongruent goals, and methods of the groups involved in consumer affairs.

Chapter 17 considers the steps involved in the purchase process as well as the psychological phenomena impinging on the individual that create situations in which the consumer is disadvantaged. It proposes that there is hardly ever a "best" buy—one generally gets what one pays for. However, there are "better" buys.

Chapter 18 deals with issues and complaints, and attributes such matters to the incongruent goals and different perceptions that business and consumers have toward each other. As a result government becomes involved. Health and safety reflect more serious issues than evidenced by product dissatisfaction.

Chapter 19 reviews a variety of consumer organizations as well as research reports, especially those put out by Consumer's Union.

Chapter 20 is based on a single interactional workshop with a sampling of consumer leaders. A strong inference exists that there is a need to change either the leaders or their characteristics.

Chapter 21 decribes the different approaches of the AFL-CIO and the UAW toward consumer affairs and points to their involvement in consumer affairs as being peripheral rather than primary. The brevity of the chapter emphasizes this void.

Chapter 22 describes some of the good and the bad as business approaches the emerging field of consumer affairs. Business must learn to sincerely use its power for more comprehensive goals than it now appears to have.

Chapter 23 treats advertising in the context of socially significant questions, one of which is the effects of advertising on children; another is the problem of associating advertising with fakery—which it need not be.

Chapter 24 describes the developing role of government on all levels in consumer affairs and the wide variety of issues and conflicts that have arisen as a result of this development.

Chapter 25 considers utopia and suggests one possible way of getting there.

Acknowledgments

The cooperation of the University of Miami and Florida International University made the cosponsorship of the Consumer Affairs Institute most feasible and was the most important single event that led to the formulation of many of the ideas presented in this book. Also of great importance is the recognition of Mr. and Mrs. Abraham Rosenberg and the Guttman Foundation. Their support is deeply appreciated.

Two of my colleagues were of great help. John B. Stewart, professor of marketing at the University of Miami, and I worked closely over many years, and our exchange of views has been most valuable to me. Ronald S. Tikofsky, who chairs the Psychology Department at Florida International University, encouraged me to teach a course in consumer psychology as well as a field course in which students not only are taught the vagaries of consumer research but also come to grips with consumer issues.

My associate Ruth Kuestner ran many workshops, analyzed many tapes, and was helpful in putting this book together. The editorial comments of George Middendorf proved that he is an executive editor.

To single out the one person who *really* made this book possible, I must recognize the important role of my wife Naomi, who served as consumer, shopper, and editor. If this book is judged as creditable, then she deserves the credit.

Milton L. Blum, Ph.D.

Coral Gables, Florida

1
PSYCHOLOGY AND CONSUMER AFFAIRS

To achieve an understanding of the psychology of consumer affairs one must be familiar with at least five major topics or areas of psychology. As a result of the understanding and insights thus obtained, one may become more aware of the incongruent goals of the individuals and groups concerned with the societal problems known as consumer affairs.

The primary reason for starting the book with a section on psychology is to "set the record straight." Not all that is presented as psychology is psychological, and not all psychology is related to consumer affairs.

These chapters set the foundations and parameters for the intermingling of psychology and consumer affairs.

1

Consumer affairs and psychology

In graphic terms, a triangle best describes the topological framework of consumer affairs. However, some of the conflicts implied by this triangle could be reduced if consumers became better informed in the area of consumer psychology.

With this knowledge a framework could be constructed that allows consumers to be the masters of their destiny rather than the victims of manipulation. Such a framework would also allow the consumer to feel less useless and powerless in conflict situations.

The problems of consumer affairs are not a result of maladjusted or dissatisfied consumers. They are a result of the incongruent goals of such diverse groups as business, government, and labor as they attempt to offer "protection" to the consumer rather than really working on solving the problems and reducing the conflicts that confront the consumer.

The question is not what percentage of consumers may or may not have been "ripped off." The problem is the effect of the great variety of transactions that occur each day on the life styles of individuals. Changes in life style can create severe and serious emotional, health, and safety problems, leaving few, if any, members of society immune. To be brief and blunt, many societal problems are directly traceable to the mishandling of problems in the realm of consumer affairs.

Consumer affairs involves four major segments of society

(listed alphabetically to establish objectivity): business, consumers, government, and labor. One must immediately recognize that these groups perceive consumer affairs, and the solution to some of its problems, from drastically different viewpoints.

Consumer affairs is not a namby-pamby name for something that will go away if nothing is done about it. It represents a set of hard-core problems that must be solved.

Consumer psychology is a study of people who buy and use a variety of products and services. It deals with their motives, their expected and actual satisfactions, and the many environmental and inner influences that contribute to their purchase decisions. It also involves interactions with the individuals, groups, and institutions that, for better or worse, have more or less recognized the need to protect, represent, or help the consumer. These include business, government on all levels, organized labor, and those consumers who sometimes prefer to be known as activists.

To state this somewhat more academically, consumer psychology involves not only the body of knowledge of psychology and its application but also the interactions of people both as individuals and as members of groups. Sometimes these people are members of a formal group; at other times the group is informal. There are even times when people may not be aware that others have labeled them as members of a group.

Consumer psychology, therefore, includes the study and the consciousness of people as consumers.

The current issues and problems of consumer psychology, as in most if not all other bodies of knowledge, are in the majority of instances not really new. Many have been with us for a long time. But there is a tendency to continually overemphasize the present, even though it changes day by day.

A plausible explanation for the common emphasis on the problems of the day is that it makes the existing time frame important because it concentrates on the most acceptable form of reality—the here and now. Dealing with the present also centers the problem on the individual and enhances his/her ego. One is challenged to contend with a problem *now*. One can even elevate the particular problem to a crisis. Crises are more dramatic and threatening than problems. They add the melodrama that makes the individual important—now—as the crises are being resolved (or at least talked about).

Emphasizing the problems of today, for many, fills a need for ego enhancement. After all, we don't *really* know the future; in addition, we may be misinterpreting or forgetting the past. And so we tend to emphasize the problems of today to a greater extent than other problems removed in time.

It is a helpful learning experience to recognize that many problems that exist in the present have existed in the past and will exist in the future, and with little variation. In other words, we keep re-solving problems—sometimes we even reinvent the wheel.

With reference to, and emphasis on, the consumer, the following poem is worth reading. Perhaps it can offer a broader perspective on consumer problems as we begin this excursion into consumer psychology and consumer affairs.

CHEER FOR THE CONSUMER

By Nixon Waterman

I'm only a consumer, and it really doesn't matter
If you crowd me in the street cars till I couldn't well be flatter;
I'm only a consumer, and the strikers may go striking,
For it's mine to end my living if it isn't to my liking.
I am a sort of parasite without a special mission
Except to pay the damages—mine is a queer position:
The Fates unite to squeeze me till I couldn't well be flatter,
For I'm only a consumer, and it really doesn't matter.
The baker tilts the price of bread upon the vaguest rumor
Of damage to the wheat crop, but I'm only a consumer,
So it really doesn't matter, for there's no law that compels me
To pay added charges on the loaf of bread he sells me.
The iceman leaves a smaller piece when days are growing hotter,
But I'm only a consumer, and I do not need iced water:
My business is to pay the bills and keep in a good humor,
And it really doesn't matter, for I'm only a consumer.

The milkman waters milk for me; there's garlic in my butter,
But I'm only a consumer, and it does no good to mutter;
I know that coal is going up and beef is getting higher,
But I'm only a consumer, and I have no need for fire;
While beefsteak is a luxury that wealth alone is needing,
I'm only a consumer, and what need have I for feeding?
My business is to pay the bills and keep in a good humor,
And it really doesn't matter, since I'm only a consumer.

The grocer sells me addled eggs; the tailor sells me shoddy,
I'm only a consumer, and I am not anybody.
The cobbler pegs me paper soles, the dairyman short-weights me,
I'm only a consumer, and most everybody hates me.
There's turnip in my pumpkin pie and ashes in my pepper,
The world's my lazaretto, and I'm nothing but a leper;

So lay me in my lonely grave and tread the turf down flatter,
I'm only a consumer, and it really doesn't matter.

This poem by Nixon Waterman appeared in "The Wit and Humor of America, Volume IV," published just after the turn of the century.

New York Times, August 24, 1973

This book intends to present and integrate consumer affairs and psychology. Its purpose is to provoke thinking, planning, and then action, all calculated to reduce consumer conflicts and lead to more appropriate behavior in solving existing consumer problems. It will unabashedly present the problems that confront consumers and will not waste time on soporifics that postpone or deny the need to do better in resolving consumer conflicts.

Consumer psychology is a specialized branch of psychology that includes principles, generalizations, concepts, and theories that are intended to explain or predict human behavior in buyer-seller-maker transactions involving both products and services. It also recognizes the need to study the antecedents as well as the consequences of such transactions not only as they are related to the individuals involved but, in turn, as they affect society as a whole.

Consumer psychology requires the use of scientific methods that emphasize acceptable research procedures as the means of gathering and interpreting data before reaching generalizations or conclusions.

Further clarification and understanding of the term *consumer psychology* may be gained by considering each word separately. A *consumer* is a buyer or user of products and services. But not all people are consumers all of the time. Rather, all people are consumers some of the time. People are consumers when they are buying or using products or services. They are not consumers when they are selling, making, or providing products or services. For that matter, they are not consumers when they are passing or enforcing laws. The notion that the President, a mechanic, or a policeman is a consumer is partially correct. It is correct when such a person is buying or using a product or service; at other times the person is something else.

Psychology is the study of human behavior, both normal and abnormal. Its goal is to understand and predict behavior as well as its antecedents and consequences. This includes mental, physical, overt, covert, conscious, or unconscious behavior. It attempts to do this by using scientific methods.

Scientific methods are those that use objective, replicable, and unbiased techniques of experimentation to gather factual data. Although psychology generally confines its conclusions to facts and data, it encourages hypotheses and theories as tentative or generally acceptable explanations of behavior.

The science of psychology has several subdivisions or branches. Although each shares a common core, each also has special methods and concerns. Clinical, social, community, industrial, and educational psychology are among the more widely known applied fields of psychology. Psychologists contribute to knowledge of as well as solutions to problems by applying psychological methods in these areas.

It is also advisable to know who or what a psychologist is. A psychologist is a person who, as a result of training, meets three sets of criteria or, to say it somewhat differently, has three basic characteristics.

The first characteristic is that he/she has completed an academic program leading to a Ph.D. in psychology. The second characteristic is a by-product of the first via osmosis or absorption: In the course of completing a Ph.D. a person attains discipline, especially as it relates to methods of gathering and interpreting data. The third characteristic has to do with standards that are equivalent to a code of ethics. It implies that the psychologist has a responsibility to the people he/she works with or for, as well as to society. The psychologist is very often involved in modifying the behavior of others or at least providing the means for such modification and, therefore, must be aware of, as well as concerned about, the implications and consequences of such actions.

Another aspect of the professionalism of psychology is that almost all the states in the United States award either certification or licenses to psychologists based on education, experience, and the passing of examinations. The preceding description portrays who and what psychologists are. It is not intended to paint a "holier than thou" picture. There is considerable overlap in subject matter between psychology and other sciences, social sciences, and other subjects normally taught in graduate schools.

To summarize, all psychologists, whether their specialty is clinical, consumer, or industrial, have by virtue of their training a common core of knowledge, discipline, and ethics.

Psychologists have "no corner on the market," and so it is with consumer psychologists. This body of knowledge is related to and overlaps with such fields as consumer affairs, consumerism, and marketing, among others. Consumer affairs includes the relations, interactions, problems, and issues that result from the transactions involving products or services.

The term *consumerism* is generally used to represent the point of view of the consumer. It has also become an emotionally toned word with political significance.

Consumer psychology also overlaps in subject matter with the "other side of the fence." This includes the areas of business that are directly involved in the distribution process, including sales, advertising, marketing, and marketing research.

Whether it is fortunate or unfortunate, business spends large sums of money for research on consumer behavior. It often uses the data obtained to draw conclusions, and it generally does so in a privileged and confidential fashion. Business is interested in and sponsors studies of the characteristics of users as well as nonusers of products and services. These studies are most often conducted by a company in order to give it a competitive advantage over another company. There is nothing wrong with this, but herein lies the great difference between market research, which also studies consumer behavior, and consumer psychology.

To clear up rather than confuse the situation, psychologists may work in the field of market research, but so do people from other disciplines—statistics, sociology, marketing, and the like. The market researcher conducts research in behalf of a business or an industry.

As has been stated, in addition to consumers and business, others—government and labor—are also involved. Government on all levels—state, local, and federal—is very much a part of consumer affairs. In any discussion of the dynamics and interactions of consumer affairs, government must certainly be considered for the sake of completeness. Government manifests its role through its legislative, regulatory, and enforcement functions and is becoming increasingly involved in consumer affairs. At any one time, on all levels of government, there are literally hundreds of bills in the legislative hopper. What must be kept in mind is that the proposed legislation is never initiated in a vacuum. The proposed bills reflect the pressures exerted by the special interests of business, labor, and consumer groups; this is popularly known as lobbying.

Consumer issues involve different degrees of interest and participation as well as different viewpoints and proposed solutions by consumers, business, government, and labor. An incomplete listing of the issues (not in any order of priority) would include inflation, shortages, fraud, deceit, misinformation, health, safety, grade labeling, date labeling, cans vs. bottles for beverages, advertising to children, unit pricing, and meat packaging.

From an operational point of view, consumer psychology uses the methods of psychology to study in an objective fashion the issues of consumer affairs. By its very objectivity it adds to more complete knowledge and, it is hoped, better solutions than the often one-sided, narrow, and even incorrect solutions sometimes proposed separately by business, government, or consumers.

Fundamentally, it is obviously necessary to reduce or prevent fraud and deceit, which often threaten the health and safety of consumers. Unequivocally preventing goods and services from harming consumers is a must. Consumer psychology must dedicate itself to this goal, not through lip service but by reporting the results of research even when doing so means "blowing the whistle" on a particular product. However, consumer psychology must be concerned not only with the short run but also with the long run. This requires coming face to face with ecology or at least recognizing the basic need for pure or clean air and water, regardless of whether shortages really exist or are contrived. The long-run problems must be considered in the context of the tendency to emphasize today's problems.

A major assignment undertaken in clinical psychology is to relieve conflicts in individuals and thereby allow them to live better-adjusted, happier lives. In related fashion, in consumer psychology a major assignment is to help relieve consumer conflicts.

Inevitably there is a battle for the individual consumer's mind and purse. It takes place along three fronts: business, government, and the consumer "advocates." Each segment sees things quite differently and, as a result, too often aids and abets the conflict. The point is not necessarily who is right or wrong. The point is that the groups themselves sometimes intensify conflicts and prevent or postpone solutions.

The problems and issues of consumer affairs are interpreted —or perceived—quite differently by government, business, and consumers.

There are those who believe consumer problems are caused by business forcing people to buy what they don't want or misrepresenting products and services. This probably happens to some of us some of the time, but surely not to all of us all of the time. Then there are those who favor a totally "free system" based on the assumption that consumers always have free choice in making buying decisions because they know what is best. Surely this, too, is not true for all of us all of the time. Chances are, the truth lies somewhere between these two extremes, and progress toward a solution to the issues of consumer affairs can result if we avoid such extremisms. A solution can probably occur if we stop our persistent striving to maintain the status quo and preserve special interests.

The issues confronting consumers are real and must be faced realistically. Some representatives of business act as if consumer issues were not real and suggest that these issues are manufactured by agitators who deliberately misrepresent.

Observing businesses and their trade association representatives, one notes a peculiar ambivalence. At times they appear to favor a totally unrestricted atmosphere, but at other times they favor restrictions and protection from what they believe would otherwise create unfair competition. It is no wonder that they contribute to the confusion of a government that needs little encouragement to be confused.

Another confusion generated by business occurs when barely noticeable differences among products are conjured up and then magnified in the false belief that the magnification process will somehow reveal greater differences than actually exist.

A serious impediment to progress is the resistance to justifiable changes suggested by others, even when the changes are necessary and inevitable. Chances are that any advertising agency, credit company, door-to-door sales company, purveyor of franchises, manufacturer of food or appliances, or retailer knows the three or four things it is doing that most need change if consumer affairs are to be improved.

But does business take the initiative to clean its own house? Generally it does not, even though it strongly favors "volunteerism." As a form of self regulation and self control to improve situations and solve problems, business has constructed an alter ego in the form of trade associations to lobby for protectionism or freedom, whichever happens to best promote its myopic viewpoint.

For example, when business states that "the consumer is king" and that people are free to choose in the open marketplace, it is either deliberately misleading or has an incorrect point of view. Such an appeal is probably intended to falsely flatter the ego or mislead the consumer. In reality, it overlooks or oversimplifies the complexities that exist in the buyer-seller-maker world.

Business, through its trade associations, has been in favor of and in fact has promoted many laws in the past. It still does. However, not many of these laws have been favorable or beneficial to the consumer. On the other hand, the same groups will staunchly oppose laws introduced by others and argue that such laws are not in the best interests of the country or will raise prices, if not wreck the total economy. As an aside one must ask,

How can these self-appointed prophets know so much about the future?

An example of emotionally toned testimony is the following, from a spokesman for the National Association of Manufacturers (1). These three excerpts illustrate the not-so-benign technique that surely must intensify conflicts.

> There is much evidence that Government will be aligning itself with parties less interested in the satisfaction of consumers and the personal relations between merchants and their customers, than with mass actions concerned with our political and economic system. (page 3)
>
> In the light of the organized criticism today directed against the business community, it is inevitable that complaints will be generated in volume by dedicated organizations and individuals, seeking their special goals. Where the stakes are enormous, unscrupulous competitors might find the encouragement of complaints the easiest route to undermine the market for a competing product. (page 16)
>
> In conclusion, we believe that the preferred role of Federal Government is to work with all elements of the marketplace, including consumer bodies, to seek solutions through leadership in voluntary procedures, rather than through compulsion and by assuming for itself the private decision-making processes. Business is, in the end, the only force which can "make consumer protection work." (page 23)

Such statements must confuse the issues and intensify conflicts. One wonders whether a person who makes statements of the kind just quoted can possibly believe what he is saying. Surely he must never have listened to the other side of the issue.

Progress can occur when all sides listen more carefully to each other and talk to each other more truthfully. It should be recognized and remembered that intense and narrow beliefs prevent understanding. One must be aware that there are at least two sides to any issue; otherwise the issue would not exist.

Now let us look at government and its part in consumer affairs. The game it plays is politics, and in this respect the issues of consumerism serve its purpose very well. Both the executive and legislative branches of government seek at times to protect the consumer against the onslaughts of the consumer's exploiter, business. In other words, government's role in consumer affairs combines some altruism with a large dose of politics. However, government should be given credit for working on the issues that business tries to duck. In many instances the issues it finds are the same ones that business knows it should be doing something about. When government finds them, it conducts hearings, introduces a multiplicity of overlapping bills, and eventually passes some laws intended to protect the consumer. At the same time, business tries to raise a set of different issues such as restrictive oppression, unfair interference in free enterprise, the whittling away of democracy, and so forth.

The problem with government's role in consumer affairs is that sometimes its representatives act as if they had some mysterious, omniscient, and almost holy way of dedicating themselves to protecting the consumer. If government is to protect the consumer, it should do so on the basis of research in consumer psychology. Knowing what protection the consumer really needs can lead to better and more appropriate legislation.

The consumer is also protected by consumer groups. The sad fact is that despite the many consumer issues, no single strong consumer group has emerged as a strong and truly representative leader of consumers. As a poor substitute, it appears that some self-appointed leaders have become spokesmen for the amorphous consumer.

Bauer and Greyser (2) make the meaningful point that business and government spokesmen, even those who espouse dialogue, more often conduct a sequence of monologues. They suggest, and correctly so, that more meaningful and effective business-government interaction is needed. This also applies to consumer dialogues. To achieve this, they suggest the following:

1. Thoughtful business and government leaders.
2. Marketers and their critics who take the time to consider and to understand (even if they do not agree with) each other's premises and assumptions.
3. Those who engage in meaningful dialogue oriented to fact finding rather than fault finding.
4. Those on both sides who address themselves to solving the problems of the real, rather than the presumed, public. (page 2)

Three of the participants in the controversies and conflicts that surround consumer affairs are the consumer activist-advocate, the business spokesman, and the government official. To borrow a page from Eric Berne (3), who, in turn, borrowed a few pages from Sigmund Freud, an analogy can be drawn that can lead to some insights as to why the roles are played the way they are.

First, emphasis must be placed on the contributing roles of the various applied fields of psychology. Consumer psychology is aided and abetted by clinical psychology. In fact, many problems that are helped by counseling or psychotherapy have their roots in or are exasperated by the tensions of the growing-up process, by interpersonal relations, and by those tensions created in the marketplace.

Just as a transaction takes place between a buyer and a seller, so, in life, transactions take place as a result of the interactions of people. Berne has attempted to add insight and understanding by referring to the roles of child, parent, and adult that can be found at almost any time in any of us as we are involved in interpersonal transactions. The child is more concerned with sensual or hedonic gratifications; the parent is concerned with rules, especially those that set "standards" for what we should do; the adult role is the most rational of the three because it stresses accountability.

To be sure, none of us is the adult to the degree that our self-perceptions allow us to believe. It may be that we are more often the child. What is of interest is that business, government, and consumers could develop either a better tolerance (or at least a sense of humor) or a higher degree of understanding if each would see more clearly the role it is playing—child, parent, or adult.

The consumer activist-advocate, who is often self-designated, assumes and would have you believe that he/she is a special representative of consumers. In Berne's system such a person is the fault-finding *parent*. The business spokesman who speaks for his own interests and then assigns them altruistic motives or slogans such as "the consumer is king" believes he is the accountable *adult*. The government official plays the *child*, who apparently finds great satisfaction in playing cops and robbers.

To further extrapolate from Berne, the "parent" (consumer activist or business activist) may become excited or distressed by the "child's" (government's) fantasies; and the "child" is particularly sensitive to inhibitory stimuli from the "parent." In other words, one may look at the problems that surround consumer affairs as generated by groups playing roles that do not lead to the resolution of problems. Quite to the contrary, the roles tend to befog and obscure the issues. The excited adversary activist who sets in motion the cops and robber game of the government official should use better avenues of access.

Serious dialogue is needed; action must follow *listening*. The present system, which intensifies advocacy, encourages the continuation of strife and conflict. If each group played an "adult" role, more progress would be made toward solving the issues of consumer affairs.

Consumer psychology must recognize the serious social, moral, and ethical aspects of buyer-seller-maker transactions as well as their broader consequences. Every buyer of a product or service reacts with degrees of satisfaction, neutrality, or dissatisfaction to the service, the product, the retail outlet, or the manufacturer directly or indirectly involved in the transaction. The issue is not merely the relation between expectation and performance of the product or service, but also the way buyers as well as sellers evaluate other human beings. The degrees of pleasure or annoyance are not correlated solely with the price tag of the product. More often, they are manifestations of the feeling of having been "had" or "ripped off." What is more, it does not matter whether the feeling is a result of fact or fantasy.

The facts and conclusions garnered by the study of all sides, that is, buyer, seller, and maker, can lead to conflict reduction when the findings are applied to rectify existing wrongs and better balance the various shares of freedom.

Satisfaction with a product or service does relate to the degree of expectation of performance. When the expectation is matched, then satisfaction exists. When the performance is less than expected, then dissatisfaction exists. It matters little whether the expectation is a fault of false presentments or a lack of knowledge on the part of the buyer; the end product of the mismatch of performance and expectation is dissatisfaction.

That is the subject matter to be considered in this book.

BIBLIOGRAPHY

1. *Should Congress Federalize Consumerism*, Washington, D.C. National Association of Manufacturers, 45 (1971).
2. BAUER, R. A., and GREYSER, S. A., "The Dialogue That Never Happens," *Harvard Business Review*, 45 (1967): 2–12
3. BERNE, ERIC, *Transactional Analysis in Psychotherapy*, (Castle Books, 1961).

2
Perception— help or hindrance?

The subject areas normally included under the label "psychology" include perception, attitude, motivation, learning, and personality. Knowledge of these topics is a prerequisite for an understanding of consumer psychology.

It is important to recognize that in the field of psychology, as well as in other bodies of knowledge, ultimate knowledge does not yet exist; in fact, the incontrovertible truth may well be a long way off. Accordingly, it is important to recognize that as a result of research, hypotheses, and theories, certain "facts" are regarded, for the present, as truths. Whether such existing truths will in any way resemble ultimate truth remains to be seen; it is likely that in many instances they will not. Nevertheless, accepting, believing, and applying and questioning what is available is helpful. That is what leads to progress and additional knowledge.

Accordingly, some psychologists may not agree with the positions stated in this book, and more humorously, many who are not psychologists may even deny that the presentments made are in the province of consumer psychology. Still others may believe that the material presented in this chapter is not even related to consumer affairs. Nevertheless, the purpose of this chapter is to attempt to understand perception as part of the subject matter of psychology as it relates to the interactions of buyer, seller, and maker as transactions take place.

Perception is the meaning or understanding an individual

has as a result of some form of energy or stimulus in the environment activating an appropriate sense organ. Perceptions may or may not reflect reality. A perceptual response is not uniform from individual to individual or, for that matter, uniform within the same individual at different times.

The definition of perception involves a number of concepts; these include a *stimulus* or *stimuli* in the environment, which is the part of the world impinging upon a person's sensory organs. This impingement results in some translation of the activity in the physical world into changes in the individual's neural activity.

The physical characteristics of a stimulus (e.g., light) activates the sense modalities, and these are neurological in nature. While we are not personally aware of the neurology, we are aware of the effects (e.g., the difference when we enter a dark room from a well-lighted room, or the difficulty in driving due west in late afternoon).

The organism, however, adapts or adjusts to the physical changes that take place as a result of stimuli acting upon the sense modality in the organism. Whereas part of the response is physiological, another part of the response relates to the adjustment of understanding, or *perception*, that occurs. Ultimately, then, the perceptual response is an individual's understanding or interpretation of the stimulus impinging on that individual's organism. This is an oversimplified statement of what perception is all about. Perception is the process of attaching meaning to the stimuli that act upon the organism.

Perceptions may differ because of physiological differences within the organism. For example, a person may be nearsighted or colorblind. Another example is the person who is very sensitive to pain and therefore perceives the stimulus of a bee sting quite differently from the person who thinks of himself as a stoic.

In addition, perceptions differ as a result of the interpretation or understanding of the individual. You may perceive a friend quite differently from someone who does not regard that person as a friend. Chances are, you attach positive attributes to the individual, whereas another person attaches more neutral or negative attributes to the same individual. To take this one step further, it is a good thing marriage usually involves romance and love. These constitute to quite a degree the reasons that a potential mate is perceived as more intelligent, more attractive, much more everything else than your friend may perceive the same person.

In this earlier stage you rationalize the difference in perception by believing that your friend is jealous and you are lucky.

Somewhat later the perception may change. At this point unhappiness may develop since a different perspective on reality changes your perceptions.

In similar fashion the same applies to products or services. There are people who "fall in love" with a newly purchased product, which acquires, or has attributed to it, qualities of "perfection" not seen by others—even one's friends. Somewhat later these perceptions may change.

Perceptions, then, are meanings and interpretations that may or may not be agreed upon by two or more people. Perception is not necessarily the essence of objectivity. In fact, perception may be the opposite of reality, as the following illusions illustrate. *Illusions* are misinterpretations of stimuli leading to false perceptions.

Five illusions are presented in Figure 2.1. The first is known as the Jastrow illusion. The bottom figure is invariably seen as larger than the top one. However, place a ruler parallel to the edge of the book but at a point where the figures end and it is clear that seeing is not always believing.

The two lines in the Muller-Lyer illusion are equal despite the "distortion" of the inward or outward lines attached. Checking the Poggendorff illusion with a ruler will prove that the line "through" the rectangle is straight. And the Zollner and Herring figures illustrate the "distortion" of parallel lines.

Illusions also apply to what can be called the hefting process. For example, lifting two objects such as two very different-sized cans will generally result in the judgment that one is heavier than the other. Our previous experience indicates that, other things being equal, when two items look alike but one is larger, the larger object will be heavier. However, if the smaller object is weighted with lead so both weigh the same, then, since the small one is expected to be lighter, less of a "hefting" movement is involved. As a result practically all individuals will judge the smaller can to be the heavier one.

The reader can construct a "do it yourself" test. All that is needed is two different-sized vegetable cans. The smaller one should be weighted to match the larger one. Now lift each can one at a time. The size-weight illusion will be clearly demonstrated.

The size-weight illusion is but one illustration that perception is at the root of many of the problems related to consumer psychology. One example involves package design and appearance creating the illusion that a package is bigger and therefore contains more items or weighs more. Outward appearance as well as packaging can influence judgments of product quality

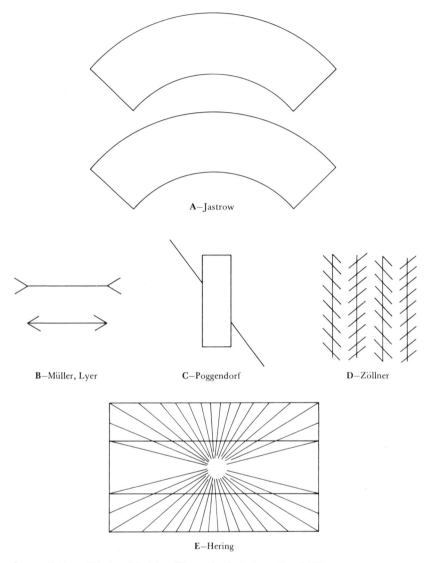

A—Jastrow

B—Müller, Lyer   C—Poggendorf   D—Zöllner

E—Hering

Source: S. Howard Bartley, *Principles of Perception*, 2nd ed; pp. 25 and 238.

FIGURE 2.1

merely because the package looks better or more attractive—an example is gift packaging vs. brown-bag packaging. This causes people to believe the product itself is different or better. Often the boxes that contain toys and cereals are larger than would appear to be necessary based on the actual contents of the box. Can the purpose be to create the illusion that the bigger the package, the more you get for your money?

In other words, illusions or the misinterpretation of stimuli can cause individuals to quite consistently misinterpret reality. Since those of us who want to be "normal" need to have good contact with reality, we defend these misinterpretations as if they were reality. When this is carried to an extreme a person is very sick and is described as psychotic.

Sometimes the adage "good things come in small packages" takes the place of "the larger the better." Again we are up against the problems of individual perceptions. When solid state was introduced into home electronics, smaller radios, even those that fit into pockets, suddenly acquired personal value. For a while a small radio had an advantage over a large one and sound became less important. Another illustration of relative size perception and value is the relationship between price and perfume quality. In one study men and women were asked to judge the quality of perfume in smaller or larger bottles. Women, more often than men, tended to judge that the higher-quality perfume was in the smaller bottles.

Consumer psychology is concerned not only with distortions and misinterpretation of size but with such attributes as quality, status, and prestige. Advertisers often attempt to have an individual associate a product with such attributes. This could apply to automobiles such as a Cadillac or a Mercedes, a department store such as Neiman-Marcus, or a restaurant that has won the *Holiday* Magazine award.

Not to be overlooked in the buyer-seller-maker transaction is color and its perception. This is not only a matter of an individual's like or dislike of a color but also includes color expectations in relation to a particular object. This applies especially to foods. For example, butter is yellow. Butter colored green or blue might not be as readily acceptable, not only because of its looks but possibly because of the taste attributed to it. In fact, the butter interests objected strenuously to the efforts of the oleomargarine group to make margarine yellow and, thus, indistinguishable from butter. Some years ago, at least in New York, margarine was sold in its natural white color, but included in the package was a yellow gel that, when mixed in, made the margarine look more like butter. Now butter and margarine look alike.

Depending on where the meat is bought, consumers are often surprised to find that the meat they have bought is less red and "healthy" looking when they get it home. The reason is the artificial lighting that creates an illusion by changing the color of the meat in the meat counter.

The influence of lighting as an aid to facial makeup is well known. The cosmetic mirror allows a woman to change the lighting as she applies her cosmetics so that she can be "made-up" for office, day, or evening.

Surely all if not most of us have had a surprise when we bought an item of clothing and found that the color of the fabric in natural or outdoor lighting was quite different from the way it appeared in the store with its artificial lighting.

The fact that colors such as red and blue can be judged as equal in brightness in daylight and unequal in brightness in twilight vision is known as the Purkinje phenomenon. The differences are due to the rods and cones in the eye and to the fact that daylight vision is colored and night vision colorless.

Another series of perceptions concerns taste and smell either separately or in combination. Much of the attractiveness or unattractiveness of foods is due to smell as well as taste. A liking for a food can be changed to a dislike if one happens to be present when that food is being cooked. Few people like the cooking smell of cabbage, Brussels sprouts, or cauliflower.

Smell does add to the use as well as acceptance of a wide variety of products from deodorants to soap, from furniture polish to air fresheners. Considering two competitive products with equal functional performance, people will often knowingly pay more for the one with a fragrance even though its basic function is the same as that of a product without the fragrance.

With a little suggestion, some people believe they and their clothing can "smell clean." In other words, advertisments try to add value to products by encouraging associations between smell and quality. More often than not, smell and quality have no relationship.

Intimately related to the laws of perception is *preparatory set,* also known as *set* or *readiness.* This term labels an individual's predisposition to perceive an object or other type of stimulus in a certain way. Very often the conditions prevailing are conducive to the establishment of a preparatory set, and this, more often than the stimulus itself, determines the perception.

Sellers and makers expend much energy and money to attribute special qualities to their products so that the buyer will perceive them as better than they really are. This is accomplished by creating favorable sets or predispositions in the buyer. As a result the consumer is often disadvantaged. When the perception changes and conforms closer to reality, the consumer's set also changes. This different set manifests itself in a greater degree of dissatisfaction. The perception of the product, retailer, or maker becomes quite different. Its qualities and characteristics become more negative in the mind of the consumer.

So the conditions under which the preparatory set takes place mainly involve whether one perceives the stimulus in the direction in which it is intended. For example, all of us have had the experience of waiting in a specific place for a person we know very well. After 5 minutes of waiting, quite a few people begin to look like that person. After 20 minutes, almost everyone does.

Set or expectancy can to a great extent determine perceptual response. Transfering all this to a buyer-seller-maker situation is quite easy. The buyer, after some involvement in the purchase process, finally sees the item that he/she "cannot live without." The person selling automobiles, negligees, carpeting, wines, or whatever offers information that suggests that this product will make you thinner, taller, younger, happier, or what have you and, once again, expectations are unfulfilled.

Perception both involves and is aided by the process of classification. Perceptions of differences in size, shape, quality, and value are based to a large degree on some arbitrary or standardized process that delineates differences that are meaningful to the individual. In fact, efforts to standardize differences and assign appropriate names to the differences in the items being classified are important and desirable from the point of view of the consumer. Without standardization and classification, the consumer might never be able to make any judgments regarding value received. Eggs offer a simple example. According to the U.S. Department of Agriculture, supermarkets must classify their eggs uniformly. Eggs are classified into five sizes: jumbo (30 oz.), extra large (27 oz.), large (24 oz.), medium (21 oz.), and small (18 oz.). The name applied to the size of the egg is related to the minimum weight per dozen eggs. Of course the consumer must know the quality of the egg, but most supermarkets sell only grade A eggs. The point is that one can now compare egg price by size category from store to store and determine the best buy. Because of competition, overzealousness, or sometimes just plain larceny, were it not for the requirement that the size of eggs be classified in a standardized fashion some stores might call their small eggs "large" and their large eggs "giants," as is done with practically all products except those for which standardization requirements exist.

The consumer is helped whenever there is some standard classification process, regardless of the product—be it toothpaste, detergent, or even grapefruit. (The term *family size* or *economy size,* for example, is absolutely meaningless in helping a consumer perceive product characteristics.) But who is to set the standards of classification as well as the terminology? Obviously business could hardly be expected to agree to set the same standards and terminology across such widely varied products as appliances, foods, and clothing. Well, then, what about government? A report by Miller (1) reveals the utter hopelessness and confusion that exist within government, at least as far as standard-setting terminology is concerned. Table 2.1 presents the three highest grades and the terms used to describe them for five food items. Such differences in language go beyond irrationality. If one has trouble understanding why these different nomenclatures have been adopted, and as a result is confused, then one has joined the ranks of the majority.

It is important to recognize that standardization helps form reference points that stabilize perceptions. This is what most clinicians would regard as a condition necessary to establish the concept of "normal." It is clear that Table 2.1 defies reality and normality: It defies the need for language that helps understanding and makes for uniformity of meaning.

Insofar as consumers are concerned, the attributes of an object about to be bought, whether it be size, quality, or any other attribute, can be perceived variously by different people. Sometimes the perceptions are unreal. These false perceptions are aided and abetted by uninformed consumers as well as misinformation by sellers and makers.

In consumer psychology the perceptions of consumers as well as the actions of sellers influence product characteristics. Sometimes more money is spent on the package than on the product. Sometimes undiscernible product differences are emphasized in order to make the buyer really believe that differences exist. Do they really exist in brands of gasoline, cigarettes, tis-

TABLE 2.1   Grading of various foods by government standards

	Beef	Canned Peas	Dry Peas	Poultry	Lima Beans
Highest	U.S.D.A. Prime	U.S. Choice Handpicked	U.S. No. 1	U.S. Grade A	U.S. Extra No. 1
Second	U.S.D.A. Choice	U.S. Prime Handpicked	U.S. No. 2	U.S. Grade B	U.S. No. 1
Third	U.S.D.A. Good	U.S. No. 1	U.S. No. 3	U.S. Grade C	U.S. No. 2

SOURCE: Modified from paper delivered by Dr. John A. Miller at 1975 American Psychological Association meeting in Chicago. A more complete discussion of grades and standards appears in Chapter 24 of Leland J. Gordon and Stewart M. Lee, *Economics for Consumers,* 6th ed. (New York: Van Nostrand, 1975).

sues, and the like? If and when they exist in automobile tires, how can the consumer really know when the difference makes a difference?

One must remember that consumer psychology, like any other body of knowledge, can be used either to benefit mankind or to harm or destroy mankind. Even when a scientist makes a discovery that could benefit mankind, someone always comes along to misapply the results. In such circumstances the consumer is often misled. Consumers remain befuddled because it is difficult to know who is telling the truth. An example is strip mining of coal: Is it as harmful to the environment as we are told by conservationists? Are its effects as insignificant as we are led to believe by mining interests? The point is that we rely on our perceptions without always knowing when perception is or is not reality.

With reference to the serious matter of survival, the most outstanding example is that of atomic energy. Its power can be used to enhance civilization or to destroy it. The consumer should know the complete truth about atomic energy and safety.

Although the people who market most products do not have the immediate destructive potential of the people who market nuclear reactors or even the guns known as Saturday night specials, there is no question but that the body of knowledge known as consumer psychology can be either used or misused. The question is whether business, government, or consumers equally and correctly perceive what they or others are doing and whether their actions truly benefit the consumer.

Consumer psychology makes it quite clear that each group perceives mankind's benefits quite differently. A knowledge of perception as well as the influences that determine a specific buyer's perception are an important part not only of the buyer-seller-maker transaction but of its consequences as well.

The buyer should be able to know as much about such items as toys, foods, and drugs as the seller or maker. This would put all three on a more equitable basis. It would surely promote consumer perceptions of products that would be closer to reality.

A term closely related to perception is *image*. Its application in consumer psychology is widespread and of consequence. Too often the word is loosely used and probably means many different things to different people. It is a convenient "handle."

For practical purposes, four questions about image need to be answered: What is an image? How does it come about? Does it change? What does one do with it?

People have needs and motives that are both physical and

psychological. Characteristics and motives combine in various ways and contribute to a total configuration. This configuration creates an impression on others, and this impression becomes known more or less as the person's image.

Images, although measurable, often exist in the minds of others without any measurements being taken but, rather, as a result of observations that are usually biased. A major difficulty with bias is that its possessor does not often recognize its existence. So here again we have a factor producing incorrect perceptions.

Once an image is formed, others act toward the person as if the image were a reality. As in the case of perceptions, sometimes the image is a reflection of reality and sometimes it is not.

What applies to a person also applies to communities of people and geographic places; just as one conjures an image of a person, it is equally easy to conjure an image of New Englanders, Southerners, PTAs, Lions, Elks, and Masons.

Without measurement but with a lot of conjuring, who is to say that image is a reflection of reality or a revealer of misinformation. In either case the image holder is likely to behave in accordance with the dictates of the image as it is perceived.

Because people freely project their own physical and psychological characteristics onto others, we also find an extension of image to products and corporations. In other words, a person's image of a product is that person's perception of the physical and psychological attributes or characteristics of that product. The perceptions may be factual, but they may also be reflections that are distorted because "the stream has ripples or the mirror has imperfections."

Images, however, must be taken seriously whether they are valid or not. Images result in product labels or characterizations. In the instance of a favorable image, it has attributed to it such characteristics as high quality, good performance, attractiveness, and compactness. On the other hand, a product may be given a negative image. It then has ascribed to it such characteristics as gaudiness, bulkiness, cheapness, or shoddiness.

Deserving or not, the product with a good image has to maintain this image, and the product with a poor image must either change its image or disappear from the competitive scene.

Many factors contribute to image formation. To better understand how an image is formed, we will consider the following: personal experience, advertising, word of mouth, dealers and servicemen, and design.

People perceive favorable or unfavorable characteristics of

products on the basis of past experience. Generally, the better the perceived physical qualities of a product, the greater the likelihood of favorable experiences. However, when psychological attributes of products are perceived negatively this can prevent any future personal experience with the product.

The product image can be negative because of unfavorable perceptions in spite of lack of personal experience. An example is the employer who refuses to hire anyone from a certain minority group even though he has never had any experience with that group in the past. Another would be never eating artichokes because you don't like what artichokes look like. Surely many people have intense dislikes for a certain color, while others may like the same color. Whether past experiences with that color ever occurred or are not remembered is not as important as the rejection of the physical stimulus by one person and not another.

An advertisement, even as a single stimulus source, can be effective. Combining ads into a series results in further stimuli and more awareness. Continuous advertising creates a multiplicity of stimuli that, when associated and accumulated, create a configuration of the characteristics of the product or business. Like it or not, advertising is effective in contributing to the image of anything from Florida oranges to airlines and even politicians.

Word of mouth is a much-overlooked but important factor contributing to image. It results from the need for people to inform or be informed. It is advisable to evaluate who is doing the talking and why in order to better understand the potent role of word of mouth as a factor contributing to image.

Dealers or servicemen sometimes elevate themselves or are elevated by unsuspecting buyers to the role of expert. Often such a person is not an expert at all. Nevertheless, dealers' or servicemen's recommendations contribute to the image of a product. Quite a few appliance ads reflect this view, including the ad depicting the serviceman who rarely if ever gets service calls.

The role of design, as it contributes to product appearance, is another often overlooked but important factor as it contributes to the image of a product or company. Quite frequently, under the heavy competitive forces operating in some areas, many companies are able to match each other in the technical development and engineering characteristics of a product. What is often the only significant characteristic differentiating one product from another is its looks. This, it is hoped, creates the configuration "all is good." For example, research has indicated that a consumer believes a good-looking radio is a good-sounding one. Radios that have equal sound quality may be judged as having better or poorer sound, depending on their design and appearance. So a person's image of a product or a retail outlet is nothing else but the perception, or the meaning, the product or retail outlet has for the individual. Sometimes retail outlets attempt to change their image—department stores sometimes want to become known as discount stores and vice versa. The reason: Each thinks the other conveys a better image.

Closely related to the topic of perception is attitude, and at various points it seems as if the topics fuse. For example, the attributes of a product often include quality and value. Whether justified or not, most consumers want to believe that their purchase decisions are based on a price-value-quality relationship that results in a "best" buy. When the stark realization occurs that their perception of a "best" buy was incorrect, some individuals prefer to blame the product rather than themselves.

It is important, if consumer psychology is to be understood and problems solved, that one not simply take the side of business, consumers, government, or labor. It is important to study the four groups and make available to all parties information gathered by objective means.

BIBLIOGRAPHY

1. MILLER, J., "Are Mandated Disclosures Deceptive Advertising," paper delivered to the American Psychological Association, Chicago, 1975.

Attitudes are or are not behavior predictors

Just as industrial psychology concerns itself with job satisfaction, consumer psychology concerns itself with consumer satisfaction. Historically, however, business has accepted the importance of employee relations more often than it has recognized the value of good relations with buyers or users, who are the company's consumers and contribute to its success or failure.

Since an important goal of psychology is to reduce conflict, it follows that a goal of consumer psychology is to reduce consumer conflict and thereby increase consumer satisfaction. Adequate complaint handling is one way of increasing satisfaction, but that may be "too little too late."

A more appropriate way of increasing consumer satisfaction is to recognize the large role attitudes play in effecting it. Other major contributors to consumer satisfaction are product or service attributes such as physical characteristics, durability, and performance as well as the meaning the product or service has for the individual, especially in relation to expectations.

An important component in an understanding of the consumer is the awareness and study of *attitudes*. Attitudes reflect an individual's beliefs or feelings. They can influence action or predispositions to action on the part of a person or group toward objects, ideas, or people. They result in tendencies to respond positively or negatively to products, services, retailers, and manufacturers.

Of course attitudes are learned or acquired. However, sometimes the learning process is so subtle that a person may not even recognize its existence as a factor related to his/her feeling or predispositions toward a product.

Similar attitudes can be held by a variety of people, some of whom may have a factual basis for their attitudes while others may not. In addition, a person's attitudes are not necessarily related to intelligence. Regardless of information or intelligence, all, or most, people are likely to have attitudes toward ecology, advertising, the use of additives in food, the question of bottles vs. cans for beverages, and so forth.

Differences in attitude are the manifestations of consumer issues. For any individual, one's attitudes, intelligence or behavior may or may not be congruent. People's attitudes are often independent of such factors. But attitudes, by themselves, play a most important role in consumer affairs.

Attitudes can be described as a part of our hedonistic life. Beginning with simple sensory feelings of pleasantness or unpleasantness, we develop likes and dislikes. We also learn to show our feelings through our behavior. But we also learn to conceal our feelings through behavior. When we have an attitude it is about or toward a person, product, or service, among other things. The attitude reflects our like or dislike. The feelings accompanying the attitude may well be deep and intense. These feelings vary according to the individual's perception of his/her attitudes.

Attitudes can accompany passive behavior, intense behavior, or no behavior at all. Watching an athletic contest generally results in displays of positive or negative feelings toward one team or the other. This display reveals the spectator's attitude as well as its expressions. This is what makes it so easy for a spectator with a seat on the 20-yard line, and quite a distance from where the play took place, to decide that the referee has ruled incorrectly. The fact that the referee was right on top of the play means little to the avid fan. It only proves that the referee is "blind."

Similarly, one may never go to a certain store because of a feeling that the store "always cheats."

Even though perceptions are cognitive and attitudes are affective, they are often intertwined. While this adds to the richness of life, it also adds to confusion in explaining consumer behavior.

Attitudes as well as perceptions can be rational or irrational. The person with a specific attitude toward coffee, or a certain make of automobile, too often believes that attitude is the only one that is rational. It may not be. When attitudes are irrational they are often strongly, even violently, defended via rationalization or self-justification. The fact that feelings, which are the essense of attitudes, are within the mind of the individual and not necessarily in the attributes of the stimulus, must be recognized. Accordingly, people's attitudes toward a product can vary while the product does not.

Why people have attitudes is a most interesting question, and one must hasten to add that the answer is complicated. People have attitudes because of their knowledge or lack of it. They also have attitudes for a diversity of other reasons.

Attitudes often express or epitomize a person's value system and life style. The attitudes of a religious person, a penurious person, or a profligate will be quite different toward many issues of the day.

Another aspect of attitude is that in many respects it summarizes one's entire feeling tone toward many involved and complicated matters and institutions. It affects our feelings toward toys, overcooked eggs, political parties, retail outlets, and the facial expressions of salespeople.

Attitudes help summarize and simplify the way we express our feelings toward almost anything. They can also serve the purpose of conveying our lack of understanding of the issues while still allowing us to vent our feelings. Similar attitudes can be shared by many different people with different personalities and degrees of intelligence.

Labels are often used to signify the collection of beliefs that comprise an attitude. Examples of labels that reflect attitudes are "conservative," "liberal," "women's libber," and "male chauvinist pig." Such labeling is apparently much easier than explaining the implied concept. Further, the label enables the holder of an attitude to accuse, judge, or "explain" the behavior of others, especially since their attitudes are different.

In one way attitudes, which sometimes do reflect an entire life style, are also labels. The problem is to differentiate the life style of the environmentalist or vegetarian, for example, from the label, which is often attached to a person in an attempt to put him down. An attitude can be quite consistent even when the basis of the attitude is inconsistent or irrational.

The attitudes of peers, family, or neighbors influence our own opinions. They can have powerful negative or positive effects on the way we dress, the foods we eat—and the products or services we use. A further look into attitudes and their formation can lead to some understanding of why they have such an important effect on our lives.

A person's attitudes have been developing from his/her earliest days. The earliest force influencing attitudes are the parents, both the mother and the father but especially the mother. Then there is the family, which basically includes brothers and sisters, both older and younger; from the immediate family constellation it spreads to grandparents, aunts, uncles, and other relatives. The neighborhood and then the schools are further factors contributing to attitude formation. These factors make the process more complex.

Children playing with other children are involved in peer groups, and quite often the peer group members can exert greater influence on the behavior of an individual than either the parents or the school. An example of such influence relates to smoking, whether it be tobacco or marijuana. The advice or influence of parents is likely to be rejected and that of peer groups accepted.

For a while it was popular to refer to a "generation gap." Probably all that was involved was the frequent lack of communication between age groups because of strong attitudinal differences.

Attitudes may or may not predict behavior. Nevertheless, intense attitudes can erupt into violent behavior.

People with similar attitudes are most likely to form or join groups. Attitudes about being a consumer have resulted in the emergence and crystallization of contemporary views on consumer affairs.

Lack of communication is encouraged when groups hold different attitudes and beliefs. Under such circumstances the exchange of information is difficult, even useless, because the other person or group (it is always the other) has the "wrong" attitude. For example, groups (business, government, consumers, etc.) hold different attitudes and beliefs regarding consumer affairs. Such attitudinal differences often lead to lack of communication. People talk but do not hear what is being said.

Much of the subject matter of consumer affairs is attitudinal. Anti- or pro-business attitudes often determine whether a businessperson, a consumer, or a legislator is for or against grade labeling, meat packaging, television advertising to children, and so on.

Attitude studies can contribute to a better understanding of consumer affairs in at least two ways. They can lead to the recognition that attitudes are feelings and not facts. And they can measure and report the extent or degree of feeling.

It is obviously vital in consumer affairs to obtain data that separate attitudes from facts. When this has been done, then information about products or services and their attributes can be evaluated more fairly.

There are more people trying than succeeding to change the attitudes of others. The more intense, crystallized, or extreme the attitude, the less likely it is to change. It is only when feelings and attitudes are not strong in one direction or the other that a change can more readily occur. Probably this is one of the major reasons for continually advertising soda, cigarettes, toothpaste, automobiles, and the like. A person's attitude toward a brand may be sufficiently neutral that the advertisement for a competing brand can change the attitude and hence the buying intentions and brand purchased.

Sometimes the intensity of attitudes seems to be out of proportion to the issue. To illustrate the illogic that surrounds attitudes, one need only refer to hair, its styling, and the attitudes people have toward those whose hair style is different from theirs. There are even people who believe that by observing a person's hair style they can predict that person's sex life, political views, antisocial behavior, and so on. Such beliefs are obviously irrational. If one were to look at pictures in museums or history books one would clearly see that long hair comes in and out of fashion and has done so over hundreds of years. Yet in recent times hair style has created controversy in institutions such as the armed forces as well as schools and families. It has curtailed the education of individuals who did not subscribe to the mandates of school administrators, and it has prevented people from earning a living because of discriminatory hiring practices. How can one explain the intensity of attitudes about hair? Really, one cannot!

Can one justify the intensity of attitudes in general? Hardly. The point is that much disagreement is based on differences in feelings and attitudes that reflect belief rather than knowledge or understanding or truth or fact. To repeat, the crux of many consumer problems and affairs is attitudinal.

Where to begin to unravel the problems caused by attitudinal differences is hard to decide, but a start may be made by considering the conservative-liberal dimension. An interesting approach to the conservative-liberal dimension is offered by Bellak (1). He refers to "eggheads" and "squareheads." Eggheads have attitudes of reasonable doubt, tolerance of ambiguity, and irreverence, essential to a sense of humor. Squareheads, according to Bellak, see the immediate concrete reality. They control their own aggression, are tight lipped and tight sphinctered. They become the guardians of other people's behavior in order to control their own.

Squareheads are generally sober people who take themselves quite seriously.

In brief, according to Bellak, an egghead

> is a person who has, as an intellectual, a predilection for, and a preoccupation with abstract issues. There is a tendency toward self doubt, skepticism and inquiry. The eggheads are a constant threat to the squareheads because they threaten the black and white and good/bad foundations on which alone the latter can resolve a crisis. An outspoken form of squarehead is the authoritarian personality. (page 15)

This egghead-squarehead dimension is intimately involved with the various issues of consumer affairs and their interpretation.

Considerable speculation and future research may lead one to greater insight as consumer affairs conflicts are resolved along the liberal-conservative dimension. If we can understand, identify, and differentiate the eggheads from the squareheads and vice versa, we will be able to more appropriately make applications and interpretations as a result of our insights as to why people take the stands they do on many consumer issues—whether they understand those issues or not.

Consider, for example, certain television programs. Narrow the choice to a political talk show involving a panel of people who have been chosen because they differ along the dimension of liberal vs. conservative or egghead vs. squarehead. Potential viewers will watch this program if they like the topic, the participants, or whatever. When one watches this type of program week after week, one knows, regardless of the topic, that the liberal panelists will espouse one side and the conservatives will favor the other. Whatever the topic, they are likely to disagree in a predictable fashion. Obviously, if one's attitude is negative toward one panelist and positive toward another, it is likely that this attitude is related to one's own conception of liberalism or conservativism. If you are conservative, you perceive the liberal on the program as radical, irrational, or wrong. If you are liberal. you perceive the conservative as authoritarian, incompetent, and biased. You will notice that all of these words have feeling tones attached to them. Other things being equal, it is easier for an individual to hold to his/her beliefs, and these are the essence of attitudes.

This illustration is intended to summarize the role attitudes play as reflections of likes and dislikes, which are the feelings one has toward a wide variety of topics—in fact, they can be considered one's life style. More simply stated, a person's attitudes reflect and express that person's life style and value system.

People differ in their attitudes toward the consumer movement, which can be described as amorphous, consisting of a number of issues that are vital to some and superfluous to others. Business tends rather generally to hold the attitude that consumer issues can best be solved when business acts along lines of volunteerism. In general, the prevailing business attitude is that it can protect itself and consumers too. According to this view, laws related to consumer issues, will result in price increases and as a result are unnecessary.

Consumers vary considerably in their attitudes toward what the consumer can do—if anything. Among those who strongly identify with the movement and take leadership roles in it, attitudes vary as to the best way to make progress.

Government representatives, be they elected officials or bureaucrats, manifest ambivalence in their attitudes. Some side rather strongly with business and others side equally strongly with consumers. Others sit on the fence or take no side at all. One's identification with consumers or with business seems to be related to an important attitudinal dimension, namely, liberal–conservative.

To recapitulate, a perception may be expressed in terms of the image we have of an item, a brand, or a retail outlet. A perception is a result of a stimulus that impinges on the organism, which, in turn, results in an understanding or a perceptual response. The perceptual response may or may not accurately describe the stimulus. Surely two or more people can be expected to have somewhat different perceptual responses to a stimulus. On the other hand, a person's attitude is the belief or feeling associated with an item, brand, or retail outlet. To further complicate matters, the attitude may or may not actually predict the behavioral response. During a period of rising prices and inflation, it is simple to assume that most people have an attitude that is anti-inflation. They are for holding the price line and against price increases. However, the attitude is different from the behavior of those who favor anti-inflationary measures in general but favor such specific behavioral changes as increasing postal rates, or increasing food prices, or increasing salaries to cover increased costs of living, or increasing the sales tax to cover increased government costs. The attitude and behavior regarding inflation is often not the same.

Another example is the inability of the vast majority of people, when blindfolded, to distinguish among the leading brands of colas; yet most people insist that they can tell the difference.

Taking this one step further, one can understand why packages, advertising, and product claims attempt to influence the purchase decision by trying to establish a believable difference between their product and a competing product. The purpose is to establish a preference in favor of a particular brand. The intent is to somehow coordinate the predisposing factors, which include the attitudes that will encourage the individual to buy that brand of toy or coffee or soap or clothing because of cleanliness, fashion, durability, aroma, or any of a multitude of aspects of a person's attitudes that, when accumulated, form a value system.

It is most important to know that attitudes may or may not be predictors of behavior. When attitude is predictive, then one can measure attitude and estimate or predict behavior. The difficulty is that there is no general rule that indicates when attitude and behavior are correlated.

One cannot consider the topic of attitude without considering *prejudice*, which is an attitude or series of attitudes that a person or group holds toward another person or group. The latter is differentiable from the former according to real or imaginary characteristics.

Attitudes and prejudices apply not only in our social life but also in our attempts to earn a living, to live in certain neighborhoods, and even to get mortgage money. The relation between prejudice and consumer psychology should be clear, obvious, and emphasized.

Only half seriously, a prejudice may be defined as the attitudes other people have and that we don't share. More seriously, prejudices are unfortunately more or less a part of all individuals. They are a collection of negative attitudes toward people or groups. For a variety of irrational reasons, the people and groups are assigned characteristics and qualities that make them inferior, unfair, intolerable, and so on.

The most obvious forms of prejudice are directed toward people of certain skin color, religious beliefs, or national origin. Not to be overlooked is the prejudice of sexism. To indicate that there is more sexism on the part of the male toward the female or vice versa would itself be an example of this prejudice.

And so it is with consumer psychology. There is no question but that there are people who are anti-business, who are certain that corporations are up to no good. There are also prejudices toward senior citizens, those on relief, policemen ("pigs"), and so on and on.

Prejudice manifests itself in buyer-seller transactions in terms of such basic values as who has the right to work or where one can live. It is obvious that people, regardless of sex, skin color, or religion, among other things, should have equal rights to consume as a result of the fruits of their labor.

There is no question but that business as an institution has some things that are right with it and other things that are wrong with it. When one is aware only of the things that are wrong or bad, that would seem to be indisputable evidence of prejudice. Accordingly, advertising cannot be all bad. Nor can it be all good. The same applies to different religions, different nationalities, or any arbitrary characteristic, be it demographic or genetic.

Changes in attitude are a function of the credibility and believability of the communicator or persuader as well as the perceived relationship between the communicator and the receiver. To the extent that attitudes can be influences involving behavior and decisions, it is obvious that sellers attempt to influence buyers' attitudes before they reach a decision. It is most important for the buyer to recognize this attempt well in advance so that his/her decision can be as objective as possible.

Attitudes exist and are measurable. A variety of measuring techniques or methods may be used. Which is preferred depends on one's attitude toward measurement.

One of the earliest attempts to measure attitudes was made by Thurstone (2), who devised measurements of attitudes toward topics such as war, birth control, and religion. His technique was to present a series of statements varying in degree of positiveness or negativeness toward a topic. Each statement was given a score based on its position along this continuum. The person's attitude then became a translatable numerical item and was equal to the average score of the weights assigned to each item. Obviously, this method can be applied to a wide variety of topics.

Later, Likert (3) used a five-point scale (strongly agree, agree, undecided, disagree, strongly disagree) to measure a person's attitudes toward a series of statements. Another technique was proposed by Guttman (4). Very briefly, he suggests the arrangement of items in a unidimension scale on a topical area in such a fashion that any person who agrees with a given item will agree with all less extreme items and will disagree with all more extreme items.

Osgood (5) proposed a semantic scale of attitude measurement. Usually two words denoting opposites are separated by a seven-space scale and the space reflecting the person's views or attitudes is marked. It might be marked in the center, which reflects neutrality, or more or less toward either of the extremes ($+3$ to -3), as may be seen in the following example:

good ————————————————————— bad
active ————————————————————— passive

Other, more qualitative, measures would include sentence completion, free association, and group discussion.

A theory that has been given considerable attention is known as *cognitive dissonance*. As formulated by Festinger (6), it states that psychological inconsistencies in a person cause activated and directional behavior or attitudes to reduce the unpleasantness produced by the inconsistency. The dissonance exists when cognitive elements or items of knowledge conflict. In a buyer-seller situation, an individual is confronted with cognitive dissonance when trying to decide whether to buy a European or American car, to smoke or stop smoking, to take a cruise or buy furniture, and so on.

Often the decision to buy, or to do one thing rather than another, needs some reinforcement in order to bolster the ego of the individual. This is how attitudes toward a product or service become crystallized and people assume postures ranging from irrational defensiveness to the need to obtain approval from others.

A major problem is whether it is more important to produce a behavioral change (to get a person to buy a different brand) or to change a buyer's attitude toward an older product (without necessarily changing the purchase pattern).

For the consumer the important thing is to examine and become more aware of one's own attitudes. It is also of value to learn more about their origins. This applies to products, brands, retail outlets, manufacturers, and so forth. Having noted the attitude, check the facts. This can change irrational attitudes and make one a better consumer. By the same token, it might do businessmen a lot of good to check their attitudes toward consumers against the facts. They may find they do not have the facts to support their attitudes.

BIBLIOGRAPHY

1. BELLAK, L., *Overload—The New Human Condition* (New York: Human Science Press, 1975).
2. THURSTONE, L. L., and CHAVE, E. J., *The Measurement of Attitude* (Chicago: University of Chicago Press, 1929).
3. LIKERT, R. A., "A Technique for the Measurement of Attitudes," *Archives of Psychology*, 140 (1932): 43–53.
4. GUTTMAN, L. A., "A Basis for Scaling Qualitative Data," *American Sociological Review*, 9 (1944): 139–150.
5. OSGOOD, C. E., SUCI, G. J., and TANNENBAUM, P. H., *The Measurement of Meaning* (Urbana: University of Illinois Press, 1957).
6. FESTINGER, L., "Informal Social Communication," *Psychological Review*, 57 (1950): 282, 771.

4
Motivation: by whom and for what?

Probably one of the better ways to relate consumer psychology to the issues, problems, and conflicts of consumer affairs is to refer to Maslow (1), who stated that "after the period of happiness, excitement and fulfillment comes the inevitable taking it all for granted, and becoming restless and discontented again for *more!*" This statement is basic to understanding ourselves and others, whether we are consumers, retailers, or makers. In other words, asking the question, "Why aren't *they* satisfied?" is futile most of the time. The answer is *more*. At the core of motivation is drive, fulfillment, and then *more*.

Accordingly, the issues of consumer affairs are based on the incongruent goals or motives of business and consumers, each not only holding onto what he/she already has but wanting *more*. The presence of groups with incongruent goals means that not everyone can have more. Nevertheless, most people keep trying.

Maslow's theory of human motivation is quite adequate to explain the motivations involved in buyer-seller-maker transactions as well as their antecedents and consequences. A most important part of the Maslow theory is that basic human needs are organized into a hierarchy of relative prepotency. The implication is that gratification is as important a concept as deprivation.

Listed first among the basic needs are the physiological ones. Maslow believes it is impossible, as well as useless, to make any listing of fundamental physiological needs. However, he recognizes that the physiological needs are the most prepotent of all. When all needs are unsatisfied, then the organism is dominated by physiological needs. Quite basic is hunger; the absolutely hungry person is dominated by the need for food to the exclusion of all other needs. As Maslow puts it, "it is quite true that man lives by bread alone—when there is no bread." But when there is bread, other, higher needs emerge.

On the average, consumers in the United States have the capacity to satisfy their basic physiological needs, so the foods advertised or stocked in food stores generally appeal to appetite, taste, or convenience rather than hunger. It almost seems as if there are more advertisements for balanced and nutritious pet foods.

Thirst appeals are often social. Water has only recently been advertised for sale; formerly it was taken for granted as pure and healthful just from the kitchen tap. The colas, the beers, the alcoholic beverages all appeal to many motives and rarely are advertised on the basis of satisfying a need for thirst alone.

Sleep and sex are only partly physiological. They easily become "higher needs." Mattresses allow you to sleep more and better. Pills bought over the counter can help induce sleep or keep one awake. As for sex, all of us have been encouraged to believe the importance of using health and beauty aids to achieve a good sex life.

Having illustrated the relative importance of physiological needs, as consumers we can go on to the second group of needs, those concerned with safety. These become established as the physiological needs are gratified. Included in the category of safety, according to Maslow, are security, protection, and freedom from fear, anxiety, and chaos, as well as the need for structure, order, and law. Whereas infants and to a degree children react to danger with little or no inhibition, adults are taught to inhibit their reactions.

Most adult manifestations of anxiety are expressed in the need for job security, insurance, and a savings account for a "rainy day." With crime rates increasing in both cities and suburbs, threats to personal safety have increased. Rape, assault, burglary, and mugging create fear, and many adults now consider themselves more threatened than ever before. As a result the need for safety is expressed more strongly.

The normal response to danger is emphasis on safety. The threatened consumer avoids shopping in downtown areas, buys a watchdog, and acquires special locks and protective systems. Some also buy guns. The threatened person wants the protection of law and order, which, in turn, can threaten normal civil liberties—and this can make people feel unsafe. A few decide to take the law into their own hands.

The third group of needs to emerge, assuming reasonable satisfaction of the first two, includes "love and affection and belongingness needs." According to Maslow, a person hungers for affectionate relations with people in general and, in particular, for a place in his/her group or family. Further, Maslow believes this important need is not given the recognition it deserves.

Maslow stresses that love and sex are not synonymous. Sexual behavior is determined not only by sexual needs but by other needs such as love and affection. Most important, love needs involve both giving and receiving.

The need for "belongingness" can be satisfied by friends, religious groups, clubs of all varieties, and especially families, neighborhoods, even political parties. Much of belonging, as well as love and affection, is demonstrated by voluntary work to help others, in which love and affection can be exchanged in ever-increasing amounts. Not to be overlooked as part of belonging are clubs without meetings (e.g., Diners Club). In some cases dues or annual membership charges add snob appeal. In others, almost anybody can join and there are no dues or yearly fees.

Fourth in the hierarchy is the need for esteem, which Maslow classifies into two subsidiary sets: "the desire for strength, for achievement, for adequacy, for mastery and competence, for confidence in the face of the world and for independence and freedom," and "the desire for reputation or prestige (defining it as respect or esteem from other people), status, fame and glory, dominance, recognition, attention, importance, dignity or appreciation."

It is very likely that this need for esteem is at the root of the disadvantaged buyer's behavior in the buyer-seller-maker transaction. On the one hand, the buyer's desire for achievement, competence, and so forth induces him/her to believe too willingly and often incorrectly in the seller's knowledge and judgment about the product choice. On the other hand, the seller offers recognition, status, and attention to the buyer for having the "competence" to make the "best" judgment. While self-esteem and deserved respect are important in life's satisfactions, they can be detrimental in an ordinary transaction. For the consumer it is better to avoid the trap of believing that one's self-esteem is enhanced by responding to the flattery of the salesperson. In the buying situation the buyer should play it the other way. The buyer should emphasize his/her own competence to judge and not accept the supposed recognition and attention bestowed by the salesperson. If when doing so, the buyer may have an "even chance," or at least improve the odds.

The fifth need is self-actualization, or the desire for self-fulfillment—as Maslow says, "to become everything one is capable of becoming." This need is evidenced by a person's striving to finish college, finish graduate school, practice his/her chosen occupation, and receive recognition.

Our society attaches lots of labels to products that are "evidence" of self-fulfillment for the consumer. These include expensive cars, prestige neighborhoods, fancy vacations, fashionable and costly clothing, and hopelessly expensive French restaurants. Many people who are not otherwise shallow succumb to this stuff and really believe they have "achieved" through such indulgences.

While Maslow's hierarchy is useful, one should not believe that it unfolds in the same order for all people. Maslow makes it quite clear that this is not the case. The exceptions are many. They relate to habituation, or what one gets used to, and also to having had one's basic needs satisfied throughout one's life, especially in the younger years. The former seems to make people better able to adjust to continued deprivation, and the latter leads to increased tolerance for frustration.

This shifting of needs means viability rather than rigidity and contributes to the confusion in consumer affairs. Some people adjust to much lower self-actualization than others, and still others will even go hungry to fight for an ideal.

It is clear that people's motives differ in kind and intensity. The greater the intensity, the more persistent the behavior that results. Under such circumstances we say the individual is highly motivated. It is also true that we may incorrectly attribute a motive to the behavior observed. We know from clinical psychology that people cannot always state exactly what their motives are, especially when a combination of motives is involved.

Human behavior is more often complex than simple. In addition to temporary or transient chemical or physiological deficiencies that provoke behavior, there are also social situations and the pressures of society, particularly peer pressure.

At this point it is not extraneous to mention that too often it seems that the most acceptable form of behavior in peer groups is that which most closely matches the "lowest common denominator." This tends to lower rather than raise behavioral standards within the group.

Another factor that must be considered in any discussion of motivation is the role of anxiety; this will be discussed further when we examine the purchase process. A major function in the purchase process is the lack of balance until a decision is made. This is akin to anxiety. In other words, the social atmosphere can create an imbalance, and the individual, in attempting to achieve balance within the peer group, can become anxious.

This topic may be illustrated by asking people who smoke why they do so and getting them to remember the first time they smoked. Most people indicate that they started to smoke either because of peer pressure or to make it appear that they shared the characteristics of a group they wanted to belong to. One way to obtain acceptance was by doing as the group did—including smoking. Chances are, similar illustrations can be offered for marijuana, alcohol, manner of dress, even the restaurants where one wants to be seen.

A better understanding of the buyer-seller-maker transaction may be gained by referring to the system sponsored by Ellis (2) while keeping in mind Maslow's hierarchy of needs. Figure 4.1 presents a diagramatic view of the dynamics involved in the buyer-seller-maker transaction from the buyer's point of view. It is intended to show why and when things go right or wrong.

The A, B, C, D and E in the diagram is explained as follows: A may be a product, service, advertisement, or any other stimulus in the environment that activates the buyer-seller-maker transaction. B is belief. This is the opinion or perception the individual has about the product, store, or service. It may be rational or irrational, but it results in the decision to buy or not to buy. C is the consequence of the purchase, resulting in satisfaction or dissatisfaction with the product or service. When it is satisfactory all is well. When it is not satisfactory, then the individual is likely to blame the activator, that is, the store, product, or service, for being inadequate rather than becoming aware that his/her belief about the activator is what caused the problem. If the buyer had taken the time to find out what he/she needed to know, he/she would not have made the purchase.

Under such circumstances it is necessary to add D and E. D is disputing the false and irrational belief, that is, saying there was no rational basis to believe the advertisement or the retailer or the manufacturer. This leads to E, or effect. When D is successful, there are changes in the consequences—not buying the product, not believing the guarantee, not trusting the salesperson or store policy.

The value of applying this system to buyer-seller-maker transactions is that it can encourage modification of behavior based on rational growth. It places more responsibility for the

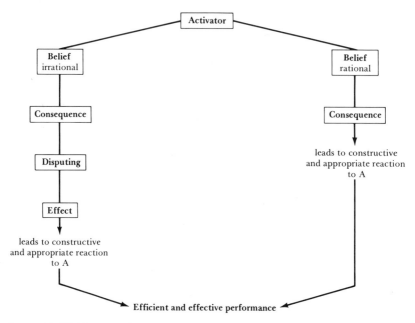

Source: Modified from A. Ellis, *Reason and Emotion in Psychotherapy*, New York: Lyle Stewart
1962, chap. 4, p. 77

FIGURE 4.1   The ABC's of Purchases

consequences on the buyer and makes him/her act in a more
aware and alert fashion.

The belief that an individual must be perfect should be recognized as irrational. No one is, or ever has been, perfect. Next to
this is the myth that you must be the best or buy the best or get
the best deal. Such goal-directed behavior is unrealistic for most
people. After all, if only one individual or company can be on top,
it doesn't mean everyone else has failed.

From the point of view of the consumer, goal-directed behavior should be more rational. It is much more realistic to get a
"good" buy. Chances are you cannot get the "best" buy within the
limits of time and money, let alone limited knowledge and personal energy costs. More realistically, chances are the "best" buy
does not exist; rather, quite a few equally "good" buys exist.

It is important to recognize that self-actualization is achieved
in relation to one's own abilities. Realistically, there is no such
thing as dreaming the impossible dream, and there is no such
thing as achieving the impossible achievement.

Maslow's theory recognizes that at any one time a person's behavior is dominated by any one of the five basic need classifications, usually the lowest one in the hierarchy that is unfilled.

In an affluent society most people are not hungry most of the time. However, it is true that all people are hungry some of the time. Some are hungrier than others because of either appetite or economic deprivation. When an individual's behavior is dominated by the need for food, then it is useless to talk about realizing his full potential. Individuals who are distraught by the lack of food are not likely to listen to such appeals. They are more likely to look for food.

For most of us, however, we generally eat because it is the time that we usually eat. What we eat is influenced by the time we have, the money we have, our habits, and our attitudes. We eat primarily for reasons other than hunger per se.

To oversimplify, consider why people buy meat, poultry, or fish. People's reasons for eating one or the other vary depending on many factors. However a better buy results when the unit price of meat, fish, or poultry is considered in relation to nutritional value. This varies with sales, supply, and season. More careful shopping can result in more nutritional meals in relation to the price paid. A good exercise in shopping would be to go to a supermarket and calculate the price per ounce for all varieties of all three items. One will probably be surprised to learn that, regardless of the nutrition value and regardless of store pricing policies, the difference between the lowest cost per ounce of any of the three items and the highest cost per ounce is likely to be quite large.

Along similar lines, the average person is unlikely to be aware of the costliness of some dry cereals compared to others. The size and appearance of the carton often mislead the consumer regarding content and weight. Prices are likely to vary with no apparent nutritional difference in favor of the higher-priced cereal. Not so amazingly, it often turns out that the higher the price, the lower the nutrition value.

The point to be emphasized in terms of consumer psychology is that it is not enough merely to state a theory of motivation. It is more important to encourage the individual to know more about him/her self and apply this knowledge to buyer-seller-maker transactions.

Maslow's theory, supplemented with the Ellis diagram, can offer a valuable growth experience. From the viewpoint of consumer psychology, the consumer should strive to reach category 5 in Maslow's theory—self-actualization. Probably the reason people flounder is that they are subjected to outside pressures and look for others to hand them self-actualization on a silver platter.

As mentioned earlier, word of mouth has great potency. Next in value to helping oneself is for peers to exchange information and be able to admit when a mistake has been made or a product does not meet expectations. Too often people conceal their mistakes, do not communicate, and thereby allow others to make the same wrong purchase decisions. What is needed is more word of mouth or consumer-to-consumer communication.

The misinformation offered by peers, salespeople, and advertising influence the consumer to make wrong decisions. Whatever it is that contributes to a product expectation that is out of line with reality, this is the basic cause of dissatisfaction. Why was the expectation too great? What lack of information or incorrect information contributed to this situation? In what way was all this related to the motives of the individual in making the purchase?

An important aspect of consumer psychology related to motivation is the fact that products and services may or may not become the objects of goal-directed behavior. The individual must realistically attempt to determine the degree to which the product or service is capable of fulfilling his/her expectations. More important, the individual should determine which is out of line, the expectation or the product.

When things are out of line it is much easier to blame others. It is at this point that business blames labor, the consumer activist blames business, and government passes laws that may or may not be related to either the problem or the solution.

The first step, then, is for the consumer to become better informed and more independent—to put it bluntly, more mature. It would be well to recognize that consumer-to-consumer communication as well as consumer-business transactions can be a considerable factor in the consumer's being misled. The individual must be more realistic in his expectations regarding products and must understand that personal motives may push the real product characteristics into false and imaginary ones.

Two illustrations may help. Regardless of whether he/she is buying a new car or a used one, and regardless of whether it is his/her first car purchase or nineteenth, somehow the buyer expects this situation to be different. Somehow the salesperson is believed to be more honest and the car is expected to be more perfect. This sort of expectation exceeds reality because neither the salesperson nor the car is likely to have better qualities than ever before. It is more realistic to recognize that one is trading different varieties of frustration along with the car purchase. It is less realistic to believe, as most people do, that one's present car is frustrating and the new car will not be.

The question is, What can the consumer do about it? How can expectations conform more to reality? Equally important is the question, When or how can the characteristics and performance of the car conform to reasonable expectations?

The second illustration relates to diets. What is there about dieting that allows magazines to publish a different diet every month and certain authors to sell diet books out of proportion to their effectiveness? The motives for going on a diet are endless. Referring to Maslow's hierarchy, one sees in dieting the attempt to achieve self-esteem and then self-actualization, in addition to the confusion between hunger and appetite.

When we do not understand our motives or others influence them disproportionately, we may be prevented from achieving self-actualization. Expectations of achievement rarely bring about achievement itself. In other words, in consumer psychology self-actualization means nothing more or less than the degree of adjustment or balance achieved by the individual in relation to his/her purposes and goals. Accepting what one is doing without being unhappy about it, rather than having the gnawing feeling that it could have been done differently or better, is at the core of adjustment. Such acceptance prevents feelings of anxiety. There is justification in the belief that one can make a better buy, but there is very little reason to believe one can make the best buy. There is every reason to take the initiative to obtain information before making a purchase. The purchase should be related to self-actualization rather than suggestions or even incorrect information coming from others with different goals and motives. Ultimately, then, self-actualization is the achievement or realization of the motives that allow an individual to live rationally and reasonably and with appropriate degrees of satisfaction or happiness. This can be achieved by the consumer through personal efforts much more readily than by waiting for someone else —government, consumer activists, advertising, salespeople, or what have you—to bring it about.

One cannot, however, end a chapter on motivation in consumer psychology with the hope that the consumer can be reasonably expected to achieve self-actualization on his/her own. The world and quite a few people in it can effectively block such an achievement. When this happens, then anger, aggression, frustration, and fear are the results.

In 1975, with inflation rampant and recession looking more like depression, quite a few supermarkets indulged in the practice of repricing or remarking food items—upward. They did this by the simple expedient of remarking merchandise already priced and on the shelves. Their explanation was that rising prices forced them to reprice. Consumers had trouble following this "logic." They tended to believe that the supermarket, knowing its costs and overhead, had probably priced the items correctly the first time. The supermarket managements said "not so"—that they were justified in repricing because they were paying more for the merchandise they were about to buy.

Needless to say, this resulted in some serious negative reactions on the part of consumers, including disbelief, lack of confidence, and mistrust. The general effects of inflation were causing consumers to feel anxious, resentful, and unable to cope. Their reactions to multiple pricing led to expressions of anger, outrage, and aggression. Some quotes from an interactional workshop reveal quite clearly the intensity of consumer feelings:

> "I'd like to punch out the grocer—just to get rid of that feeling of anxiety that I have after shopping."

> "I just get so angry and they're forever marking things up."

> "My feeling is one of outrage and I feel angry enough to tear at things in stores."

In other words, the buyer, especially of groceries, is tormented beyond the possible short-term gain achieved by supermarkets in repricing items already priced, especially since most grocery items have a high rate of turnover.

Thus, in essence, when expectations are not fulfilled one can predict hostility, aggression, anger, and frustration. Good business sense would seem to dictate that customers deserve better treatment—even if it is only for the good of business.

BIBLIOGRAPHY

1. MASLOW, A. H., *Motivation and Personality*, 2d ed. (New York: Harper & Row, 1970).
2. ELLIS, A., *Reason and Emotion in Psychotherapy* (New York: Lyle Stewart, 1962).

5
Learning to be a consumer

This chapter is intended to enable the reader to learn to modify his/her present attitudes and behavior in consumer affairs. Such learning can also enable the buyer to gain a better position in the typical buyer-seller-maker transaction. But first it is necessary to consider what the psychologist has to say about learning. Learning is evidenced by a change or a modification in a person's behavior or performance. It is different from other changes in behavior in that it can be performed repeatedly. Further evidence that learning has taken place occurs when the behavior change results in improved performance. Such performance is either smoother or better (a qualitative manifestation) or faster (a quantitative indicator).

In other words, an individual has learned something when a modified form of behavior can be repeated in a smoother, better, or faster manner. This applies to dressing, writing, skating, fishing, and cooking, as well as shopping. It also applies to abstract types of knowledge of the nonperformance variety usually called mental processes. These include subjects taught in school, such as languages, chemistry, consumer psychology, law, and economics.

Learning often facilitates thinking, reasoning, and problem solving, which, in turn, facilitate other individual performances.

Learning takes place in a variety of ways. Psychologists have made much of different theories of learning. But most agree that no one theory is distinctly superior to the others. They are in general agreement that different points are emphasized in different theories. One may learn by *association,* that is, associating A and B with each other, or one may learn by *contiguity,* that is, A and B are learned because they occur in close time proximity. One may also learn as a result of being rewarded for certain responses. This tends to reinforce the correct response, especially when incorrect responses are not rewarded.

One of the most popular terms used in theories of learning is *conditioning.* Briefly, conditioning has taken place when a stimulus evokes a response that ordinarily would not be the response to that stimulus. The classical example is the work of Pavlov. Food as a stimulus evokes the response, salivary flow. A bell sound presented prior to the giving of food, when repeated, can result in salivary flow. The stimulus (bell sound) now evokes the response (salivary flow). Ordinarily a bell sound would not evoke such a response; it now does so because of its sequential relation to the original stimulus, food.

In essence, learning takes place when stimulus and response relationships are strengthened.

An important component of learning is the prerequisite of motivation. One learns little without it. This is essentially true of the higher or more complex forms of learning. In addition to motivation, other terms and concepts are important. Concepts such as thinking and imagination and reasoning play a role. A combination of learning, thinking, reasoning, imagination, and a certain amount of fantasy leads to what can be regarded as the ultimate learning—creativity.

It is important to know that as a result of these higher mental processes, individuals can create new and improved means of communication. These, in turn, add greatly to knowledge. Thus learning has a dual significance. It is not only the ability to reproduce that which has been taught but also an additive process as new insights are gained. This is what leads to the creative process. For example, one will have learned about consumer psychology if one can repeat and understand the principles considered in this book. One will also have evidenced learning if one modifies one's behavior as a result of these principles. One shows the greatest degree of learning when one is able to add newer and more meaningful concepts to those that have already been learned.

Surely learning about consumer affairs, especially as it currently exists, can lead to improvements. Learning also implies greater ability to solve problems and, accordingly, reduce conflicts. In the buying situation, a person will manifest learning to the extent that the modification of behavior leads to better purchase decisions, thereby reducing the anxiety that can accompany the purchase process.

While considering learning one must not forget to consider *forgetting*, which is the deterioration of performance or the disappearance of knowledge that existed previously.

Psychologists who work in laboratories with animals or humans conduct experiments and, when successful, reach conclusions that describe more efficient ways to learn. They then label such findings in various ways. Four such concepts will be discussed here: *conditioning, reward, reinforcement,* and *response shaping.* These concepts are emphasized by many contemporary learning theorists. Each can have a direct bearing on modifying consumer behavior through the elimination or reduction of many extraneous factors that make the consumer a poor shopper because of deceitful or misleading advertising, overwhelming displays, false price reductions, and the like.

Operant conditioning is the likelihood of a voluntary response recurring because of an appropriate reinforcing event. Although Skinner (1) has worked for many years with rats and pigeons, he and others are totally aware of the varied possibilities of this form of learning.

With reference to the consumer, the voluntary response is buying a brand of canned goods that is marked down in price. The appropriate reinforcing event is that the food, when cooked, is just as tasty as it would be at its original price. Continuing to buy only marked-down cans of food, then, is the recurring response, which is always reinforced by the appropriate event—the equally tasty food.

How does this apply to the buyer of canned goods in a supermarket? Quite directly. The buyer's behavior is modified, since he/she buys only canned goods that are legitimately marked down in a retail outlet that honestly presents the original price and the reduced or sale price. Each time the buyer visits the store, only the sale or marked-down items are bought.

Whether or not one uses the term *operant conditioning* is unimportant. What is important is that a modification of behavior that is rewarding to the buyer has occurred.

Two other terms emphasized by psychologists in considering learning are *reward* and *reinforcement.* Offering rewards to people who learn—higher grades, compliments on a better casserole, expressions of how well you look—can create conditions that encourage faster and more effective modification of behavior.

Reinforcement is essentially the presentation of a sought

response that encourages the repetition of a voluntary response; an example is continuing to buy tasty food at lower prices after being complimented for this achievement.

The fourth concept is *response shaping,* the rewarding of responses that approximate the desired final response. For example, the buyer reads the food ads in the local newspaper and makes a list of advertised prices, equating for size, brand, and so on. This shapes the response, and the person shops at the store with the lowest prices. In the case of appliances, liquor, mattresses, or any other item where brands play an important role, the preferred brand may be bought at the outlet with the cheapest price or, if one judges various brands to be comparable, the lowest-priced brand may be bought.

Little or nothing has been done to educate people as consumers. Much confusion results from the general belief that experience is the best teacher. The problem is that experience may or may not result in learning.

For example, continually buying the same brand because one has had a favorable experience with that brand may or may not be justified. It is justified if nothing new has appeared that is better. It is not justified if a new, better, more economical item appears. This may apply, for instance, to preferences for coffee beans, ground coffee, or instant. Such preferences may be justified on the basis of experience, whereas blindfold tests may prove that these preferences really do not exist.

The typical shopper repeating the same shopping experience in the same ineffective manner is not demonstrating any form of learning. Whether the purchase is coffee, meat, or any other food or nonfood item, experience may have nothing to do with becoming a better shopper.

Many consumers, quite irrationally, become defensive and refuse to modify their behavior. Continually repeating a purchase because one knows the characteristics of the product may prevent learning about different or newer products. The lack of ability or willingness to modify behavior can be called nonlearning. The consumer's previous experience may tell him/her that changes in brands or retail outlets sometimes result in inefficient behavior.

There are many variables and stimuli impinging on the consumer. Why do we prefer certain brands of coffee, refrigerators, or automobiles and not others? Why do we prefer specific retail outlets and not others? Too often the answer is experience. The problem is whether the experience has been varied or complete enough to indicate the possibility of continued learning. Do we stop the learning process before it has run its full course?

Surely one semester of a foreign language is evidence of some learning; the second semester is different and broader in scope—evidence of additional learning. By the same token, if one continues to shop the same way, the learning process may have stopped; for all practical purposes one repeats the first semester over and over. One has not added scope, varied one's opportunities, or created a better way of fulfilling one's objectives as a consumer.

Intimately related to the question of consumer learning is the question of whether the consumer should learn to be dependent or independent. The "protectors" of consumer interests, be they consumer advocates, government officials, or business in general, regardless of their intentions or motives, may make the typical consumer too dependent. A dependent consumer learns less. The motives to learn tend to be dulled by the offer of an easier way out—"believe in me and I will protect you." The point to be emphasized is that the person who claims to know what is best for the consumer may be a poor substitute for the learning that the consumer needs most.

This should not be taken to imply an ulterior or unscrupulous motive on the part of the "protectors." However, it may well be that, in all innocence, they are discouraging or inhibiting learning, which is surely a growth process that must continue throughout one's life. Imagine an overly protective parent who continues to feed an infant into childhood. This would inhibit the child from learning to eat alone and result in too much dependency.

The thesis offered is that all means should be taken to develop an independent consumer who is taught to assume responsibility, especially in the realm of purchase decision making. For example, studies show that the consumer regards supermarket shopping as a chore for which he/she has little time or liking. However, other studies show that the typical consumer could save from 15 percent to 20 percent; sometimes more, on his/her food bill by learning to modify his/her buying behavior.

The following suggestions may help stretch the family budget:

1. Pay attention to newspaper advertisements of weekend specials.
2. Comparison shop; this means buying various items in two or more outlets even though it may be less convenient and more time-consuming. (Here one must balance the cost of gas against the saving in the cost of food.)
3. Pay attention to unit pricing and either shop at stores that

display unit price as well as total price or use a calculator. In addition to the battery-operated calculator, which is in the $20 price range, there are slide rule calculators that are easily used and cost very little.

4. Pay attention to date labeling for freshness and shelf life. Insist that the manager decode in the event that the chain does not openly reveal shelf life or expiration dates. If every shopper insisted that the manager decode the can to reveal its shelf life, he, in turn, would soon have to tell his boss that his managerial duties are being disrupted by requests for can decoding. The consumer has a right to have information about products, but only the consumer can insist on it. The supermarkets and food processors have reasons for not wanting to share this information.

5. Pay attention not only to nutrition labeling but to the nutritional value of different types of foods. For example, when tomatoes approach the price per pound of chuck meat, then tomatoes should not be bought.

6. Pay attention to grade labeling. Prime meats are of higher quality, are higher priced, and have a higher fat content. In the main they are not the best-priced value. Choice cuts generally offer better price values.

7. Don't buy if the price of an item or food category suddenly rises. In what is supposed to be a free economy, prices are a reflection of supply and demand. A discussion of whether or not this is true could fill another book. But in the meantime don't buy when the price is up. Remember that supermarkets must have both volume and turnover to be successful.

The suggestion that one should not buy items whose price is skyrocketing is often countered by the statement that "everything is going up." Be it food or automobiles or any other item, the consumer should learn that not buying will create a large inventory in the seller's hands. Such inventories mean overstocking, with its resulting expenses because of food spoilage or interest charges on car inventories. Sooner or later, if the consumer acts rationally, the prices come down or price rebates are offered. At that time the consumer should buy such items.

The shopper who hoards is not acting in the best interests of consumers or, for that matter, his/her own. Shortages, rumored or real, of sugar, gasoline, even toilet paper often result in buying rushes, which, in turn, can bring about a shortage that otherwise would not have existed. Besides, how much sugar can the average person buy and store, and for how long? Chances are, shortages, even if real, would disappear if consumers acted rationally and bought as little as possible rather than overbuying.

What is needed is a change in attitude and behavior as a consumer. Feelings of powerlessness must be changed to feelings of self-esteem. A change in the self must take place and efforts to influence existing conditions in the marketplace are necessary. The consumer must learn to exert more authority and not to accept the denigrating role of powerlessness.

A change in buying behavior is also required. Purchases should change with price increases, sales, and season. Buying less, or lower priced items or those without "convenience" features can exert an influence in the marketplace. Consumer self-esteem rises as one sees an ability to influence price and service in transactions.

One should also be aware that offering information does not necessarily lead to learning. Evidence of learning exists when there has been a modification of behavior and in the direction or achievement of certain goals. Accordingly, making information available to consumers or, for that matter, passing new laws will benefit consumers only if they modify their behavior as a result. If one passed a law requiring unit pricing or date labeling and consumers did not base their selections on either unit pricing or date labeling, then such laws would appear to be ineffective. (However, recent evidence has shown that food manufacturers will modify the ingredients of certain items to match those of competitors. This side effect, oddly enough, benefits the consumer who "just sits there.") In short, information leads to learning only when modification of behavior takes place.

A good example of helpful information is found in eight pamphlets put out by a supermarket chain in Florida known as PUBLIX (2). They offer shopping information on fresh fruit, fresh vegetables, outdoor eating, beef, dairy, cheese, deli, and unit pricing. Merely being aware that such pamphlets exist— even reading them—is not learning. Modifying one's purchase behavior as a result of understanding the information given is evidence of learning.

The pamphlets offer information such as the following:

1. A major point in purchasing fruit is to save money by getting it in season. Different fruits ripen at different times of the year and depending on geographic location. Other things being equal, fresh vegetables and fruits are likely to be priced in relation to their seasonality.

2. With reference to meats, the more marbling, the higher the quality and the price. Bones identify the seven groups of retail cuts of meats (e.g., rib, loin, breast). Fancy names such as London Broil or His and Her Steaks are meaningless. By law, ground beef is limited to a maximum fat content of 30 percent; it may come from the flank, shank, or loin.

3. With reference to dairy foods, milk comes in many forms such as fresh, evaporated, or dry. The evaporated and dry milks cost less. Both tend to have the same nutritional value but obviously do not have the bulk because the water has been removed.

4. Cheeses vary as much by price as by variety. Aged cheese generally costs more because of the cost in time for curing.

5. For most foods, consideration of unit pricing is a must. However, most supermarket items are priced by the package, and packages for such smaller foods as dry cereals and crackers vary considerably per ounce. For most foods the important unit is price per ounce.

While it is true that it is necessary to check grade labeling or quality against price per ounce, family taste should determine the degree to which a higher quality is more desirable than a lower quality. Taste preferences, as well as manner or style of cooking, can compensate for price and quality differences.

An interesting point about this series of pamphlets is that practically all of the information furnished is intended to benefit the consumer; only a small reference is made to the chain itself, and puffery is practically nonexistent.

Another form of consumer information that should be learned—that is, that should result in the modification of behavior—is the information in "consumer" buying guides. However, it is important for consumers to recognize the accuracy and objectivity of the source. Certain of these books or pamphlets may actually serve as helpful references, especially when purchases are being considered in which the purchase cycle is infrequent, for example, furniture or refrigerators.

An illustration of a consumer buying guide is the one published by the Better Business Bureau (3). It attempts to communicate to the consumer the fact that needs are best served by buying from reliable businessmen and suggests that consumers be wary of unusual bargains and pay careful attention to contracts before agreeing to a purchase.

The guide advises consumers to be wary of the "bait and

switch" policy of some businesses, in which they advertise low-priced items such as television sets and then advise you not to buy them and switch you to higher-priced items. It also warns consumers to be wary of statements like "we sell for less," "less than cost," "won't be undersold," and "below wholesale."

Consumer buying guides are also useful insofar as they inform the consumer of what to look for in buying furniture, carpeting, appliances, home improvements, automobiles, even clothing and dry cleaning. These services plus the *Consumers Union* and *Consumer Reports,* as well as the abundance of government publications and local consumer law enforcement agencies, are available. The consumer must learn their content and availability and modify potentially faulty behavior before making a purchase.

The extent to which businessmen are honest or dishonest should not be the basic question for debate. A fundamental of consumer psychology is the need to encourage learning or modification of consumer behavior. An independent consumer is one who takes steps to protect him/herself rather than having others do the protecting. He/she must seek out the information and make purchase decisions based on available facts. In short, he/she must *learn* to be a better and more efficient consumer instead of depending on experience alone.

BIBLIOGRAPHY

1. SKINNER, B. F., *The Behavior of Organisms* (Englewood Cliffs, N.J.: Prentice-Hall, 1938).
2. Pamphlets from Publix Supermarkets, Florida.
3. *Consumer's Buying Guide, How to Get Your Money's Worth* (New York: Rutledge Books and Benjamin, 1969).

6

Will the real personality please stand?

Part I of this book, which attempts to integrate typical psychological areas and consumer affairs, has led from perception to attitude, motivation, learning, and finally, personality. The order of presentation is related to the extent of the contribution of each topic to the field of consumer psychology.

In their study of personality psychologists have uncovered little material that can be applied to benefit consumers. In fact much has been misapplied by nonpsychologists. Nevertheless, it is valuable to review some of the theories and approaches to the study of personality to see how they may benefit consumer psychology.

An outstanding example of an exercise in futility is the attempt to relate personality traits to specific products. Scores of studies have been conducted, but not a single one has found a relationship of any consequence. In other words, attempts to relate users of certain products with particular personality traits have led nowhere.

Other researchers have attempted to find the characteristics of innovators, that is, those who are the first to use a new product or brand. While the problem is intriguing, the results are quite confusing and mainly negative. There is no known characteristic common to "innovators." The only finding of any significance is that some consumers believe certain products give them status or prestige—an example might be a Cadillac or

Mercedes. In reality, however, status and prestige, if deserved, must be obtained in other ways.

Studies of users of certain brands of cars, coffee, and so forth do not establish any findings of consequence relating the product to personality traits. In fact the personality trait approach may itself be sterile. Quite a few psychologists no longer believe in the trait approach as a basis for understanding personality.

What is known is that brands become more or less popular over time. Not so long ago Colgate was the largest-selling brand of toothpaste. Now it is not. It would be futile to believe that people's personalities changed. It would be more logical to believe that another toothpaste came along that appealed to their anxieties better than Colgate. What brand will be tomorrow's best seller? It may well be one that is not on the market today.

Another example relates to supermarkets. Not so long ago the Great Atlantic and Pacific Tea Company, better known as the A&P, was quite important in many cities, but now these stores are losing market share in many areas. Should this change be attributed to new, more appealing retailing techniques on the part of other chains, with the A&P falling behind because it hasn't changed, or to personality changes among consumers? In fact, supermarkets as we know them may not be here forever. Thus any attempt to establish a relationship between personality and brand (or retailer) just does not work—and probably never will. What does seem to work for the seller is an attempt to either increase or decrease an individual's anxiety about a particular product. As the consumer becomes more rational and mature, this will not work either.

The advertiser attempts to discover and use appeals that are related to such conflicts. They ferret out people's anxieties and hope the consumer will believe that by using a particular brand he/she will be able to reduce those anxieties. This approach is fairly successful, even though a particular toothpaste, coffee, car, or what have you will not change personality characteristics or even match them.

Advertisers also attempt to recognize trends. For example, large mass magazines such as *Life* and *Look* have, for all practical purposes, disappeared; more specialized types of magazines seem to be more popular. Once again, this change has probably occurred because of the role of other mass media—especially color television—rather than changes in personality.

An individual is continually changing whether awake or asleep. Chemical, physical, physiological, and social conditions, separately or in combination, make the person somewhat different from one day to the next. The individual is continuously bombarded by stimuli; knowingly or unknowingly, he/she makes positive or negative judgments related to these stimuli. Watch some prime-time television and count the commercials. There are as many as 15 or 20 per hour. One can begin to see the pressure to use one or another headache remedy, buy one or another dog food, toy, appliance, and so on.

In considering the purchase process, it is important to recognize that the products and services others want us to use are (supposedly) related to our own needs, hopes, wants, and expectations. We have seen that knowledge of consumer psychology can lead to a better understanding of oneself as well as a better knowledge of the uses and claims of products and services. This understanding can be valuable in reducing the conflicts induced by advertising and should allow the personality to be normal or at least able to dismiss certain appeals as inappropriate.

The interplay between business and its products on the one hand and the individual's needs on the other does create anxiety. Foods to make you thin, detergents to get things whiter, toothpastes to make you popular, or cosmetics to make you smell either nice or different are more or less playing on that anxiety.

Just think of the array of products and appeals. In clothing, you can run a complete gamut from diapers to mink coats; in toys, a complete range from rattles to golf carts. Many products are advertised as offering continuous and excessive happiness. Take pleasure boats, for example. But boats break down just like anything else. An individual who is unhappy, and believes a boat can make him happy can buy a boat—and with it an additional cause of unhappiness: the boat that needs repair.

It is important for the consumer to recognize that products and services will basically do very little to change one's personality to any degree or for any appreciable time. This is not to suggest that we should all go back to Thoreau's Walden, but we can obtain satisfaction from products and services provided that we are able to recognize the relationship between the reality of the product or service and our expectation of the degree to which that product or service will be satisfactory.

Most of us want to maintain a sanitary and healthy posture as well as to be accepted and loved, so we prefer not to be dirty or smelly. However, the products that claim to get things whiter, prevent bad smells, or create good smells seem to be pushing beyond rationality by creating anxiety in people. When successful from the point of view of product sale, they create oversensitivity and fear. Products that claim they prevent body odors do sell. People with and without body odors do buy them. The latter group does so because of concern, fear, or anxiety. Such appeals cater to the insecurities in people and may even create personality problems that otherwise might not exist. Advertising does a disservice when it creates worry, fear, or anxiety.

The lonely and unhappy person who expects a dance course, cruise, or new house to solve his/her personal problems may be in for more conflict, more loneliness, and more unhappiness. A maladjusted individual may benefit by the use of appropriate acquisitions, but the new acquisition is hardly ever equal to psychotherapy. For example, if one needs a new car because one is being inconvenienced or even frustrated by the present one, and if one does not have the money to buy a new car, then one must decide whether the hoped-for positive features of the new car will overbalance the negative pressure of being in debt.

Too often the product or service that was supposed to change the buyer's personality may be doing damage by creating more worries and less self-esteem.

The anxiety created by indebtedness causes various personalities to react quite differently. Some people worry a great deal and others rationalize in an effort to absolve themselves from responsibility. Such conflicts are often a result of purchasing a product for the wrong reason. The product is supposed to change or improve one's personality—but the likelihood that a product can do this is exceedingly remote. Too many consumers either learn this the hard way or never seem to learn at all.

Purchasing a product and going into debt illustrates confusion of cause and effect. The buyer hopes the product will make him/her more popular—a car, for example, is supposed to promote dating possibilities. But suppose the car does not attract dates and the debt creates serious conflicts. Then things are worse, not better.

Anxiety is a diffuse or persistent state of apprehension. Too often the cause is not known but the feeling or state is present and painful. Very often people say "I feel anxious" and indicate that they do not know what they feel anxious about. To a degree, the popular word *anxious* is the equivalent of the technical word *anxiety*.

It is quite possible that a full-blown state of anxiety results in the most severe and painful neurosis an individual can suffer. A normal person, aware of conflicts and their attendant anxieties, learns to adjust and relieve the conflict. According to Hoch and Zubin (1), anxiety is the most pervasive psychological phenomenon of our time; as Levitt (2) points out, it begins in infancy with a fear of the unknown and concludes with a fear of the unknown that is death.

Words like *stress* and *tension* are not too different in usage from the term *anxiety* except that they refer to a description of the physical condition accompanying anxiety rather than to anxiety itself.

It should be recognized that a lack of equilibrium exists during the purchase process. Anxiety, or a state closely resembling it, occurs until balance is restored as a result of the purchase decision. It is primarily for reasons related to what the buyer-seller-maker transaction does to the consumer's personality problems that it is advisable to include personality in a study of consumer psychology.

Anxiety is probably at the core of personality problems in this field. In a much different context but one that is nevertheless appropriate, Freud studied the defenses individuals build to try and contend with anxiety. Two ways commonly used are avoidance and denial. In other words, a consumer builds defenses to relieve anxiety. An illustration of avoidance has a shopper avoiding a visit to his/her favorite department store. This prevents or avoids the fear of buying another item of clothing.

An illustration of denial is refusing to recognize the situation or event that provokes the anxiety. An example of denial is when a person refuses to fly in a plane. Obviously this denial is related to the fear of death as a result of an accident while flying. Why do people avoid wearing seat belts? It may well be that not wearing seat belts on the trip from home to the supermarket is a denial that an accident is likely to occur on such a short trip in such familiar surroundings. The denial of the possibility of accident is encouraged by not wearing a seat belt, which is an assumption of safety, or the opposite of the anxiety that fear of an accident provokes. However, there are many other defenses, such as compulsiveness, which occurs in an exaggeration of miserliness that is not justified by one's financial situation. On the other hand, anxiety may not be all that bad. Its presence can modify behavior, as in learning to shop more efficiently.

Anxiety in individuals can spread from one to another. An anxious person can provoke others, and so a fear that there may not be enough sugar or gasoline can cause a panic. The opposite is cooperative, calm, reasoned behavior.

Not buying perishables such as meat or vegetables can cause prices to go down. Anxiety resulting in the premature fear of "starving" will result in excessive buying, and this generally results in rising prices.

Another concept related to personality deserving of serious attention in any study of consumer psychology is the view that frustration can produce aggression (3). This idea presents a most interesting hypothesis that is too often overlooked as a contemporary explanation of a phenomenon found in many walks of life from the behavior of minorities in or out of ghettos to the behavior of consumers. Simply stated, it recognizes that frustration can produce aggression as well as withdrawal or depression. People who are frustrated by denial or are unable to cope with a challenge may withdraw or become depressed. In other words, they may give up. Searching for the food or clothes one can afford during a period of inflation or unemployment may often result in feelings of depression because one cannot afford to make the needed purchase. On the other hand, it can result in aggressive behavior. A mild form is illustrated by the person who honks his/her horn in stalled traffic. More serious would be attacking people or property because one's minimum needs cannot be fulfilled.

A supermarket shopping study on pricing indicated that consumers frustrated by rising prices felt or acted aggressively rather than becoming apathetic and withdrawn. Although people differ in aggressiveness, even nonaggressive people may, under certain circumstances, demonstrate aggressive behavior.

To be sure, there are many theories that explain the contemporary development of personality, but in a book on consumer psychology it is not necessary to look at all of these theories. In general terms, the unfolding of personality is probably related to parental acceptance—primarily by the mother but also by the father. When there is parental acceptance there is generally a basic trust in the self and the world, and this type of relationship develops security.

It is important for a consumer to know about personality and personality development. A more complete knowledge will help him/her better understand the needs and behaviors of others if not the self. In other words, not every salesperson should be believed. Further, the nonsensical appeals of some ads should be laughed at rather than taken seriously.

Some of the personality theories that have attracted considerable attention include Freud's (psychoanalysis), Jung's (analytic), Adler's (individual), and Sullivan's (interpersonal), among others. These, along with Maslow and Ellis, can give the consumer considerable insight.

As is well known, Freud created a specific type of therapy, known as psychoanalysis, that recognized that present personality problems have their roots in the past. His view was that problems could be better understood by paying attention to dreams, manifestations of the unconscious, and the role of sex, which is manifested in various ways from the earliest years of life. For a while "motivation research" was popular in market research; it was supposed to have come from Freud and his emphasis on the unconscious.

Jung was one of the many followers of Freud to break away and offer his own theory of personality. His contributions include the concept of opposites, such as the introvert-extrovert dimension, and some that are more esoteric, such as the collective unconscious and the archetype.

Adler was another who broke with Freud. He emphasized the individual's striving toward superiority or perfection and the resulting inferiority feelings as the individual failed to achieve his goals. Much advertising directly or indirectly plays on this theme.

Sullivan's work emphasizes interpersonal relations, and much of what is accepted in current therapies can be traced to Sullivan's work. Sullivan considered dynamisms to be recurring behavior patterns, especially as they involve other human beings.

One could describe many additional contributors to personality theory. However, from the point of view of consumer psychology the views just presented should provide sufficient understanding of the term *personality* as it relates to consumer psychology and consumer affairs.

Assuming that a worthy pursuit in the development of an individual is a mature personality, then it is necessary to recognize the *affects* as well as *effects* of prior events on the present status of the personality involved. It is also necessary to recognize one's present role and the degree to which that role produces satisfaction or dissatisfaction.

The recognition of various dichotomies—introvert-extrovert, egghead-squarehead, buyer-seller—must also be recognized as contributing to individual differences as people relate, for better or worse, to each other. Such awareness helps in understanding some of the conflicts that exist in the marketplace.

To summarize, personality describes the characteristics an individual possesses which attributes to a uniqueness that differentiates a person from all others. In addition to traits, such factors as affect, role, and dichotomy must also be considered an integral part. Affect describes the feelings and expressions of the individual as a result of the kinds of interactions involved with products, services, and people. A person reacts differently even to the identical stimulus presented on two different occasions. This often depends on the affective state as it is related to price increases, product failure, poor service, sales tactics, and advertising appeals or degree of frustration whether it be actual or perceived. This explains why one person explodes while on a food stamp line or why another person explodes while on line for a plane ticket. Furthermore, it is not always the same person who explodes.

Role and personality are also intertwined. The roles we assume or are assigned often predetermine the way we are described or act. The consumer should initiate role changes as frequently as a chameleon changes color.

Polarization is the intensification and final result of reacting too literally to dichotomies that are offered to explain degrees of difference. The results of polarization either increase conflict or break communication; they never reduce conflict.

Consumers differ. There are as many different personalities as there are consumers. Since personalities are involved in market transactions, an understanding of the manifestations of personality can increase effectiveness for the consumer.

A better understanding of personality can promote further insights into oneself as well as others. When this understanding is successfully applied, then fewer and fewer ads that promise personality "improvements" will be successful. In addition, salespeople playing on the same theme will be less effective.

It is normal for individuals to want to be accepted and loved. However, the consumer must unequivocally understand that such needs are not likely to be fulfilled by products or services.

Further, buyers, sellers, and makers have incongruent goals. Each seeks his/her own satisfaction, quite often to the exclusion of others'. This is at the root of the conflicts that exist in the marketplace.

It is necessary for the consumer to have a better understanding of his/her own personality as well as that of others. He/she also should gain greater insight into the degree to which products relate to personality. Most important, the consumer should make purchase decisions on the basis of functional and realistic needs.

BIBLIOGRAPHY

1. HOCH, P. H., and J. ZUBIN, eds., *Anxiety* (New York: Grune & Stratton, 1950).
2. LEVITT, E. E., *The Psychology of Anxiety* (Indianapolis: Bobbs-Merrill, 1967).
3. DOLLARD, J., et al., *Frustration and Aggression* (New Haven, Conn.: Yale University Press, 1939).

2

RESEARCH
AS A TOOL

The findings of psychology in general, and consumer psychology in particular, rely heavily on research. The research methods in many of the social sciences both overlap and differ, and the same goes for marketing research and consumer research.

This section is intended primarily to indicate why research is necessary in consumer psychology and to describe three quite different methods: observation, interactional workshops of a qualitative nature, and quantitative research.

The following four chapters will not turn the reader into a researcher. They are intended to be descriptive and illustrative. Other sources treat this subject in greater depth. For the person whose goal is to become a better consumer, these chapters are intended to offer some information as well as an opportunity to enhance a better understanding of the research process.

7

Why consumer research?

Consumer research should be conducted for both general and specific reasons. The general purpose of research is to gather facts leading to conclusions and, it is hoped, principles, laws, or generalizations. Research can also aid in determining the cost effectiveness of various policies and practices.

The specific reason for conducting consumer research is to help consumers, business, and government by obtaining facts that can help solve problems, reduce conflicts, and lead to a better understanding of consumer affairs.

More specifically, consumer research should furnish needed information to the consumer to aid in buying decisions as well as to establish appropriate standards in order to preserve health and safety.

For government, consumer research should weigh heavily in the establishment and modification of information used in setting public policy.

For business, at long last, there should be a clear and unequivocal differentiation between market research and consumer research. Business needs to conduct consumer research in order to better understand the issues involved in consumer affairs, especially as these issues are perceived by consumers. A total consumer research program involves far more than handling complaints.

What consumer research should emphasize is not a study

of past conflicts and problems but, rather, the development of ways to solve emerging problems before they become serious.

Consumer research should study the policies and practices of sellers and makers as well as their products and services. This information, if made available to consumers, would make the odds in the buying "game" somewhat more even. To a degree *Consumer Reports* does this.

The fact that we live in a marketing and service society creates certain problems. In some instances the public health or safety may be jeopardized. In other instances consumers may be deceived or otherwise put at a disadvantage.

It would be valuable to establish a list of priorities focusing attention on the problems most in need of solution. In other words, it is important to recognize the unfulfilled needs of the consumer. Surely there is a need to measure consumer satisfaction on a broad and comprehensive scale. Surprisingly little is known about the consumer's view of the purchase process itself. Such knowledge requires more than a study at the moment of purchase. It must include pre- as well as post-purchase attitudes and behavior on a longitudinal rather than a one-shot basis.

The problem of improving the environment by eliminating air and water pollution will become an increasingly intense issue illustrating the frictions of business and public interaction. The solutions offered will be many, but research can obtain data on the priorities in the minds of the public. Such surveys can measure the intensity of feelings on the part of the consumer as well as the perceptions of business. In turn, business would do well to learn the extent to which its pronouncements are believed. If in some instances it is not believed, then it should "tell it like it is."

There are a host of issues affecting the interaction between business and the consumer, but many can be generalized as resulting from business' emphasis on marketing. This emphasis has led to mistrust on the part of consumers, and it becomes increasingly urgent to know the extent to which they are dissatisfied, defrauded, or damaged. In some instances the deleterious effects may be greater than in others. Surely a survey of consumer issues and consumer reactions should attempt to place in relative perspective such factors as unit pricing, packaging, guarantees, product servicing, credit cards, sales policies (door to door, mail, etc.), advertising, and games, premiums, or giveaways.

Solving complex social problems generally results in the creation of new problems in need of solution. It is for this reason that changes in attitudes and behavior, especially following changes in codes, laws, and practices, must be known. There is a need to know how change can affect behavior, but we hardly ever take the time to measure any change that has taken place. Further, studies to determine the needs and priorities of the poor, the affluent, the young, the aged, and so forth, would be helpful.

Research should be done for the purpose of benefiting society as a whole. Consumer research, if properly conducted, can help. Possible subjects include the effects and use of drugs, the effects of misrepresentation—short of fraud—as well as the need for convenience as a style of life.

It is for these reasons that consumer research is necessary. When some businesses develop consumer affairs departments to better understand the consumer, a small step will have been taken. When business actually researches its customers' problems from the point of view of the consumer, in addition to studying its own marketing problems, it will have taken a bigger step.

When funds and facilities are available for consumer groups to conduct their own independent research, no matter where the funds come from, the biggest step of all will have been taken. The primary need is that the research be directly related to consumer affairs and issues.

The next three chapters will describe observational, qualitative, and quantitative research techniques as they relate to consumer research and psychology. In the remainder of this chapter we will discuss the question, What is wrong with research? The answer is simple but shocking. One would expect research to be the height of honesty. The naive person cannot believe that sound scientific methods can lead to unsound conclusions. Unfortunately, however, they can and they do.

The two major sins of research are just plain stupidity and downright dishonesty. One does not have to pass a test of ethics, honesty, or intelligence to conduct research. Using inappropriate methods, ignorantly asking the wrong questions, or misapplying or stretching the findings can be a result of stupidity. However, deliberately asking leading questions or doing the research in order to justify currently held views is dishonest or borders on dishonesty. The alleged conclusions of some market research studies that the consumer sees popularized on television are quite unreal. In addition, magazine audience research leaves much to be desired. Sometimes it seems as if everyone wins except the consumer.

Years ago, a misapplication of intelligence test results suggested that the average adult had a mental age of 14. Some of the "tests" on television allow the viewer to infer that the average consumer also has a mental age of 14.

The point is that almost anything can be used for good or bad purposes. This applies to market research in the guise of consumer research. Research used dishonestly debases all research to the extent that many consumers form prejudices, overgeneralize, and deny that any research is honest.

Whereas it might be hoped that research could lead one out of the morass of intensifying conflict by objectively gathering data and reporting the results, in fact it is sometimes deliberately used to further confuse the issues.

When attitude measures are represented as behavior or assumed to be predictors of behavior we have either confusion, stupidity, or dishonesty. Thus lobbyists use research to further their own means and ends. The consumer must be trained to be cautious, wary, and also to challenge those who falsify research or bias their findings in a predetermined direction.

The truth is that research is no panacea. Not all research measures up to scientific standards or, for that matter, is equally in quest of knowledge. Some of it deliberately misleads the consumer.

Market research is conducted to gain a competitive advantage, but consumer research is, or should be, conducted to reduce the conflicts and dissatisfactions of consumers. In this connection one should not overlook the potential ethical dilemmas of consumer research. It is especially important that consumer research not be biased or directed. And it is important to be aware that many things called consumer research simply are not.

Anyone conducting ethical research has to be responsible for that research. Sometimes research is planned so that it leads to biased and erroneous conclusions by taking advantage of the favorable image of research.

Another ethical issue arises in connection with the source of financial support. The issue is whether the acceptance of financial support associates the researcher with the goal of the sponsor, be it a company, a government agency, or a foundation.

Conflicts resulting from consumer research can be avoided if a simple code is followed. First, the client must understand and agree that the researcher will be solely responsible for the design of the methodology, the selection of subjects, the interpretation of data, and the drawing of conclusions. Further, the sponsor must agree that beyond reporting the results no further use of the findings may be made without the knowledge and consent of the researcher.

In addition to establishing the need for ethical research, it is important to include some illustrations of the variety of research included in the category of consumer research. A most valuable paper is offered by Ross (1), whose bibliography includes close to 150 articles. He is a fair critic in pointing up the shortcomings of the methods as well as conclusions of many of the research studies he analyzes in his quest for ways to make research play a more important and meaningful role. The following quote deserves attention:

> Consumer behavior theory and empirical findings in the general case of consumer information handling has not been systematically applied to researchable questions raised by current and proposed public policy affecting consumer behavior. What we do know about consumer information handling should suggest to us that most of the questions raised require a much richer, more complex research approach than those which have been employed in the material reviewed here. No doubt the fact that public or private research support is difficult to obtain in magnitude sufficient to execute high quality research is a partial explanation of our lack of apparent research effort, for, as in all surges of applications of the behavioral sciences to real world problems, the research goes where the money is." (page 59)

Ross perceives a research need in consumer information to be a function of protection. He conceptualizes it in three ways: "more and better information with which consumers can make decisions, product safety/quality, and better 'post purchase' treatment in the event of dissatisfaction." He organizes his review of the literature into two main categories, consumer information handling and its application to public policy. He is polite but firm in indicating the gaps as well as, at times, the inappropriateness or unrelatedness of the findings. He points out that "empirical studies have generally not addressed the problem of the *quality* of the consumer's information seeking and handling."

With reference to public policy, Ross reviews the literature covering such topics as unit pricing, nutrient labeling, open dating of foods, other packaging and labeling issues, disclosure of interest rates, corrective advertising, counteradvertising, deceptive advertising, other advertising issues, and the use and value of consumer product-rating publications.

A most valuable technique used by Ross is the presentation and comparison of six studies on unit pricing. Table 7.1 presents his data.

TABLE 7.1 Summary of unit-pricing studies

Source	Bureau of Advertising (1971) (New York City)	Lamont and Rothe (1971) (King Sooper, Denver)	Coyle (1971) (Jewel Tea, Chicago)
Sample	222 women shoppers in various supermarkets in four boroughs of NYC. Biased upward in age and education. Personal interviews	2330 households, telephone sample, and 177 mail responses from metro Denver	517 personal interviews one month after intro and 429 three months after intro
Time Period	6/5/71, four days after effective date of NYC's unit-pricing regulation	telephone survey 2 mos. after intro of unit-pricing (9/22/70), mail survey soon afterwards	1 month and 3 months after intro of unit-pricing (on 3/70)
% Aware and Attributes	69% aware—those with college backgrounds and those younger were more aware	After 2 mos., 68% were aware (82% for those already King Sooper shoppers); more awareness in high occup. and income	47% aware 1 mo. after and 63% aware 3 mos. after; 99% aware in "white collar neighborhood" but only 29% in black neighborhood
Degree of Understanding of Unit-Pricing	Of total shoppers, 43% had "complete" understanding and 16% had "possible" understanding; after brief explanation, almost all able to understand	—	—
Usage of Unit-Pricing in Buying	About half of those aware reported usage. Those spending more on trip reported more usage	53% King Sooper shoppers reported having used info; "users" were younger, higher occup., less store loyal, and motives were quality and price rather than service or convenience	44% had used 1 mo. after and 45% 3 mos. after (30% used "regularly"). More usage in high educ. and income: 72% used in white collar neighborhood; 14% in black.
Consumer Evaluation of Unit-Pricing	Majority who used said it was helpful; of those aware, 68% said "very important" and only 18% said "not so important"	—	41% considered it worthwhile
Other Findings	—	of those reporting use of info, 38% used to change package sizes and 28% to change brands. 8% of King Sooper shoppers had switched to them to use unit-pricing information	5% switched shopping decision (brand, package, etc.) as a result of unit-pricing. No aggregate evidence of move toward larger sizes or private labels

	McCullough and Padberg (1971) (Kroger, Toledo?)	Friedman (1971b)	Monroe and LaPlaca (1972), Morse (1971) (3 chains in D.C.)
Source			
Sample	About 2400 personal interviews of shoppers in ten stores	About 1000 personal interviews in two stores	Telephone survey among 500 shoppers
Time Period	During last week of 16 week study (4 mos. after intro in Feb., 1970)	5 mos. and 7 mos. after intro at beginning of 1970	Late March 1971, 1–8 months following intro in 3 supermarket chains
% Aware and Attributes	65.5% aware; more awareness among high educ. and income and among whites and among younger shoppers	—	Of those who shopped in a unit-priced chain, 64.5% aware
Degree of Understanding of Unit-Pricing	48.5% of total shoppers correctly understood unit-pricing information	—	—
Usage of Unit-Pricing in Buying	64% of those who understood had used it (31% of total shoppers used it); those more inclined to use, *if* they understood it, were blacks and households with young children	31% reported usage; usage higher in suburban store (38%) than in inner-city store (20%). However, these %'s when adjusted for respondent error showed that usage was probably greater in inner-city (17%) than in suburban (11.5%) store	Of those who shopped in unit-priced store, 47.3% had used when shopping at least once and 37.5% had used in one-half or more of products purchased
Consumer Evaluation of Unit-Pricing	Over half of those who understood unit-pricing had favorable attitude toward it	—	—
Other Findings	75.5% of those using unit-pricing reported saving money; at least 28% switched from their regular brand or size	—	No net change in switching to **or** from chains which had unit-pricing

SOURCE: I. Ross, "Applications of Consumer Information to Public Policy Decisions," working paper #7, University of Minnesota, November 1972.

His candor and objectivity are also to be commended as he reviews and comments on the studies reported in the literature. An example is the following:

> One study (Kottman [2]) demonstrated that there is low agreement among consumers about what ads are misleading, although the way in which the study was designed might better lead to the conclusion that when something (deception) is not defined, people don't agree on what it means. (page 53)

Sometimes problems create problems. For example, a new journal appeared on the scene in 1974 called *The Journal of Consumer Research* (3). The journal refers to itself as an interdisciplinary quarterly. It is cosponsored by ten different professional societies. The following is a list of some of the articles it has published:

"Federal Programs to Measure Consumer Purchase Expectations, 1946–1973: A Post-mortem"

"Commentaries on McNeil, 'Federal Programs to Measure Consumer Purchase Expectations'"

"Attitude Models Revisited: An Individual Level Analysis"

"Fear Appeals: Revisited and Revised"

"A Taxonomy of Prepurchase Information Gathering Patterns"

"Some Empirical Contributions to Buyer Behavior Theory"

"A Complementarity Model of Consumer Utility for Item Collections"

"Multiattribute Measurement Models and Multiattribute Attitude Theory: A Test of Construct Validity"

"Commentaries on Bettman et al., 'Multiattribute measurement models and multiattribute attitude theory'"

"Demand Artifacts in Laboratory Experiments in Consumer Research"

"Primary and Secondary Validity of Consumer Purchase Probabilities"

"An Empirical Test of the Fishbein Behavioral Intention Model"

"Changing Brand Attitudes Through Modification of Cognitive Structure"

"Joint Home Purchasing Decisions by Husbands and Wives"

"Social Factors in Consumer Choice: Replication and Extension"

"A Method for Investigating and Representing Implicit Theory of Social Class"

"A Comparison of Four Multi-attribute Models in the Prediction of Consumer Attitudes"
"A Path-Analytic Exploration of Retail Patronage Influences"
"Consumer Decision Making: A Comparative Analysis Using Orthogonal Regression"
"Factors Affecting Cognitive Resistance to Advertising"

Pity the average consumer who might be seeking empirical evidence in the hope of solving or reducing conflicts in consumer affairs. From the titles it would appear that lots of different things can be called consumer research but much of it may have little or nothing to do with typical consumers and their problems. The list of titles published in this scholarly journal suggests or creates a gap between the typical consumer's problems and the scientist's interests and concerns about consumer research.

BIBLIOGRAPHY

1. ROSS, I., "Applications of Consumer Information to Public Policy Decisions," working paper no. 7, University of Minnesota, November 1972.
2. KOTTMAN, E. J., "A Semantic Evaluation of Misleading Advertising," *Journal of Communication*, 14 (1964) 151.
3. *The Journal of Consumer Research*, 1, nos. 3 and 4 (1974).

8

Observational techniques as consumer aids

Many readers will be quite familiar with what takes place when a refrigerator or air conditioner is being considered for purchase. For those who have not had such an experience, it would be a good exercise to visit any outlet and observe the customer-salesperson interaction. In most instances the buyer has to consider so many variables at the same time that the characteristics of the product he finally buys may have little bearing on his actual needs.

For the consumer, this chaotic situation can be modified. The technique is to use observation under controlled conditions. Most simply, this means making up a chart in order to record more objective observations. The first step requires making preliminary observations, which allows for a listing of the important attributes of the product. For the two products already mentioned, the list might well include the following (not necessarily in order of importance): price, size, temperature maintenance, efficient use of electricity, noise, warranty, appearance, safety, and special features and their cost. These items might form the vertical column of the observation chart. A four-point rating scale (excellent, good, fair, poor) might form the horizontal column of the chart.

As one goes from store to store, model to model, or manufacturer to manufacturer, one records immediately what one has observed about each item considered for purchase. Using this form will not only prevent errors of memory but also allow for a better purchase decision because the observations made are more standardized and objective. A husband-and-wife team rating the items independently and then comparing results can often come to a decision that will satisfy the needs of the family more appropriately than if either one made the ratings alone.

One might also use a ten-point scale like the following:

Quiet - - - - - - - - - - - - - - - - - Noisy
　　　　10　9　8　7　6　5　4　3　2　1

As long as one is consistent, it is possible to make judgments based on a series of observations rather than as a result of bias, in which one attribute is favored entirely out of proportion to others and determines the purchase decision.

In addition to product characteristics, it is possible and advisable to observe the salesperson and record observations about his/her manner. For example (assuming that one has a chance to talk to the salesperson), the following items should be observed: degree of pressure to make a purchase, extent of knowledge and information about the product, degree of bias toward one brand and (inferred) reason, and reasons offered for not recommending other brands.

The form for recording observations should be prepared in advance. As for the question of whether the salesperson should be aware that you have the form, the answer is a resounding yes! If the salesperson knows you are serious about buying the product that is best for you, he/she will either back off or get down to "the facts." In the former case you may be saved much unpleasantness; in the latter, you may make a better purchase.

The use of an appropriate observation form may encourage consumers to become "researchers" and use such information in making the purchase decision.

The consumer must become more explorative and investigative if he/she expects to gain greater equality in the buyer-seller-maker transaction. The most direct way for the consumer to become more knowledgeable is to develop and apply a research-oriented point of view.

Research is neither mystical nor esoteric. It is a scientific means of gathering data to aid in the solution of a problem. Surely the typical consumer needs to become a better purchaser of products and services. The point is that research can be easy: By following a few rules the consumer can conduct valuable research on a do-it-yourself basis.

While it is true that one does not necessarily benefit by experience, it is also true that observations, when objective and standardized, can improve on experience. While experience can lead to impressions that may or may not be correct, observations under controlled conditions can enhance the meaning of the experiences one has had.

The observations of an untrained observer are casual and subjective. Untrained observers witnessing an identical incident will vary considerably in their reports of that incident. Trained observers, with the benefit of a form to record their observations, will vary much less in their reports.

Casual observations may be spurious, whereas controlled and objective observations can be accurate recordings of reality. Such observations are likely to reduce or eliminate an individual's bias and prejudice not only in the social world but in the world of consumer transactions.

What is needed is increased objectivity, which, in turn, leads to reliable, accurate data. Such data can result in greater correctness in the decision-making process. This is especially applicable to the buying situation. Accurate observations are often obscured by habit. Continually reaching for the same brand as one scurries down the supermarket aisle prevents seeing other items that may be better buys. Such habits, when entrenched, prevent consideration of alternatives.

The consumer needs to use more standardized and objective methods of observation. Admittedly, resolutions will not work. Changes in behavior will, provided that one takes the time necessary to train oneself in the "powers" of observation. Reality is observing facts, situations, or conditions the way they really are —without embellishment.

One way of developing the ability to make one's observations more objective is to work with others. A form to make one's observations more standardized and complete is a great aid. Otherwise it is possible that those observations may be invalid or at least not as objective as they might be. A helpful training device is to have two, three, or more people use the same observation form and observe the same situation independently. By comparing the resulting observations for similarities and differences one may sharpen one's ability to observe accurately.

For example, in any shopping area different people have different beliefs as to which supermarket has the lowest prices. The way to decide would be to have a few people with identical shopping lists record the prices in various supermarkets. Such observations will lead directly and accurately to an answer, whereas casual impressions will not. The data may indicate that one store does have lower prices or that supermarket prices vary by department—one has lower produce prices and another has lower meat or dairy prices.

The point is that two or more people working together can teach each other to observe more objectively. More important, standardized and objective observations can be recorded and replicated, allowing for better decision making than is possible using casual, subjective impressions.

Many additional examples can be offered. Assuming that marketers and merchandisers know what they are doing, it follows that they will have on display or in their windows items that are current, fashionable, and appropriately priced for that particular type of retail outlet. Now suppose one plans to buy a dress, a suit, shoes, sportswear, a radio, a minicalculator, or a can of paint. Whatever the item, objective observations will allow for such conclusions as which color is most popular, what style is shown most and is therefore more fashionable, as well as the probable "best" buy in terms of price and so on.

As another example, suppose one decides to buy an electronic telephone-answering device or a minicalculator for either personal or business reasons. In addition to reading consumer reports or learning about the experiences of friends, the thing to do is make a list of four or five retail outlets likely to sell the item. Include a variety of stores—specialty shops, discount stores, department stores—and then visit each one. The name of the store and the items available should be recorded on the form. List such factors as brand, model number, features, and price. You may find little to choose from or quite a variety. In any case the formal observation process results in factual data; the purchase decision can then be based on a comparative analysis of the product and its characteristics in relation to the needs of the buyer.

Developing an objective basis for observations prior to purchase and sharing it with others with mutual interests can give one the satisfaction of "researching" one's purchase as well as a high probability of buying a better-quality product.

A series of examples will be offered here in which groups of people with common purchase interests can help each other. The group might consist of parents with young children. Suppose they agree that each will independently shop for a particular toy and record the following observations:

Store shopped _____
Why that store? _____
Toy most preferred, brand _____ price _____
Description (size, color, etc.) _____
Advantages _____
Disadvantages _____
Toy least preferred, brand _____ price _____
Description _____

Reason(s) ―――――――――――――――――――
Role of salesperson ―――――――――――――――――

It should be obvious that two, three, or more parents meeting and sharing their shopping experiences can be helpful in teaching each other more about toys than they might have known if each did his/her shopping under conditions of casual observation.

Another example deals with items that have high price tags. The item might be any of a variety of electronic home entertainment items, such as a television, stereo, or radio. It might also be any of the so-called home appliances—vacuum cleaners, toasters, irons, electric can openers. In such cases it may be a little more difficult to have neighbors and friends shop independently for you, but many people, once involved, like the technique. They readily admit that they learn not only about the product but also about becoming better shoppers. This increases self-esteem as well as making one more efficient.

The form developed might look like this:

APPLIANCE OBSERVATION FORM

List each manufacturer or brand on display ――――――――
――――――――――――――――――――――

Manufacturer with largest display ―――――――――――
Nature of labels and visual displays for each item ――――――
――――――――――――――――――――

Brand (if any) salesperson tried hardest to sell ――――――
(Inferred) Reason ――――――――――――――――
Extent of belief in salesperson's knowledge ―――――――――
Extent of belief in salesperson's integrity ――――――――――
Feature(s) most liked ―――――――――――――――
Feature(s) most emphasized by salesperson ――――――――――
Feature(s) most disliked ―――――――――――――――
Brands presented negatively by salesperson ――――――――――
(Inferred) Reason ――――――――――――――――
Rate as excellent, good, fair, or poor three preferred items re:
    Price   ――――――   ――――――   ――――――
    Appearance ――――――   ――――――   ――――――
    Performance ――――――   ――――――   ――――――
    Warranty   ――――――   ――――――   ――――――

Again, if this observational exercise is followed a better buy is likely.

In short, using controlled and standardized observations while shopping allows the consumer to be a "researcher" or at least use an acceptable scientific method in order to increase the odds in favor of a better, more appropriate purchase.

9

Interactional workshops

Interactional workshops involve a group of peers who share information on a common topic, product, service, or combination of related items. They are helped by a leader who keeps the flow of information going without resorting to the role of teacher, lecturer, or expert.

In many respects an interactional workshop is a form of qualitative research technique that emphasizes the dynamics that take place in a group discussion. When interactional workshops are understood and used correctly, they can be a most useful measuring instrument in consumer psychology. Unfortunately, and much too often, sound qualitative research is either distorted or misused, or it is avoided by those who have a bias toward frequency or large numbers of respondents. Among the latter are those who believe there is safety in numbers. This may not be true at all.

The interactional workshop, as described and explained in this chapter, leads to an optimal amount of understanding and problem solving in a reasonably short period. On the other hand, it is no "quick and dirty," a term generally used to describe shady research techniques. The technique encompasses the use of experimental design and the opportunity for replication of data. Interactional workshops involve a group of people sharing views on a topic of common interest. It is a method that meets scientific standards by incorporating within it the experimental method.

Experiments can be conducted in a laboratory or under exist-ing conditions in the field. The experiment has the advantage of "forcing" data by planning the conditions that will enable observa-tions to be made more objectively and accurately than would be likely if one had to wait for the situation to present itself under naturally unfolding conditions.

For example, if one wanted to learn about people's attitudes toward inflation, the need for specific legislation to change or improve the service given by utilities, or whether shoppers should be able to see the underside of meat that is prepackaged and sold in supermarkets, one could plan an experiment to gather the data. One method would be to convene two groups of people with known characteristics, for example, upper-income and lower-income people, utility executives and users of utilities, or older vs. younger purchasers of meat. Each group, depending on the topic, might be asked to indicate its perception of existing condi-tions, ways to improve things (if any), projections as to how "the others" think, and so forth. By comparing the differences one could make inferences and reach conclusions about the reasons for existing conditions and the ways to improve or change them.

Accordingly, interactional workshops are thoroughly capable of gathering data under controlled conditions. In other words, the experimental method, which is a basic scientific methodology, can be used to gather information about groups and about indi-viduals in groups with equal effectiveness.

Probably the most important dichotomy with reference to the psychologist's research methodology is the quantitative-quali-tative dimension. Each is appropriate in its place, and often the findings of each are complementary to those of the other.

Qualitative research is valuable in constructing hypotheses, checking hypotheses, or gaining ideas that begin to explain the attitudes or behavior of people. In fact it may be very useful as a preliminary to quantitative research. Qualitative methods tend to probe more intensively into the reasons for the attitude or be-havior in question. The quantitative method includes large num-bers of respondents and tends to accept their answers as stated.

In short, quantitative research involves larger numbers of respondents and indicates the extent to which they favor the question at hand. Qualitative research deals with smaller num-bers of people and indicates *why* the question is favored or not favored.

The roots of interactional workshops, which emphasize the group discussion technique, are found in the theories of group dynamics and group psychotherapy. Using a group technique allows for an understanding of the beliefs of the individuals who compose the group as well as group interaction.

This technique should not be confused with the "focus interview" that is popular in market research. It seems that there are as many varieties of focus interviews as there are people who claim to use them. Those who run focus groups are often undisciplined and untrained. They sometimes manipulate their methods to influence findings—too often to please the client. The very term *focus interview* implies that the interview is focused on a topic or result. By contrast, a qualitative group discussion involves verbalizations and interactions about areas for discussion; the leader of the group does no focusing.

To reiterate, research using the interactional workshop method is qualitative. It differs from quantitative research insofar as it emphasizes to a much greater degree the exploration and analysis of ideas, attitudes, opinions, and behavior. A major characteristic of this type of research is its use of small samples, but it allows the individuals involved to respond in greater depth and with more feeling. Qualitative research allows for not only an in-depth analysis of the responses of an individual but also interplay of ideas, attitudes, and opinions among the participants.

It is a truism in psychology, as well as in other areas of knowledge, that anything that exists can be measured. Different kinds of measuring units are used for qualitative and quantitative data. However, it is expected that the findings will be similar, especially insofar as conclusions are concerned. For example, while yards and meters are different they nevertheless bear a definite relationship to each other. Similarly, qualitative and quantitative measurements are related. Both techniques are equally valid measures provided that equally rigorous standards are used.

In order to lead to reliable and valid findings, an interactional workshop must meet a set of predetermined requirements. For example, a trained and experienced discussion leader must exactly follow a series of rules and regulations. The responses elicited from the group must be the spontaneous and varied reactions of the individuals in the group, and the discussion leader can furnish no information beyond that which was originally planned.

The leader must also keep the discussion on schedule and on target and be certain that all participants, regardless of their individual differences and characteristics, have an opportunity to express their views. The leader must have sensitivity and insight and must know when to probe for further depth and when to encourage responses that may in fact be suggesting new and creative ideas. The leader must also allow for ample differences in the views expressed without allowing such differences to erupt into personal attacks.

The discussion leader must offer all participants an approximately equal opportunity to talk. In any group of 8, 10, or 12 people there will be many individual differences. Any group is likely to include a "noisy one," a "quiet one," an "attention getter," a "funny one," an "insecure one," and so on.

There may be "born leaders," but there are *no* "born discussion leaders." All discussion leaders *must* be trained. Some learn faster than others. Sad to say, some never learn.

When the confused, insecure, or structure-seeking participant asks "What do you mean?" or says "I can't answer because I don't understand," the leader may only reread the question and ask others to volunteer an answer. When the leader is asked for additional information he/she must not be trapped into playing the role of "expert." He/she must answer "I don't know!" Soon there will be a "good samaritan" in the group who comes to the leader's aid.

Another important part of leading a workshop is to be sure everyone in the group has a chance to talk. Different members of the group should be encouraged to start the various discussions. While the leader should encourage interaction within the group by allowing participants to ask each other questions, he/she must nevertheless maintain control.

For variety, it is occasionally appropriate to use the "around the table" technique, in which each person speaks in turn. This often provides the balance that can sometimes be overlooked in a totally free discussion situation in which the "quiet one" says too little and the "noisy one" is too vociferous.

The reason the leader should present the discussion material uniformly is that all groups should have the same information. One group should not be advantaged or disadvantaged in comparison with other groups because certain individuals in the group unknowingly try to modify the procedure.

The leader must use judgment in determining whether the discussion is wandering far afield or serendipity is on the threshold. Keeping the group to a planned schedule is recommended, yet there is no room for the hopeless compulsiveness in which time becomes more important than the gathering of meaningful information.

Also of great importance is knowing when and how to probe. *Probing* is asking for clarification or further information. For example, "I like it" is an uninformative answer. One must learn why.

In brief, the leader is the one who elicits the responses by alternating between acting as a "sponge" and stimulating the thoughts, ideas, attitudes, and opinions of the members of the group.

At times, prior to the discussion of a specific question, the participants are asked to record their answers on a questionnaire. This technique is used to ensure that each respondent is reacting individually and not because of the influence of others in the group. After the individual responses have been recorded and the members have had a chance to interact, one often clearly sees the influences of individuals on one another. This technique allows one to better understand the influences that effect changes in attitudes and opinions as various points are raised.

The findings obtained from interactional workshops are based on analysis of the content of the various members' comments. Such analyses include both the manifest and latent content of the discussions.

A decided advantage of this technique is that all the data are available and based on a single tape recording of all that took place. This allows those who are interested to obtain all the primary data. The recorded discussions reveal not only the nature of the members' opinions but also the intensity of the feelings expressed. In other words, the data are directly on the tapes, unlike the data of quantitative research, which consist of the interviewer's report, impressions, or interpretations of what the respondents said.

An important aid in conducting a successful interactional workshop is the creation of a proper atmosphere. In this connection the participants should be seated at a round table. This is important. Any other shape—oblong, square, U-shaped, etc.—is inferior to the round table. A round table does not put the discussion leader at the head of the table. Moreover, the participants are all relatively close to the leader; this prevents those who would otherwise be at the end of the table from feeling removed from the mainstream of conversation. Each can see the other participants better when seated at a round table. The round table helps keep the group together and the discussion flowing.

Three important characteristics of an interactional workshop technique are the size of the group, the manner of selecting the group, and the decision as to the number of groups to conduct.

There is no set number of people in a group. From experience, 8 to 10 seems to be most appropriate. However, the number can drop to 6 or increase to 12 and still be highly rewarding, although it is generally more difficult to conduct.

Since some individuals appear for the workshop half an

hour early and some five or ten minutes late, it is important that all be kept at ease in a friendly and sociable atmosphere but discouraged from talking about the announced topic. Groups quite frequently are made up of women. Whether they are married or single or have children or not depends on the nature of the problem being investigated. However, for complete information in many areas men must also be included.

Prior to recruiting the participants a grid is constructed consisting of nine cells. Along the vertical axis might be three socioeconomic levels; along the horizontal axis might be three age ranges. Accordingly, the nine group members (or eight or ten) might represent a rather wide age range as well as variations in family income.

One should never run interactional workshops with existing groups such as church groups or PTAs. This merely maintains the social pecking order that has already been established. Rather, it is important that the participants not be acquainted with anyone else in the group. Optimally, this would mean gathering a group of strangers. If by chance two people already know each other they should not sit next to each other.

Recruiting participants is difficult. It is best to have one person in charge who uses three or four others to do the recruiting. Indeed, one pays the recruiter as well as those who attend. A fair price is about $10.00 for a two-hour session. Whether to hold morning, afternoon, or evening sessions depends on a number of factors, one of which is economy of scheduling.

Conducting interactional workshops in a hotel or motel suite is much better than conducting them in either a home or an office. Such a setting lends itself to sociability and is businesslike as well, without over- or under-doing it.

It is necessary to tape record the sessions so that an accurate content and theme analysis can be made. To avoid invasion of privacy, the microphone should be visible and the plan to tape the discussion must be explained in advance. Sometimes one-way screens are used and people, unknown to the group, listen and watch. This is a form of bugging and not an ethical practice. One-way screens, at best, are a gimmick; tape, on the other hand, is a full record of what took place. If a one-way screen is used, the participants should be told.

Some workshops use closed-circuit television so clients can be part of the sophisticated electronic world. One-way screens and closed-circuit television have the same appeal as dog and pony shows. The point is that showmanship has no place in responsible research.

Running two independent sessions with participants who have similar characteristics is advisable. When the sessions are removed in time and space and recurring themes are arrived at independently, one can be confident that the theme is an important one. Many times, because of the variables involved in an experiment, three to six groups may be needed to obtain sufficient data.

Before beginning the workshop the leader sets the stage by explaining the need to follow certain rules. In a friendly, conversational tone the discussion leader says:

We are going to be having a workshop, and there are just a few simple rules.

We want your candid, frank, and honest opinions. Please remember there is no such thing as a right answer or a wrong answer. It is your opinion that counts; therefore feel free to say what you think. In addition, feel free to disagree with any of the opinions already expressed. Just because someone expressed a view before you did does not mean that it is any more right than your view.

Because we are on tape [point to the microphone] and we will be analyzing the discussion at a later time, please talk only one at a time. Also would you please avoid whispering and private conversations with your neighbors.

Talk loud enough for the group to hear you and for the tape to pick it up.

Just one more thing: From time to time you will be filling in your answers on a questionnaire before discussing them. Please do this according to the way *you* think.

A variation of these instructions is used when the group is more sophisticated and might interpret the former as "talking down." Its format is as follows:

In conducting this session I will ask you to please observe a few rules:

1. As you see, we are taping the session for analysis and report purposes, so please speak *one* at a time and *loud* enough for us to have your "gems of wisdom" recorded.
2. Avoid private and whispered conversations. We pick them up and sometimes hear what is not on the agenda.
3. Try and cooperate by considering the other participants and allowing for equal time.
4. Feel free to agree, disagree, change your mind, and register doubts, but please state your views in relation to the topic.
5. Recognize that my job as discussion leader is to keep on track and on time, so state your points fully, but no speeches, please.

Obviously, the key to the value of the data to be obtained is in the construction of the guide that is used. The guide requires very complete and careful planning. The problem being discussed must be separated into a series of unfolding discussion areas. The questions must include a delicate balance between structure and lack of structure so that the participants can interpret the question or topic in accordance with their own views. This elicits differences of opinion. Further, the questions must not be phrased in such a way as to encourage the respondents to answer in a particular way. Whenever a participant asks for clarification it is important for the group leader not to assume the role of expert or explainer. Rather, the group leader must parry with "What do you think?"

The following are examples of questions that might be asked:

Will you tell me what you thought about as you paid the person at the checkout counter the last time you were in a supermarket?

Considering all the toys your child plays with, will you tell me what his/her favorite is?

How important would you say toys like trucks and cars are in your child's play activity? Would you say they are very, somewhat, or not at all important? What did you answer and why did you answer the way you did?

Considering an ideal radio for your needs, would you tell me how many bands it should have and what those bands are?

Will you tell me where you do most of your meat buying and why you buy there?

The questions are important only to get the discussion going. The discussion determines not only the participants' attitudes and reasons but also their familiarity with the subject. Further, it determines, regardless of whether they are correct or not, the intensity of the views held. During an interactional workshop one can see and hear changes in views as they take place. Data of this sort can help predict, if one adjusts to change, the degree to which a new law, meat package, or what have you will be popular.

Another subject worthy of probing is the concept of "psychological pricing." By asking people what they expect something to cost or what they would be willing to pay for an item, one can form an estimate of that item's real value to an individual. If the price is estimated as considerably less than the item would cost, one can infer that such an item would have less value for that person. More important than the "guesstimate" are the reasons offered. This concept is more valuable in understanding a person's values than in predicting market share. The latter is a concern of market research; the former is a concern of consumer psychology.

When one group member has estimated a lower price and another has estimated a higher price, it is informative as well as fascinating to see who "gives ground" and why. Such discussions indicate the values people attach to ideas or things.

To illustrate this technique, excerpts from different studies are offered in the remainder of this chapter. The topics include unit pricing, meat packaging, and multiple pricing of items on supermarket shelves. These studies also illustrate important research areas in consumer affairs.

A study on unit pricing was conducted in Hartford, Connecticut, in 1970. Two examples from the report are presented to indicate the accuracy of the findings as well as the predictions.

Not a single consumer in the two Hartford panels had heard of unit pricing. Accordingly, they did not know what it was, and encouraging them to guess only led to varied and confused responses. Few were able to infer that unit pricing might be related to price per ounce.

Therefore without a definition of unit pricing their answers as to whether they were for or against unit pricing or whether they believed unit pricing would affect the cost of merchandise would have little value. What is clear is that an educational campaign must accompany unit pricing if and when unit pricing is introduced. Without this education confusion would abound:

> Isn't this some "kickup" in Washington? I'm guessing, but it seems that somewhere I heard that there was some kind of legislation introduced about—what is it? Bess Meyerson—or whoever it was that runs it—said something about so the housewife can really know what she's paying for everything.

Another thought this was right and said "but the manufacturers are against it."

> It sounds like you go into a store and you have to buy what they want you to buy, and not what you want to buy and how much you want to buy.
>
> If they put the cost per ounce on the boxes, I'm 100 percent for it!

One woman felt that everything is based on competition and "more important than how much they get per box is how many boxes they sell." She also felt that placing the price per ounce on

packages would "make them become more aware . . . of competition; it would be less easy to fool you and they might be more
concerned with getting your business."

At this point in the workshop, a definition of unit pricing—
"items you buy that show the cost per ounce or per pound or per
pint"—was offered; the participants were then asked to estimate
whether they would prefer to shop in a chain that had unit pricing
or in one that did not. Eighteen of the 19 participants said they
would prefer to shop in the store that had unit pricing. Their
reasons varied, but they were all related to getting what you pay
for and removing deception, if and when it exists: "It would be
more difficult for a store to put something over on you." Such
answers indicate a general receptiveness to unit pricing on the
part of the consumer:

> If you want to get the best buy you can do it, the price per
> ounce is there for you.
>
> I feel that perhaps in the long run we might be able to save
> ourselves a few cents here and there knowing how much it is.

It must be emphasized that research limited to two groups
must be considered exploratory and qualitative, not definitive.
Within this context, however, a number of plausible suggestions
leading to hypotheses do emerge:

1. Consumers show shopping patterns, and in most cases the
   pattern is highly repetitive, resembling a habit.
2. The consumer often buys the brands that, on the basis of
   experience, are most likely to result in satisfaction and minimum risk.
3. Reasons for purchasing particular grocery items are varied,
   but buying to please the family or serve what they like and
   will eat is of paramount importance.
4. The consumer is greatly influenced by specials at reduced
   prices, especially when they are items that would normally
   be bought anyway. At such times he/she is likely to increase
   the quantity of those purchases, provided that money and
   storage space are available.
5. The consumer tends to regard purchases of meat as more
   important than purchases of other food items insofar as
   he/she feels that he/she can really save more money on this
   item in the grocery basket, yet insists on the quality of meat
   that he/she normally expects.

Unit Pricing, therefore, has to be considered in the context of the consumer's typical shopping pattern, with the following in mind:

6. Consumers in Hartford are almost totally unfamiliar with unit pricing.
7. When the consumer is provided with a definition of unit pricing he/she is favorably disposed to the idea.
8. The consumer is price conscious but is used to the prices of the items he/she habitually buys. He/she can recognize a price reduction when it occurs.
9. Changing the consumer's shopping pattern from price per item to price per unit will require an adjustment on the part of the consumer.
10. Consumers generally do not compute price per ounce for themselves; if they do, they are not sure this information is important to them.
11. If unit pricing is to be introduced, the consumer will have to be reeducated.
12. Attempting to predict behavior, that is, changes in shopping patterns, is not possible from the research undertaken. However, the following can be inferred:
    a. The consumer is favorably disposed to unit pricing.
    b. He/she is most likely to accept the concept of unit pricing if it occurs in the outlet where one normally shops and includes the items normally bought.
    c. Shifts to other retail outlets and changes in the brands purchased probably will not occur quickly. A period of trial and error will be necessary during which unit pricing as an influence on specific purchases is evaluated against the consumer's present shopping pattern, which is based on familiarity with present brands and retail outlets.

In summary, unit pricing should not be regarded as a panacea but is worth further experimentation.

Now for the second example. In Dade County, Florida, an ordinance was passed requiring that meat be sold in packages allowing at least 70 percent visibility through the bottom of the tray. The intent of the ordinance was to prevent the packaging of meat in such a way that fat, bone, and gristle would be hidden on the underside of the tray holding the meat.

The dispute was over whether a certain type of pulp tray would afford adequate visibility.

To obtain some research data an experiment was conducted. Interactional workshops were held in which two roasts, two packages of chops, and two packages of chopped beef were shown in pairs and passed around the table for each person to examine closely. The participants were told (and shown) that one item in each pair was packaged in a plastic tray and the other was packaged in a pulp tray. They were asked to indicate whether there was more, less, or the same amount of fat, bone, or gristle in one or the other of the packages. To avoid bias, they were first asked to indicate whether there was more, less, or the same amount in the plastic tray; this was done when they were shown the two packages of roast. When they were shown the chops they were asked to indicate whether there was more, less, or the same amount in the pulp tray. In the third comparison they were shown chopped beef and asked to indicate whether there was more, less, or the same amount of fat in the plastic tray. What these people were *not* told was that the butcher had been instructed to select pairs that were equal in fat, bone, and gristle (or as close as possible based on his experience).

In examining the three sets of trays, not a single person indicated that he/she could not make a judgment because the pulp tray did not provide enough visibility. Because of the small number of people involved in this experiment ($N = 14$), it would be unwise to draw any definitive conclusion as to whether plastic or pulp trays show meat to have more, less, or the same amount of fat, bone, or gristle. Nevertheless, the findings are revealing.

In the case of the chops, the pulp tray was judged to contain chops with less fat. It would be unwise to draw any other conclusion except that when instructed to determine which package had more, less, or the same amount of bone, fat, or gristle, no one indicated that a judgment was impossible because the pulp tray did not provide enough visibility. This conclusion strongly supports the earlier results reported, in which the pulp tray apparently does provide sufficient visibility to make accurate judgments about the meat. The following quotes illustrate the findings of this study:

> I think they were cut at the same time off the same cut of meat.
>
> I would say less. In the pulp tray the meat was lighter in color, there was more fat in it.
>
> I put more in the plastic, but not a big difference. But on the top of the meat, on the top of the package, I could see more fat than I thought I could see in the pulp.
>
> I put more—the bone seems to be just about the same, but there is a little bit more fat in that plastic.

I said less, because B had that bone all the way across—bone, gristle, and fat—and I judged it on that basis.

In another study in Boston, three groups of consumers were required, as a condition for attending the sessions, to select and purchase a top round steak weighing between one and two pounds. The three groups differed primarily in the chain (A, B, or C) where they bought the meat. The three chains were selected because of differences in their meat packaging. Chain A used plastic. Chain B used pulp. (Both plastic and pulp are see-through materials.) Chain C used foam, which is solid material.

A comparison test was used in each of the groups. The plastic tray users preferred plastic to pulp by a 6-to-4 ratio. The foam tray users preferred plastic by a score of 10 to 0. The pulp tray users also preferred their tray to a foam tray by a 10-to-0 score.

A big difference between the plastic and pulp trays is that the former do not absorb the meat juices and the latter do.

Consumers tend to be ambivalent, confused, and generally uninformed about meat juices. From the point of view of esthetics, "blood" is rejected. They say it looks messy and sometimes smells.

With reference to the value of meat juices, most consumers have no knowledge and quite a few admit that they "have not thought about it before." The reasoning for or against the accumulation or absorption of meat juices is just as likely to be irrational as rational. For example, some believe the juices are a necessary part of the meat. But even among these there are some who dispose of the juices. There are some who believe that when a tray absorbs the juices it dries out the meat. Still others pour the juices over the meat at the time of cooking. Others believe freezing meat takes out the vitamins and does not preserve the juices. Still others believe the presence of juices in a meat tray suggests that the meat is not fresh, but on the other hand they do not regard the pulp tray, which absorbs the juices, as esthetically pleasant either.

It appears from these findings that a valuable contribution could be made if factual information were provided to the consumer about the pros and cons of meat juices. Incidentally, it is interesting to note that women consistently use the word *juices* and hate to use the word *blood*.

Here are some quotes illustrating the different points of view:

I prefer to call it meat juices. I hate the word *blood*. It's making me sick thinking about it.

I don't ever think I've had a piece of meat that had an excessive amount of blood or juice in the tray, and I do pour it on the meat too.

It really adds flavor to the gravy.

I never really thought of it as having any value.

I agree, a little bit of juice is fine until it starts dripping all over your hands.

I leave it in the pan when I'm making gravy. It helps to brown and it helps to flavor.

I don't think it's appetizing looking. I throw it right out.

Our fourth illustration of the use of interactional workshops relates to the Dade County, Florida, ordinance prohibiting the repricing of items previously priced by supermarkets except under certain special conditions. In general, the sessions revealed that anger, outrage, aggression, and anxiety were building up as consumers realized that a food item might be priced two or more times and that each time they shopped the price was higher. The following quotes are presented as illustrations:

I always feel very angry, and especially the sale items are not always marked. Sometimes the girls go through them very fast and I say "Slow down, that's that and this is that" and I say "It's not your fault, honey, but someone is making a lot of money off these extra prices." I really feel very strong about it and I always get a chance to talk to the manager, especially the increases over the previous prices. It is very annoying and I know the individuals in the store aren't responsible for it but I get a very angry feeling. It's hurting my health.

I'm just outraged. I don't think that anybody can walk into any place now where you're not terribly conscious of how much more everything costs—everything.

I thought I spent $60 and I really don't have enough food for two weeks—not nice meals. I have to give my husband soup and eggs. I can't buy meat with the money I have to spend.

I shopped a few days ago and I didn't have too much money on me and I thought, "I wonder if I'm going to make it"—and I ended up writing a check. I hadn't bought too many items and it was more than I had figured on so I wrote a check. I had about $7.00 on me and I would have been short. I bought that baby beef, and peppers, onions, a few potatoes, and a quart of milk.

I think the resentment I have is when I see them marking things up. The things are on the shelf and some of them have been marked and some haven't and they mark them up maybe 5¢, 7¢, even 10¢. That's my biggest gripe really. Another thing that I find is that I don't shop as often—if I don't shop often I can do without things and that's what I do. I just get so angry and they're forever marking things up. I feel that they should not be able to mark things up, because they have bought it at the old cost and they should give the customers that benefit really. Then keep it back and when they're almost all cleared off, then put the higher-priced merchandise out. But not to have them almost insult your intelligence marking that darn stuff up. You see, I get mad.

10

Quantitative research, or head counting

Quantitative research is more widely used, more popular, and for many, less questionable as a research technique than either of the techniques referred to in the previous two chapters. Somehow the buyers and sellers of research are happiest when they have large numbers of respondents. As a result the inadequacies and inaccuracies of many quantitative studies are masked or unrecognized.

Studies with large numbers of respondents are not equally valid; some are (either purposely or ignorantly) so poorly designed as to be misleading or untrue. Too often the results of quantitative research are given credence out of proportion to their value, and too often the questions that should be asked are overlooked.

"Quantitative research" is taken to be synonymous with "scientific research." One even hears news commentators reporting that "our survey" is unscientific. What is meant by "scientific" in the case of surveys is that the sampling technique used makes it possible to project the findings to the entire population ostensibly being studied rather than only the part of the population that has been sampled.

The U.S. Census figures provide basic information on the demographic characteristics of the total population in this country. In quantitative research the sample is drawn to resemble the total population, or *universe*. The calculations are done by computer; in fact the computer corrects for variations in the sample obtained, so that the corrected sample does replicate the universe. This technique is widely used in market research, political polling, and public opinion surveys. In consumer affairs, the little research that is being done also tends to favor quantitative methods.

The image of survey research is such that if it is not quantitative it is not "scientific." This is naive and often dangerously erroneous.

The basic "goodness" of quantitative research hinges on two factors. The first is the sample and its ability to project to the total population. The second is the method of inquiry, which is usually a questionnaire.

The major pollsters, whether they study attitudes toward soap, Presidential candidates, or the future of the economy, have established methods of obtaining the minimum number of interviews necessary to be able to project and forecast. The techniques developed are sufficiently refined so that most often, and depending on the survey outfit, the number of respondents in the total sample usually ranges from 1000 to 2000. It is with the use of such techniques, as well as computer programing, that pollsters can predict election winners on the basis of early returns, which means a sample that can be accurately projected.

Based on statistical inferences, which, in turn, are based on "laws of probability," the probable error of a sample reporting certain results is readily established. This then allows one to say that in 90 or 95 cases out of 100 the results will not vary by more than 2 percent or 5 percent. However, a number of factors in addition to sample size account for the validity and reliability of the conclusions. The probable error of the findings is important, but it would seem that it has been overemphasized.

Based on statistical inferences the probable error is reduced as sample size increases; but unless other factors are considered, the "minimum probable error" can be very misleading with reference to drawing valid conclusions from the data.

To name only a few factors, one should consider the actual sample of respondents obtained, along with the nature and manner of drawing the sample. Most "scientific" samples obtained vary from that which should have been obtained; "statistical corrections" are made to compensate for such variations.

The sample obtained includes all respondents who have furnished answers and completed the inquiry. However, the sample also includes the break-offs and the nonrespondents. Obtaining the *highest* possible percentage of completed interviews is basic. Nonrespondents can never be assumed to resemble respondents.

In fact, it is always safer to assume that nonrespondents are different. By the same token, respondents who are "uncertain" or "do not know" or do not complete the interview are different from those who answer with a yes or a no.

With reference to consumer research, the undecideds should never be treated like the "yes" or "no" respondents. As they get additional information, they may become quite different from those who have already responded. In other words, responses are valid as a function of the respondent's knowledge of the subject matter covered by the question, but the responses of the uninformed also count.

The greatest problem of quantitative research, and one that does not surface too often, is the integrity of the interviewers as well as the accuracy with which they record the responses, which include the demographic information as well as the answers themselves. The basic unit of measurement in quantitative research is the individual response and its accuracy as indicated on the questionnaire. When the unit of measurement is imperfect, it would appear that multiplying this imperfection by 1000 or 2000 respondents will increase the amount of nonsensical data rather than decrease it. Obviously, a number of careless or dishonest interviewers can complicate matters even more, and this can affect the validity of the study.

The second factor on which the validity of the results hinges is the questionnaire used. The types of questions asked may vary, depending on whether the respondent is contacted in person, by phone, or by mail. The questions and the responses they elicit create a pattern and actually determine the nature of the findings.

Characteristic of most quantitative studies is the closed-end question, in which a number of responses are included and the respondent selects the one that is most appropriate. Some studies include a few open-end questions, and then it is up to the interviewer or the respondent to write out the response. Such questions require classification of responses. Open-end questions are also useful for probes, that is, asking for reasons, clarification, or additional information related to a response already furnished.

Few quantitative studies do much probing, and a great many avoid open-end questions. It seems as if the simpler and more sterile the answers are, the better. In quantitative research it appears that all that matters is which candidate, soap, advertisement, or what have you is preferred. Another concern is to obtain the relation between the preferred response and the age, income, education, geographic region, and other characteristics of the respondent.

Since quantitative research is so widely used and accepted, it can be safely assumed that the reader has already come in contact with its methods and findings. Polls are widespread and are often syndicated by newspapers, magazines, and other media. Surveys conducted by market research companies for clients may or may not be made public, depending on the preferences of the client. Because of the overwhelming popularity of quantitative research, three studies will be referred to here and an attempt made to emphasize their different points of view.

The first study is a good example of consumer research and presents a careful and thoughtful interpretation of the findings. The second is an example of "loading the deck" and biasing the research toward business. The third is a legitimate study and illustrates how some studies can be useful in both market research and consumer research.

Lenahan et al. (1) are aware, based on previous research, that "consumer information programs often gather more in the way of generalized flavor than concrete use." Accordingly, they conducted a two-part study. The first part used a national probability sample (same size–N=2195) to obtain projected attitudes toward nutritional labeling. The second part included a less intensive interview with 4435 shoppers in several cities where various supermarket chains were operating a test of the nutritional labeling program.

According to the authors,

> This study was designed to measure actual use of the labels in the purchase decision as well as the consumer's attitudes toward them. Other variables measured were the changes in customer response over time and with varying levels of promotional activity. The objectives of this research were:
> 1. to discover the form of nutritional information most useful to consumers.
> 2. to identify the rate of perception, understanding, and use of nutritional labels in actual tests.
> 3. to determine the nature and importance of non-use benefits perceived by consumers.
> The last of these objectives bears further explanation. We hypothesized that apart from the direct-use benefits of the nutritional labeling program, there might be other, non-use, benefits involved. Presumably, even if there was no use of the labels by the consumer in the purchase decision, the very existence of the labels might have some influence on the market; it might create a whole new basis of product competition. (page 1)

This study found that 26 percent of the respondents had seen the labels two months after the labeling program began. Sixteen percent stated that they understood the labels, and 9 percent indicated that they had used them at least once. However, among those who saw and understood the labels, 59 percent had used them.

After the labels were explained to the respondents, 51 percent said they would occasionally use them and 97 percent said they favored a nutritional labeling program. The study also found that consumers were more aware of the labels as the level of promotion increased. Respondents seeing the labels increased from 20 percent with limited promotion to 26 percent with medium promotion and 29 percent with extensive promotion. Lenahan and his colleagues summarized their findings as follows:

1. Consumers exhibit a clear preference for a label format expressing nutritional values as a percent of RDA.*
2. In supermarket tests, about one-fourth of the consumers were aware of the labeling, about 15 percent understood the labels, and less than 10 percent used them.
3. More intensive promotion increases perception but has little effect on understanding and use.
4. Understanding and use seem to increase with the duration of the program.
5. There is evidence of increases in nutritional knowledge and sensitivity associated with the duration of the nutritional labeling program.
6. The recognition of non-use benefits is much broader among consumers than is direct use of the labels.
7. Recognition of non-use benefits is highly correlated with education and income. (page 12)

This study should be considered quite seriously, and further research in consumer affairs may well use it as a model. Most important are the implications of the study as perceived by the authors, as may be seen from the following excerpt:

Consumer survey research of the type reported on in this study has obvious limitations if one wishes to project the long term usefulness of the nutritional labeling concept. Since a longitudinal research effort is not feasible, it is necessary to show what we believe are some important conclusions at this stage in the development of the concept. This research effort to measure the potential role of nutritional labeling as perceived by consumers both exposed to the programs in a limited manner and by a representative cross section of consumers who were exposed in a less direct fashion has revealed some new facts. By relating these facts to other studies and a general understand-

* RDA stands for recommended daily allowances.

ing of trends in the food system, one should be in a better position to understand the implications for the food industry, the consumer, and regulatory agencies.

While it is useful to know the rate of perception and use of experimental labels in supermarkets, one of the most important findings of this study is the identification of extensive non-use benefits. These findings may change our approach to policy concerning product labeling. Although this study documents widespread consumer recognition of non-use benefits it gives little explanation of why consumers react in this manner. One hypothesis is that consumers see informative nutritional labels as a part of general food industry accountability rather than an input to the purchase decision.

Although experts tend to see nutritional labels on food products as a direct input to the food purchase decision, consumers tend to see their value in a much more general way. Consumers see themselves benefitting from nutritional information because of the way its affects others—through advertising and through the accountability of food manufacturers for the nutritional quality of their food products. In addition, they find it easier to have confidence in an industry which makes open disclosure of basic facts, such as nutritional information and unit price. These non-use benefits are most significantly perceived by the more affluent and educated.

These results are surprising because we tend to take nutritional labeling at face value. We live in a society and an economy that pay great respect to experts. As functions become more sophisticated and attended by science and knowledge, they are more admired. It is hard to understand that consuming may be more admired as it is made more simple. The educated, affluent consumer may have a substantial appreciation for the value of market information, but she probably does not want to spend her time comparing food labels or counting up nutrients.

Today's food buyer goes to the supermarket with very different needs and aspirations than her mother did a generation ago. Between 1940 and 1970, per capita income (after taxes and inflation) more than doubled. The share of college-age youth attending school increased from 15 to almost 50 percent. By 1970, over 49 percent of U. S. families had incomes over $10,000. Associated changes in lifestyles and food preferences are immense. Today's food shopper has many interests beyond the household which compete for her time. Many are employed. Others have civic, humanitarian, or leisure activities to attend on some organized basis. Although her mother may have seen food shopping and preparation as a central part of her responsibility, new priorities on outside activities make them merely maintenance functions for today's consumer. Shopping is more hurried as time is more scarce and money more abundant.

Our modern shopper wants the food industries to take over as much of the burden of these maintenance activities as possible. As the functions which were central to mother's ideas of self-worth are relegated to the faceless food industries, we search for some basis for trust and confidence. In times past, we knew the grocer personally. He knew something about the limited line of products he offered and he was accountable for them. Today, the personal basis of confidence is gone. We see no one we know in the supermarket. In fact, usually we see no one at all. If we can locate some one in a supermarket, he may know where a product is located in the store, but he knows nothing about it. He is in no way accountable for the quality or nature of the product.

Consumers seem to perceive nutritional labeling (along with open code dating and unit pricing) as systems that make the faceless food industries more accountable. This automated accountability may be inferior to person-to-person accountability, but it is better than nothing. It gives security and benefits because its open disclosure disciplines the market. These benefits may accrue to all even if only a small proportion of consumers use the labels directly. Consumers see these benefits as having more important implications than the direct use benefits which accrue to the few.

Even [though] the non-use benefits seem to be most important and affect all consumers, direct use benefits should not be underestimated. In the only study done over a time span, the last survey showed over sixteen percent of the consumers using the labels in the purchase decision. It also showed a tendency for direct use to increase with program duration. Given the importance of habits in consumer purchase behavior, it is not surprising that any change is slow in coming. As the program duration extends into years, direct use benefits could be expected to reach a substantial part of the consuming population. (page 11–12)

The Lenahan study probably makes its greatest contribution by demonstrating that the incongruent goals of buyers and sellers lead them to perceive the same set of facts differently. If this were the typical market research study, it would probably offer the data as evidence that nutritional labeling is a failure. But it is not that kind of study, and therefore it can be as valuable for the seller and maker as it is for the consumer. This study is a good illustration of why consumer research, as opposed to market research, is a necessary adjunct to market research. The sooner business can recognize this, the better.

Our second example is quite different from the Lenahan study. Its title is *Government and the Consumer* (2). Three organizations are involved: The Business Roundtable, Research Strategies Corporation, and Opinion Research Corporation. The following statement indicates the basic purposes of The Business Roundtable and lists its officers and their companies (3).

> The basic purposes of The Business Roundtable are to provide a forum in which the business leadership of the nation can exchange ideas and develop policy recommendations on major business, economic and social issues; to foster a higher and more realistic public appreciation of the contributions by business to society; to obtain a better balance in labor-management relations; and to strengthen the voice of business on these problems.
>
> One of the distinguishing characteristics of the Roundtable is the dedicated involvement of the chief executives of many of its member companies. John D. Harper, board chairman of ALCOA, is chairman and chief executive officer of the Roundtable. John D. deButts, chairman of A.T.&T., and Howard J. Morgens, chairman, Executive Committee of Procter & Gamble, are Roundtable co-chairmen. Chief executives of many other member companies participate actively in the Roundtable's Executive, Policy and Operating Committees.*
>
> Roundtable Task Forces, organized to deal with the most urgent challenges currently facing the business community, are headed by the following business leaders:

Consumerism	J. B. Jackson, President
	J. C. Penney Company
Consumers Energy	Edgar B. Speer, Chairman
	U. S. Steel Corporation
Economic Concentration	Robert S. Hatfield, Chairman
	Continental Can Company
Environment	Frank R. Milliken, President
	Kennecott Copper Corporation
International Trade	J. Stanford Smith, Chairman
	International Paper Company
National Health	Henry Ford II, Chairman
	Ford Motor Company
Regulatory Agencies	Irving S. Shapiro, Chairman
	E. I. Du Pont de Nemours & Co.
Taxation	Reginald H. Jones, Chairman
	General Electric Company
Wage & Price Controls	F. Perry Wilson, Chairman
	Union Carbide Corporation

The basic purposes, as described, are laudable. But now let us look at a study paid for by the Roundtable. The following ex-

*This committee does rotate and the names change from time to time.

cerpt from the foreword is typical of quantitative research. It emphasizes matters like number of respondents and probable error. All the questions are of the closed-end variety. There are no probes—just the "facts."

> Findings in this survey are based on a total of 2,038 interviews conducted personally and individually in respondents' homes between January 10 and February 3, 1975. Interviewed was a representative sample of all adults in the continental United States 18 years of age and over.
>
> The probability sampling methods used are of the type that produces a true cross-section of the population coast to coast, rich as well as poor, occupational groups in their appropriate proportions, etc. In reading this report, a good statistical rule of thumb to keep in mind is this: When the total sample is involved in any breakdown of answers, differences of 3% and more can generally be regarded as significant; when comparisons are made of subgroupings of the total public (old vs. young, etc.), differences of 8% or more are needed. (page ii)

Earlier in this chapter we mentioned the fact that the nature of the questions has as much if not more to do with the validity of the findings as the "scientific" sampling. This study surely proves the point.

A series of questions were asked. Most dealt with the respondent's knowledge of and attitude toward government agencies; a few dealt with attitudes toward business. For example, the first question referred to in the report is as follows:

> As an American consumer, you buy a variety of things for yourself and your family. In general, how fairly do you, as a consumer, feel you are treated by business? Would you say you are almost always treated *fairly*, usually treated *fairly*, usually treated *unfairly*, or almost always treated *unfairly* by business? (page 3)

Somewhat later the following question is asked:

> Now, I would like to ask about some of the Federal Government agencies and commissions which regulate the selling and marketing of products or services sold to the American consumer. . . . For example, the Federal Office of Consumer Affairs; have you ever heard of it? (page 13)

This is followed by similar questions about the Consumer Product Safety Commission and the Environmental Protection Agency, and then the following question is asked:

> Those in favor of setting up an additional federal consumer

protection agency on top of the other agencies say it is needed because the agencies we have are not getting the job done themselves. Those who oppose setting up the additional agency say we already have plenty of government agencies to protect consumers, and it's just a matter of making them work better. How do you feel? Do you favor setting up an additional consumer protection agency over all others, or do you favor doing what is necessary to make the agencies we now have more effective in protecting consumer interests? (page 35)

Among the conclusions reported is the following:

On the direct question as to whether they are for or against setting up a Federal Consumer Protection Agency over all existing consumer-related agencies, 75% of the public vote against doing this and are in favor, instead, of making existing agencies work better and more effectively. When the 13% who vote for establishing the new agency are asked whether they still would be in favor if the costs were to be "at least $60 million for the first three years," as provided in the proposed bill (S200) under consideration in the senate, about half say they would not.

Adding these to the 75% who originally voted against setting up the new agency, the total vote comes to 81%. (page 36)

Carol Tucker Foreman, executive director of Consumer Federation of America, is reported by *Advertising Age* (4) as complaining that the question "constitutes an inexcusable and unprofessional exploitation of the unfortunate lack of information most consumers have regarding the nature and goal of the proposed Agency for Consumer Advocacy." And Senator Charles Percy cited the text of the question used by the agency's opponents as an example of a rigged poll.

We have heard from labor and government. What does a publication representing advertising and business have to say? The following editorial from *Advertising Age* speaks quite eloquently.

GREASING THE OPINION POLL

To learn that public opinion pollsters do not frame their own questions or stand behind their findings is devastating and unacceptable.

A recent poll by Opinion Research Corp. contained a question that smacks of rigging in order to make a client happy. And the aftermath of this disclosure signals some very tough times ahead for the entire research community.

The poll, unfortunately, involves Business Roundtable, made up of many of our leading business executives, which hired the highly regarded ORC to poll people about the proposed Agency

TABLE 10.1 Husbands and wives purchases and influences—food and beverages

PACKAGED PRODUCTS 7-day purchases

BASE: Purchases by Wives and Husbands in Past 7 Days

WEIGHTS REFLECTING INFLUENCE — More influential Spouse=1.00 (Read Table Across)	Purchased by		Weights Reflecting Share of Influence							
			Direct Influence				Indirect Influence			
			Prod. Dec.		Brand Dec.		Prod. Dec.		Brand Dec.	
	Wife	Husb.	Wife	Husb.	Wife	Husb.	Wife	Husb.	Wife	Husb.
Food and Beverages										
Baby Food	1.00	.21	1.00	.10	1.00	.10	1.00	.12	1.00	.12
Beverages										
Alcoholic Bev. (Except Spirits)										
Beer	.70	1.00	.27	1.00	.27	1.00	.27	1.00	.24	1.00
Wine	1.00	.93	.96	1.00	.86	1.00	1.00	.84	1.00	1.00
Coffee										
Freeze Dried Coffee	1.00	.48	1.00	.75	1.00	.62	1.00	.78	1.00	.70
Instant Coffee (Reg.)	1.00	.26	1.00	.65	1.00	.70	1.00	.86	1.00	.86
Ground Coffee (Reg.)	1.00	.35	1.00	.54	1.00	.54	1.00	.72	1.00	.67
Fruit Drinks										
Canned Fruit Drinks	1.00	.26	1.00	.38	1.00	.38	1.00	.50	1.00	.52
Powered Fruit Drinks	1.00	.23	1.00	.38	1.00	.34	1.00	.51	1.00	.45
Soft Drinks										
Carb. Soft Drinks (Diet)	1.00	.34	1.00	.33	1.00	.33	1.00	.38	1.00	.37
Carb. Soft Drinks (Non-Diet)	1.00	.42	1.00	.62	1.00	.63	1.00	.74	1.00	.74
Tea										
Regular Tea	1.00	.25	1.00	.42	1.00	.37	1.00	.61	1.00	.57
Cereals										
Cold Cereal (Unsweetened)	1.00	.19	1.00	.36	1.00	.40	1.00	.53	1.00	.50
Hot Cereal	1.00	.18	1.00	.49	1.00	.49	1.00	.59	1.00	.69
Cheese (Pkgd. American)	1.00	.22	1.00	.53	1.00	.52	1.00	.67	1.00	.62
Chewing Gum	1.00	.25	1.00	.40	1.00	.40	1.00	.44	1.00	.45

Table reads: Wives are assigned a weight of 1.00 reflecting their larger proportion of baby food purchases, and relative to the wives' weight of 1.00, husbands are weighted 21, etc.

SOURCE: Haley and Overholser and Associates, Inc., *Purchase Influence*, New Canaan, Conn., 1975.

TABLE 10.2 Husbands and wives purchases and influences—durables

DURABLE GOODS AND SERVICES 12-month purchases / SHARE OF INFLUENCE	BASE Purchases in Past 12 Months	Wife and Husband Influence on Purchases = 100% (Read Table Across)	Share of Influence											
			Purchase Decision Influence				Initiation				Information Gathering			
			Prod. Dec.		Brand Dec.		Prod. Dec.		Brand Dec.		Prod. Dec.		Brand Dec.	
			Wife	Husb.	Wife	Husb.	Wife	Husb.	Wife	Husb.	Wife	Husb.	Wife	Husb.
Automotive														
Automobiles			38	62	33	67	22	78	21	79	18	82	18	82
Automobile Tires			20	80	18	82	12	88	11	89	13	87	14	86
Appliances														
Home Entertainment														
TV Set. Black and White			50	50	49	51	58	42	45	55	48	52	45	55
TV Set. Color			46	54	42	58	38	62	30	70	41	59	37	63
Cassette Tape Recorder			48	52	42	58	48	52	41	59	44	56	45	55
Major Appliances														
Clothes Dryer			53	47	53	47	67	33	56	44	55	45	55	45
Clothes Washer			54	46	51	49	70	30	57	43	57	43	55	45
Range/Stove			52	48	52	48	66	34	45	55	54	46	51	49
Small Appliances														
Electric Blender			59	41	53	47	67	33	50	50	53	47	52	48
Coffee Maker			64	36	64	36	73	27	68	32	64	36	66	34
Vacuum Cleaner			60	40	60	40	80	20	69	31	66	34	65	35

Table reads: Wives accounted for 38% of total influence on the decision to buy the last new automobile purchased in the past 12 months, husbands 62%, etc.

SOURCE: See source for Table 10.1.

for Consumer Advocacy. The Business Roundtable opposes this federal consumer agency. So do we. But that's not the issue here. The ORC questions included stuff like this: "Do you favor setting up an additional consumer protection agency over all others, or do you favor doing what is necessary to make the agencies we now have more effective in protecting consumer interests?" Isn't that like asking: "Do you favor waste in government?"

Predictably, only 10% favored the new agency. At least one senator has termed this an example of a rigged poll, and a Senate subcommittee is investigating the matter. The question to be sure, leads the respondent, and we believe it also misrepresents the facts. When the heat began to emanate from Capitol Hill, ORC disclosed that the question was drawn up by another company, Research Strategies, and the Business Roundtable, not by the ORC staff. ORC added that this procedure is "in accordance with the ethics of the profession."

We think opinion researchers should be responsible for their entire survey, not just selected parts of it. How can the public be expected to take opinion polls seriously if it turns out that the sponsor is shopping around, buying the appropriate segments *a la carte*? In market research, it seems that questions are developed more carefully so as to be bias-free. But then, a cynic might say the stakes are higher, involving the sale of products or services, not public opinion and the governing of our country.

All research, all poll-taking activity, not only opinion surveys, has suffered a considerable setback because of this episode. And it doesn't take a survey to figure that much out.

Advertising Age, April 4, 1975

It matters little which of the three companies involved is responsible. The fact that all three could not see the implications of such a study raises serious questions.

A spokesman for Opinion Research states that "what happened here was clearly in accordance with the ethics of the profession." He goes on to say that "the client drafts the questions and purchases what he wishes." This is ethics?

The reason we refer to this study is to illustrate that all that is quantitative need not be valid. In fact, the writer has conducted some qualitative studies related to the positions of all three organizations and finds (based on unscientific sampling) that they have few defenders.

Here we see how a study purporting to conduct consumer research apparently did not do it in as fair and unbiased a manner as possible—if the comments we have selected from labor, government, and business are representative.

The third study to be referred to was conducted by Haley,

Overholser & Associates and was sponsored by five magazines: *Family Weekly, Readers Digest, Sports Illustrated, Time,* and *TV Guide.* Its title is *Purchase Influence—Measures of Husband/Wife Influence on Buying Decisions* (5).

The 46 million households headed by married couples living together constitute 84 percent of the U.S. population and 81 percent of total consumer income. The study measured the influence of husbands and wives on purchases of 87 packaged products and 21 durable goods and services. Personal interviews were conducted with 2373 wives and 1767 husbands in 2480 households. Audits were taken to confirm that the interviews were in fact conducted.

A constant sum scale was used as a measure of influence. In other words, the respondents were asked to indicate the influence exerted on a purchase by each member of the husband-wife team, for a total of 10 points. Admittedly. this measure is not a perfect one, but it is at least a candid and honest attempt.

Tables 10.1 and 10.2 illustrate the relative influence, both direct and indirect, of husbands and wives on purchases of some packaged goods, as well as the purchase decision influence, initiation, and information gathering of husbands and wives for a sample of durable goods.

Although this is a market research study and the sponsors have a very direct interest in the results, it is an example of a careful, unbiased study. From the standpoint of consumer research, this study adds credibility and validity to the way consumers actually make decisions and recognizes the "real world" in which husbands and wives are continually interacting and influencing each other. Of course this technique could be applied to many more critical issues in consumer affairs, but for the time being that is not where the money is.

BIBLIOGRAPHY

1. LENAHAN, R. J., et al., "Consumer Reaction to Nutritional Labels on Food Products," *Journal of Consumer Affairs,* 1 (Summer 1973).
2. Opinion Research Corp., *Government and the Consumer* (New Jersey, 1975).
3. The Business Roundtable, New York, 1974.
4. "Senate Unit Investigates Consumer Agency Poll," *Advertising Age,* April 7, 1975.
5. Haley, Overholser & Associates, Inc., *Purchase Influence—Measures of Husband/Wife Influence on Buying Decisions* (Connecticut, 1975).

3

SOCIALIZATION—
THE PROCESS
OF BECOMING
A CONSUMER

If consumer affairs were limited to buyers, sellers, makers, and (depending on one's point of view) the help or intrusion of government and labor, the problem would not be so foreboding. The severity of the problem is that too many people have overlooked for too long the fact that the buyer-seller-maker transaction, its antecedents, and its consequences may ultimately rock the very foundations of both democracy and capitalism.

How long can a disadvantaged consumer endure this situation?

This section of the book raises such general and fundamental social issues as freedom and change while looking at the process of socialization and the very special problems of overlooked consumer groups (because of their apparent lack of consuming resources) such as the ghetto dweller, the young, and the old.

11

Books as vignettes of societal problems

In general, the issues related to consumer affairs rarely attract as much attention in the media or in the minds of the public as the issues of sex, war, crime, and politics. From time to time a consumer issue will draw attention, but then it goes away to come back some other day.

In contemporary thought, all social movements attempt to raise the consciousness of ever-increasing numbers of people. This, it is hoped, will result in the success of the movement.

And so it is with consumer affairs: The need is to raise the consciousness of consumers. It is interesting to note that this has sometimes happened as a result of the impact of a book on society. Every now and then the printed page can help people focus on an issue to a greater extent than riots, overreaction to picketing, and other forms of confrontation or violence. It is good to know that books can lay the foundation for progress, growth, and change.

In this chapter we will discuss four books that have had an important influence on consumer affairs. In some respects these books may even be considered classics, if one accepts the definition that a "classic" is a book that is talked about more than it is read. Since these books all attempt to call to the reader's attention an existing conflict and a hoped-for reduction in that conflict, they obviously contribute to the field of consumer psychology.

Each book, in its way, describes a perilous set of conditions.

Each refers to a situation in which the consumer is obviously getting less than a fair share of freedom. To the extent that a book is able to influence concerns and action, these books have resulted in a more equitable distribution of freedom and a reduction in conflict. They have also encouraged thinking which has resulted in changes in attitude as well as changes in behavior. This is what gives some books their value.

The Jungle

The Jungle (1) was written by Upton Sinclair in 1905. To gather the factual information on which this novel is based, Sinclair spent about seven weeks wandering through the stockyards dressed as a worker. The book's content was and still is quite provoking. As often happens in such instances, the publication of the book was controversial. A Chicago paper sent an "impartial reporter," who declared that almost everything in the book was false. There was a slight hitch, however: The "reporter" turned out to be a publicity man for Armour, the meat packer. (One might add that this was not the first of such "dirty tricks," nor have we seen the last. The point is to not be gullible and accept "high sources" as factual. It is necessary to ferret out who, what, where, and why—at the very least. Over the years "dirty tricks" have been especially popular in the area of consumer affairs. One must be cautious in evaluating what side is saying what—if it is saying anything at all.)

The Jungle is a sad, human, and picturesque portrayal of life among industrial workers at the turn of the century. Its stark reality in revealing substandard, even inhuman, conditions led first to shock, horror, and concern and then to action and change. It can be unequivocally stated that *The Jungle* instigated a series of investigations and revelations that continue to the present day. It surely was responsible for a series of laws that now, somewhat reasonably, guarantee pure foods in order to protect our health and safety.

Although *The Jungle* is a novel, its description of the sordid working and living conditions of the stockyards is realistically unfolded. Slaughtering is an ugly mess at best, but the conditions of slaughtering were matched by the living conditions of the slaughterers. The prevailing "law of the jungle" seemed to be to slaughter every animal regardless of its condition. Further, this mess was accompanied by a prevailing system of corruption. Workers generally paid tribute to their "bosses" or to local politicians either in the form of money or, at times, even by allowing their own bodies to be part of the "deal." Corruption, graft, and special privileges were the order of the day, and the most blatant political shenanigans abounded. It was clear that the workers were powerless and that a few "bosses" sustained their power by exploiting the workers' fear of unemployment.

Although at that time U.S. government inspectors certified that all diseased cattle were kept in the state of Illinois, it was equally true that this did not prevent meat from diseased cattle from being sold in Chicago. Further, there was evidence that diseased meats were processed while the inspectors had their attention distracted and, as a result, could be sold anywhere.

The book also refers to the early attempts to organize the workers and the resulting spying, threats, and strike-breaking tactics. It is a story of despair. In the main, the individual's primary struggle was merely to survive; the issue of freedom was too much of an abstraction. Yet these workers, who were immigrants, learned ways of protecting themselves while at the same time developing principles that eventually brought about a change in fundamental living and working conditions that many of us now take for granted as an undeniable right. The tragedy is that almost three-quarters of a century later migrants and ghetto dwellers still live and work in conditions that may not be appreciably better.

Jurgis Rudkus, the book's main character, is like thousands upon thousands of young people who are willing to work hard, raise a family, refuse to succumb to adversity, and yet, on their own, just can't seem to make it against overwhelming odds. The trade-off is what happens to the millions of people who ate ham, sausages, or beef that was bloated, and chemically treated, regardless of its condition at the time of slaughter, all with apparently little conscious concern on the part of Packing Town and its owners.

A value of this book is that Sinclair anticipated the relatedness of the right to pure food and reasonable working conditions and the need to reduce corruption. As Sinclair said, "I aimed at the public's heart and by accident I hit it in the stomach."

Unsafe at Any Speed

The current symbol of consumer advocacy, standing head and shoulders above all others in effectively resolving the issues he chooses to attack, is Ralph Nader. The words *Naderism* and *consumerism* tend to be used interchangeably.

Whether Nader's fame would be as widespread without *Un-*

safe at Any Speed (2) is a moot question. The fact is that *Unsafe at Any Speed,* written in 1965 and revised in 1972 as *Since Unsafe at Any Speed* (3), is must reading. It reveals the power of an industry that has been almost totally unregulated since its earliest days, as well as the excessive influence of lobbyists and advertising.

The book also strikes at the ineffectiveness and confusion of bureaucrats and elected officials and shows how they make ineffective the efforts of the small sprinkling of dedicated officials who really try. Nader also exposes the influence of one-sided dissemination of information on an uninformed and unsuspecting public.

Most important, the book indicates that perseverance in pursuit of truth and justice (a redistribution of freedom) in a dedicated and persistent manner *can* result in change.

Nader deserves credit, especially because he kept at it and gained his point even though the odds were most difficult. Just as Sinclair influenced the future, so has Nader. The automobile industry may never be the same again, despite its powerful position in the American economy. The impact of the automobile industry on the total economy is immense. Prior to Nader the industry seemed, for all practical purposes, impervious to regulation. It designed and manufactured cars according to its own standards and thus set the conditions that determined the safety of drivers and passengers. In a way, *Unsafe at Any Speed* is about a different sort of "jungle."

The book is much more than an exposé of General Motors' Corvair. Nader indicates that the company was aware of the car's instability both before production and at the time the car was first put on the market.

Sometimes a most unlikely set of events must coincide before insight and understanding can occur. This is the way it was for Mrs. Rose Pierini. She had just had an accident that severed her left arm. She reported to a California Highway Patrol officer that "something went wrong with my steering." It just so happened that Officer John Bortolozzo saw the car flip over and was aware that Mrs. Pierini had been driving 35 miles an hour in a 35-mile zone. He saw the car move toward the right side of the road near the shoulder, and then "all of a sudden the vehicle made a sharp cut to the left and swerved over." In the lawsuit that followed, General Motors settled the case for $70,000 rather than continuing the trial so as not to possibly attract unwanted publicity.

What is unusual (and one of the interesting points implied

by Nader) is that people are blamed for accidents whereas cars are not. Nader goes further and points out that traffic laws center on the infractions of people and seem to hold cars blameless. The book stresses the need for better engineering so that drivers would be safer.

The industry's emphasis on styling and minimal attention to machine safety had all but caused the disappearance of bumpers, with the result that one had to replace the fronts and rears of cars as well as the people—if they survived the accident. Was this done to please the buyer's esthetic preferences, or was it done to sell front and rear body parts?

Three examples should make the point clear. (1) Few car owners know that tinted windshields are inappropriate for drivers over 45 years of age because of decreased visual acuity. This little-known fact is one that should be pointed out to older drivers. (2) Further, tinted windshields interfere with night driving. There is less light available to all drivers, regardless of age. (3) Among the leading design factors contributing to accidents are such "little things" as the reflection of the instrument panel on the windshield, which results in improper driver vision. Surely these "little things" could have been corrected a long time ago.

Obviously, the manufacturers and their trade associations have not paid as much attention to safety as one might expect. A question for contemplation is whether they might be more concerned with car repairs and auto body replacements than with their customers' lives. Of course it would be useless to ask automobile executives this question. They base their emphasis on styling and appearance on market research results, and this is a tautology or a begging of the question. Of additional concern is the fact that professional societies such as those including automotive engineers seem to be one-sided in their research. By this we mean that they are oriented toward the company rather than the consumer.

Nader reports that Cornell's Automotive Crash Injury Research, which is 60 percent supported by government funds and 40 percent supported by industry funds, often allows its preliminary findings to be reviewed by the Automobile Manufacturers Association. He writes, "To permit public funds to be mixed with industry money in such a project as ACIR and to give researchers full discretion to give data to manufacturers while denying it to all others is nothing short of an abdication of the public trust."

Another issue on which the automobile industry tangles with the consumer relates to freedom to pollute the air. In 1950 Dr. Arlie Haagen-Smit stated hydrocarbon compounds produced by automobile exhaust react with oxides of nitrogen under sunlight to produce photochemical smog." Since 1950 (and for that matter before 1950) little has been done either voluntarily or through law to appreciably reduce the automobile's capacity to pollute air —which most of us need in a purer form than we now seem to be breathing. Just as attempts to curb this cause of air pollution were getting started, along came the energy crunch. Then there were more arguments for continued pollution than for purer air. Why?

The Chemical Feast

An early associate of Nader was James Turner. He, too, continues in the quest for more freedom for the consumer and less confusion generated by the pattern of industry and government working closely together.

The Chemical Feast (4) is a by-product of a Nader study group on food protection and the Food and Drug Administration (FDA). Although the title is catching, in a way it is misleading. The book is primarily an exposé of the FDA as an inefficient bureaucracy.

Based on interviews and library research, it unfolds a story of altered documents, misrepresented facts, and suppressed research within the agency. Further, it is a tale about bureaucrats and their bureaucratic habits of inefficiency and self-justification. It tells of a combination of inertia, vested interests, and insulation from exposure. It also furnishes some insight into why there is a steady procession of new appointees who start off intending to accomplish a change for the better but soon go away saddened and defeated by the entrenched bureaucracy that seems to stay on forever. In other words, bureaucracy is a formidable self-perpetuating force.

The book's introduction presents some startling statistics that should rid many readers of complacency about how well off we are as a nation. In a relatively short period (1950–1968) we dropped from fifth to thirteenth among the nations of the world in infant mortality rate. In other words, relatively speaking, more of our infants die than before. Further, according to Dr. Jean Mayer, nutrition advisor to former President Nixon, 20-year-old men in 36 countries will live longer than American men who are 20 years of age. To complete this depressing scene, 20-year old women will live longer in 21 nations than American women who are 20 years old.

The point is that life expectancy and infant mortality are

generally regarded as indicators of a nation's health and welfare. We continue to do more poorly. So when politicians tell us that we are the strongest nation in the world they must be talking about something other than life expectancy. Is it naive to believe that the strongest nation in the world is the one in which the citizens live longest?

Obviously, life and death have something to do with nutrition. Turner's study of the FDA indicates that the safeguards for retaining nutritional values in food are not operating. Further, many food additives are less than desirable. A major theme of *The Chemical Feast* is that the industrial-bureaucratic combine leaves the consumer at a decided disadvantage.

Few can disagree with the premise that a fundamental principle of food labeling should be honesty in dealing with consumers. For health and safety purposes, food labeling should be complete. Who can be opposed to this view? The answer is, many special interest groups.

The examples are all too frequent. A typical one is the efforts of Coca Cola and Dr. Pepper to prevent the labeling of caffeine as an additive in cola drinks. Somehow, after the publication of *The Chemical Feast* things changed: Caffeine labeling now appears on cola bottles.

The lack of knowledge on the part of the average consumer about many of the controversies related to nutrition and additives is appalling, and one must ask why this is the case. Surely people, if they were fully informed, would manifest normal concern for their own health and safety. It is within this context that the book refers to the long controversy over matters such as bleached flour in white bread, benzoate of soda in catsup, the use of saccharine, and until relatively recently, the presence of monosodium glutamate in baby foods as well as typical Chinese restaurant dishes.

The main thrust of the book is the series of serious questions it raises about the FDA, its performance and its failure to protect the consumer. The book reveals the power and influence of the food and drug industries and their day-to-day contact with the agency to the almost total exclusion of the public.

The agency's insidious reference to a lack of consumer interest, based on the absence of a strong and continued consumer effort, is preposterous. The consumer and, for the most part, consumer leaders do not have the resources, the influence, or the time to match the trained, well-paid lobbyists representing the food and drug industry.

Recognizing that any Nader team, such as the one that did

the research for *The Chemical Feast,* has a motive for making its investigations, just as any lobby has, it is for the consumer to decide who represents the consumer best as a result of reading this book.

To repeat an important theme, the consumer should seek out all sources of information and then independently reach a conclusion. If he/she cannot do that, then at least it should be his/her responsibility to seek out the information that will enable him/her to spend money on food that has nutritional value and is free from additives that might lead to poisoning, cancer, or malnutrition—regardless of the amount of money spent.

The Greening of America

A different approach, but in many ways an equally thought-provoking one, is found in Charles A. Reich's *The Greening of America* (5). Most simply, it states that a new revolution is coming. It recognizes that liberal reformation in the form of a corporate state has failed and that a new way of life is coming that will incorporate new values and a new culture. It rejects the conditions of impoverishment, dehumanization, and war, as well as any attempt to justify such conditions through "logic" or, as the psychologist would say, rationalization.

The book raises some interesting questions. Among them might be whether the Rockefellers, Vanderbilts, Carnegies, Harrimans and Fords were benefactors or enemies of the American people. With reference to the New Deal, Reich points out that it was responding to ills that had been diagnosed decades earlier and that it simply transferred power from the private sector (business) to "public" (government) organizations. That all was not well is evidenced by the counterattack of the right and its spokesmen, the House Unamerican Activities Committee.

Reich is a law professor, but he writes not as a lawyer but as a freewheeling speculator in the fields of philosophy, psychology, sociology, and literary interpretation. The book is imaginative, but it may well be guilty of overgeneralization. For example, the three stages of consciousness that Reich describes are more speculative than real. He writes, for example, "All that is necessary to describe the new society is to describe a new way of life." To the psychologist this means that in a do-it-yourself manner the individual somehow obtains a new style of life with new goals and activities. Not too many people can make such a drastic change and remain "adjusted." Reich's views of the liberation of the self, rejecting the concept of perfection and assuming personal responsibility, are quite well known to most therapists as well as to people who have had some therapy. They are valuable aids to a person who is trying to change.

The primary reason for referring to *The Greening of America,* beyond its provocations, is that it makes a direct reference to the worker-consumer. Reich offers the view that the overly persuaded consumer may no longer be a willing worker because of the conflict between hedonistic pleasure and the self-denials imposed by work. He says, "When advertising paints a picture of consumer hedonism and freedom, and work is considered only a means to that end, the machinery of the Corporate State begins to work toward its own destruction."

Reich refers to two forms of consumer revolt that he believes are very common. One is against inadequate public services and the other is against assaults on the environment. Thus his views extend beyond direct buyer-seller-maker transactions and recognize that consumers are beginning to demand that society provide schools, hospitals, and safety in the streets, as well as a stable environment, which includes clean rivers and air. A note of pessimism is struck with this statement: "But just as we are producing workers who are increasingly unwilling to work, so we are producing consumers who are increasingly dissatisfied, no matter what they get."

This is quite a mouthful and deserves a lengthy pause for contemplation and evaluation. Reich could very well be right. It would be good for business, government, and labor to look more closely at themselves as well as the consumer. We tend to look more critically at others than at ourselves. But as consumers we should look at ourselves and what we do. It may be too much to expect business to see us the way we really are. In turn, business would do well to look at itself. The same goes for government and labor. But all groups, and the individuals in those groups, need "cleaner glasses" to help them "see" more clearly.

Conclusion

The critical reader may well question why, among all the books related to consumer interests, *The Jungle, Unsafe at Any Speed, The Chemical Feast,* and *The Greening of America* should be singled out. There will be some who say that the author is really an activist at heart. Not true. It is important to understand all sides of a story, or at least to understand that a conflict exists between the powerful and the powerless. One can then begin to understand the issues and thereby begin to reduce the conflict.

Without such understanding one has nothing but the status quo, which often leads to decadence. After all, one never really stands still.

The Jungle is a story full of pathos. Its contribution is the reform it generated.

Nader took on General Motors. The industry may never be the same.

Turner shows up the ills of bureaucracy.

The Greening of America is a freewheeling and imaginative interpretation that, among other things, stimulates the reader to ask why the worker and the consumer, who are one and the same, are at the same time in conflict.

All four books look squarely at certain conflicts using either facts or hypotheses. With their penchant for creativity and change, they suggest or imply ways to resolve or at least reduce some of those conflicts. Accordingly, these four books have been discussed as illustrations or vignettes of consumer affairs.

BIBLIOGRAPHY

1. SINCLAIR, U., *The Jungle* (Cambridge, Mass.: Robert Bently, 1972).
2. NADER, R., *Unsafe at Any Speed* (New York: Grossman, 1965).
3. NADER, R., *Since Unsafe at Any Speed* (New York: Grossman, 1972).
4. TURNER, J. S., *The Chemical Feast* (New York: Grossman, 1970).
5. REICH, C. A., *The Greening of America* (New York: Random House, 1970).

12
Free enterprise and freedom

There are some who view consumer issues as limiting the free enterprise system. This view should be considered either biased or illogical. It would appear that the free enterprise system should include freedom for all the parties involved in a transaction.

The issues of consumer affairs are an outgrowth of the individual's right to actualize his/her needs and goals. To the extent that one of the parties in a transaction achieves its needs and goals to a greater degree than another, then different degrees of satisfaction, frustration, and power exist.

To achieve one's goals or satisfy one's needs, one must have an opportunity to be informed and make a choice. The information should be relevant to the decision, and the choice should ultimately be in accordance with the consumer's needs. The completion of a transaction should result in mutual advantage. The fact is, however, that a buyer-seller-maker transaction may be something less than "free enterprise" as each party tries to achieve its own needs and goals. Obviously, free enterprise does not mean equal freedom for all.

At the core of consumer affairs is the fact that various transactions result in varying degrees of freedom or restriction for all the parties involved, either directly or indirectly, in the transaction. Each of the parties or groups not only has different degrees of freedom but also makes different interpretations of the degree of freedom they and the others have. Simply stated, most consumer issues come down to the question of who shall have how much freedom in the pursuit of his/her needs and goals.

Business, consumers, government, and labor have incongruent goals. The actualization of each group's goals is at the center of the issue of freedom. Each group perceives quite differently the extent to which it should share their freedom with the others.

What must be recognized is that freedom is both relative and finite. It is relative because different individuals share it differently. It is finite because there is just so much of it and no more. And this applies to both individuals and groups.

The restlessness of the consumer is manifested in the demand for a greater share of freedom, which consumers have come to believe they deserve. On the other hand, business has enjoyed a greater share of freedom in terms of who, what, and how to inform. Under the auspices of "free enterprise" it chooses what products shall be available and makes itself heard quite effectively through advertising, lobbies, the media, and various government sources. Accordingly, business seems quite content with the share of freedom it exercises and prefers things the way they are. Many of its efforts are well organized to prevent any erosion of the status quo.

The consumer movement and the resulting changes must cause gains or losses in freedom for either the consumer, business, government, or labor. The degree of gain or loss depends on the way one perceives the problems and issues of consumer affairs.

Based on their perceptions, individuals wind up with the conviction that the consumer movement is either right or wrong. Some even see the movement and its by-products as a threat to democracy itself.

It is erroneous to believe that freedom is an ever-expanding thing in which more and more can exist for all. Quite to the contrary, the total amount of freedom that exists is absolute. Freedom is not something that is shared equally by all. There is just so much freedom to be shared. The more freedom one group has, the less there is for others.

One might think of freedom as a bunch of goodies in a bag. The more you get, the less someone else gets. The more freedom business has, the less freedom there is for the consumer or labor or government. To illustrate, does business have the freedom to adulterate food, manufacture unsafe products, or advertise a food or beverage as nutritious when it has no nutritional value? If it does, then the rights and freedom of consumers are impaired. Yet such practices have existed in the past and continue to exist in the present. The records of the Federal Trade Commission and the FDA make this amply clear. Such records offer clearer evidence than the accusations of consumers or the denials of business.

If business possesses considerable freedom—unless prevented by law—then the freedom of the consumer from the standpoint of health and safety is limited. For example, does a supermarket meat department have the right to package fat, bone, and gristle on the bottom of the tray, or does the consumer have the right to see through the bottom of the package to determine if the meat is the same on the bottom as it is on the top? For the consumer to see through the bottom of the tray, a law must be passed.

As another example, does business have the right to make covert credit checks on consumers, or does the consumer have the right to be protected against such an invasion of privacy?

For some, free enterprise means the freedom of business to conduct its affairs and not be subject to regulation. It would appear that free enterprise and freedom are not the same thing either in principle or in reality.

One should note that the early labor-business struggles involving unsanitary working conditions, child labor, and unreasonable work hours were also concerned with the division and distribution of freedom. The more freedom business had, the less labor had, and vice versa. In other words, the issues of consumer affairs as they exist today may well have their roots in the issues that labor was concerned about some decades ago.

Consumers have the right to be *informed* (as to food quality and nutrients, etc.), to *choose* (e.g., which brand of refrigerator actually uses less electricity, etc.), and to be heard (when complaints are seriously considered and adjusted). Most basic is the right to safety (when driving a car, using an appliance, eating canned foods, playing with toys, etc.).

When President Kennedy, in his 1962 consumer message to Congress, spoke of the right to safety, the right to be informed, the right to choose and the right to be heard, he was really declaring a bill of rights for the consumer. In many ways this is where many contemporary consumer issues came into focus. To be sure, there were many important antecedents to the need for a "consumer bill of rights." But Kennedy's message spelled out the need for freedom for the consumer more clearly than ever before. It also signaled the need to pass laws that would change the balance of forces and increase the degree of freedom consumers might enjoy.

It was easy to predict that business would resist. After all, the freedoms business enjoyed, whether appropriate or excessive, were indulgences that would not be given up freely.

Very often freedom accompanies power and influence. Freedom is easy to live with. Those who do not have an equitable share of freedom are powerless and uninfluential, and this they find difficult to live with. Officeholders, bureaucrats, and business executives have power and influence. Ghetto livers, the aged, and the uneducated are generally powerless and uninfluential.

Thus it is clear, or should be, that business wants the freedom it has traditionally enjoyed and consumers want more freedom than they now have. New laws related to consumer affairs add to the freedom of some groups and take it away from others. In other words, laws, especially as they relate to consumer problems, determine the relative degrees of freedom that groups with incongruent goals shall enjoy.

The point is that in consumer affairs a particular individual or group may well be in a favored position because it has a greater share of freedom. As it becomes clear that its goals are incongruent with those of other individuals or groups, the issue becomes one of maintaining the status quo vs. effecting change. The change may give the formerly disadvantaged group a greater amount of freedom; as a result the formerly advantaged group will have less freedom.

Obviously, the greater the share of freedom the consumer has, the less freedom business will have. Accordingly, laws either grant or restrict freedom. The chances are that any law does both at the same time, but not to the same people or groups. Thus a law restricting the sale of firearms both gives and denies freedom. A law that requires truth in lending denies the freedom to misrepresent and grants the freedom to be informed. But each side perceives what is fair quite differently. When incongruent goals place consumers and business on different sides of the fence as to whether or not a law should be passed, one hears both sides arguing the question from different points of view regarding rights and freedom. Sometimes the arguments become supercharged, excessively emotional and irrational. At such times one even hears the irrational statement that the law being considered is "unamerican" and will prevent the democratic system from functioning.

When business says that the consumer is free to choose products in the marketplace, the consumer answers, "provided that they are safe and worth choosing in the first place." When business decides unilaterally what information will be furnished, (despite its market research) the consumer sometimes finds that the information is incomplete, irrelevant, and possibly misleading. So the consumer is increasingly insistent that such information be more complete. The issue is whether the decision to furnish information will be made according to a limited definition of free enterprise. In this setting, governments on both the local and national levels pass laws in response to pressure from lobbyists who are paid to preserve or extend the freedom their side wants to gain—or not lose. Most of these laws are fundamentally related to freedom.

In the past quarter-century the consumer movement has grown at an accelerated pace. This surge has been related to the relative freedom of business and the consumer and to their incongruent goals. When it is recognized that a democratic government is or should be responsive to the issues raised by its various constituencies, then we can see quite clearly "where we are at."

FIGURE 12.1

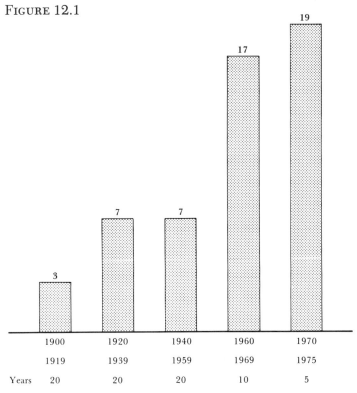

Years	1900	1920	1940	1960	1970
	1919	1939	1959	1969	1975
Years	20	20	20	10	5

Source: U.S., Department of Commerce, National Business Council for Consumer Affairs; correspondence with Edward A. Merlis, consumer counsel, Senate Commerce Committee.

In other words laws in a democratic government often reflect pressures as well as justice and degrees of freedom for some.

As Figure 12.1 shows, since 1900 a total of 53 federal consumer "problem" laws have been passed. As many laws were passed in the decade beginning in 1960 as in the previous 60 years. From 1970 through 1975, 19 laws were passed. Incidentally, before the turn of the century only one such law had been passed. No wonder one hears business suggesting that there are already too many laws and that it is being deprived of the freedom to conduct its own affairs. At the same time, we hear consumers suggesting that we really need more laws in order to have the freedom "to choose, be informed, be heard and the right to safety" not only in terms of the pursuit of happiness but also in terms of satisfaction with products and services used and consumed.

To sum up, the view that freedom is both relative and finite can increase insight and understanding, reduce conflict, and allow for the modification of attitudes and behavior.

13

Change—
the only constant
in consumer affairs

Knowledge of consumer psychology, including the problems of consumer affairs, requires awareness of change and its consequences. More cogently, it is necessary to study the phenomenon of change itself. If consumer issues are to be identified and conflicts reduced, the hoped-for solutions will depend on the ability to cope with change.

Change plays an integral part in conflict reductions that lead to solutions. It is probably the most important ingredient as one moves from a seller- and maker-oriented society to a buyer- and consumer-oriented one. The issues of consumer affairs are nothing more than a bold recognition that change must and will take place.

Change is the antithesis of four powerful inertias—the forces of habit, experience, tradition, and status quo. Inertia preserves the past without the need for adequate justification. It allows behavior to be replicated with little effort and preserves the balance of power by promoting existing inequities. Most of all, it prevents progress, and without progress there is decadence merely because the world does not stand still.

Change requires adjustment, acceptance, rejection, or coping, depending on the individual being subjected to the change. Often the initiators of a change are quite zealous. Those who did not initiate the change and will be affected by it, fearing a loss, will most often resist it. Both sides tend to overreact, prophesying the end of the world, or at least "the system," if the change takes place or does not take place.

The difference between making the efforts and adjustments involved in change and "not rocking the boat" is the difference between striving on the one hand and existing on the other.

Change is generally difficult to accept. It is a psychological challenge; it is stressful. Most important, it is a phenomenon as well as an event. To be explicit, change as an event occurs at some point in time, but change as a phenomenon is a unique experience. Briefly, change is different from something that formerly existed.

Consumer affairs involves issues whose resolution demands change. One cannot comprehend either consumer psychology or consumer affairs without considering the phenomenon of change. Issues such as zoning, credit investigation, advertising to children, and food packaging involve aspects of change and create different sides. Each predicts dire consequences if the other side wins. Too often both sides tend to overreact.

As has been mentioned, change is the antithesis of habit and experience. To be sure, habit and experience are "comfortable friends" and help one avoid making decisions. Both habit and experience encourage resistance to change. However, life *is* change. Each day is different. While it is true that in many ways today is like yesterday, in many other ways it is different.

It might be well to recognize that experience prepares us for the *past* to a greater extent than it prepares us for the future. It is equally important to recognize that we must change if we are to grow, mature, and understand the world around us. We must learn to cope with change.

Consider what change does to you and others. Its consequences are vital, whether for the better or for the worse. As has been mentioned, change and consumer psychology are intertwined in many ways. Impinging on the individual is the constant advertising of products and services, which has as its objective getting the individual to change from one thing to another. Another force impinging on both the individual and society is government and, hence, laws. In fact, a manifestation of change is the number of new laws that are consumer oriented. Previously the laws tended to be concerned with the protection of business or industry.

An extension beyond the immediate business transaction relates to the protection of the environment. Laws requiring changes in mining techniques and air and water purification are among those that have been passed or are being considered. The value of such laws is perceived quite differently by businessmen than by conservationists. These conflicts must be resolved. All of us may be seriously affected by the decisions made today, especially as they concern the future.

Most important, however, is the concept of change and how it affects the individual. Acceptance or resistance to change seems to be most closely related to whether the individual wants the change or is among those who introduce the change. Having learned to behave in a certain fashion, we expect that activities that have been successful in the past are likely to be successful in the future. Such activities can be pursued with a minimum of decision making. Business, like individuals, prefers to continue as it has in the past, especially when it can profit from doing so.

We have said that change and consumer psychology are intertwined. To be specific, each time a purchase is made, a decision also has to be made—to use the same brand or a different one; to pay more or less for the same type of item; to dress in one style or another; to wear one's hair in one fashion or another. These are among the many decisions each of us is required to make many times a day, day after day. In fact, some writers refer to "overchoice," "overload," or "overinformation." They suggest that there are more stimuli bombarding the individual than he/she can successfully cope with. This implies that life is becoming more complex and less manageable. If this is true, then we are in for more difficult times in terms of individual adjustment. The counterpart of this pessimism is to recognize more clearly the phenomenon of change and the fact that it is an integral part of life.

Children are limited by environmental and parental protection. They grow and survive under, it is hoped, friendly circumstances. Adults must learn to select from many stimuli competing for their attention. For example, corn flakes, on television commercials that show how they crunch, or the radio ad that lets you hear them. Other stimuli that have become more numerous than in the past may be seen in the great variety of materials used for clothing—both synthetic and natural—and the many different colors, styles, prices, and levels of quality available.

Making a change can induce anxiety in the individual. Changes that are made by others but affect you can also create anxiety. Accordingly, people have to learn to cope with change, its by-products, and its effects, whether they participate in the decision to make the change or the change is presented as an accomplished event.

An important factor in acceptance of change is whether the

individual is initially for or against the change. Often if the person is instrumental in initiating the change or believes it will be of benefit, then he/she is for it. If the change is imposed on the individual or there are fears or threats, then it is likely that resistance will occur.

Change is perceived variously as being a matter of small or great significance. People who are otherwise neutral can be made to fear a change if it is labeled "drastic." If it is labeled "hardly any change at all," then it is more likely to be acceptable. Change, then, in its conceptual form is the degree to which something is different or is presented as different.

All of this leads to the cliché "the more things change, the more they are the same." Alvin Toffler does not accept this notion, but there is more than a modicum of truth in it. In *Future Shock* (1) Toffler has probably explored the phenomenon of change more than anyone else. Whether or not one agrees with his conclusions, his book is unquestionably thought-provoking. It is an important book in the sense that it has made many people think along some very speculative lines. It has even been made into a television documentary but it loses its impact in comparison with the book.

Toffler makes the point that change is occurring at an ever-intensifying pace and, as a result, can be overwhelming to some people. He coined the term "future shock" to describe the shattering stress and disorientation induced in individuals who are subjected to too much change in too short a time.

One of Toffler's major points is that change is accelerating. His data and illustrations are quite convincing. However, if one considers the typical learning curve, as was suggested by Bryan and Harter as early as 1899 (2), it may well be that what we see as an accelerated rate of change is merely evidence of where we are in the total learning process taking place in our civilization. We may well be at a point where the positive slope is increasing at an accelerating rate. (See Figure 13.1.)

The learning curve shows that, for equal intervals of time, greater change takes place as the learning process continues. So it may well be that the accelerated thrust we perceive is merely a function of the stage of our development at this point in time. To state this somewhat differently, in any learning process the rate of learning over a specific time period varies. At some stage in the learning curve, the learning rate is very rapid and gradually tapers off. We may well be in the rapid learning rate period at this point in the development of knowledge.

An interesting exercise is to try to decide which of several discoveries required the greatest ingenuity. Among others, one might consider the wheel, the printing press, the polio vaccine, the atom bomb, and the moon walk. All are evidence of change, but who has the wisdom to know the extent and consequences of those changes?

Toffler also makes the point that transience allows for a "new temporariness" in everyday life. This transience is suggested not only by the prevalence of short-term personal relationships but also by the disposable and nondurable aspects of many products.

A popular notion, but probably a myth, is the belief that product obsolescence is "planned." Some products are shoddy for a variety of reasons. The requirement that more and more units be produced regardless of their durability or quality may well have led to the notion that "nothing lasts the way it used to, so let's sell or buy cheaper stuff to begin with." The existence of shortages, higher prices, poorer quality, and so forth is evidence of change in regard to products consumed. The devil himself probably could not have planned for planned obsolescence. Shoddy, hurried carelessness on top of lack of pride in production and ownership are its true causes, and it is not easy to tell how much is contributed by labor or how much by management.

Technological developments in the airplane industry, for example, have produced tremendous changes. Compare the DC-3

FIGURE 13.1   A Learning Curve for Telegraphy

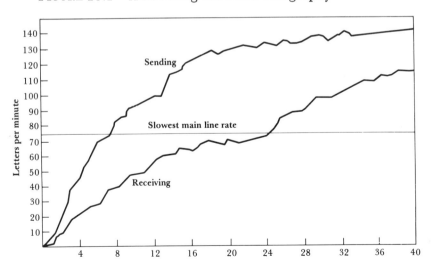

Source: From W. L. Bryan and N. Harter. "Studies in the Telegraphic Language", *Psychological Review*, 1899, 6, 346–376.

with today's jumbo jet, and add to this the dispute over whether supersonic passenger travel should be encouraged. Surely obsolescence has not been planned in this instance. The problem is one of technology advancing faster than people are willing or able to fly.

Toffler also speaks of "ad-hocracy." This is a new organizational system that is quite different from bureaucracy. In a bureaucracy an individual occupies a sharply defined slot in a vertical hierarchy that emphasizes permanence. The ad-hoc group, on the other hand, gets together to solve specific problems and then separates. The task force is supposed to be less enduring than the committee.

It is characteristic of consumer groups to get together to encourage or prevent an action—for example, a change in zoning where they live—and then disband. Angry consumers may picket a supermarket to protest high prices and then, again, disband. It may well be that one of the major reasons for the lack of progress by some consumer groups is the fact that these organizations are temporary because their reasons for existence are based on short-term issues.

Another of Toffler's major theses is that there are limits to the amount of change that the human organism can absorb. Beyond this there is "future shock," which is the human response to overstimulation. Its symptoms are anxiety, hostility, and violence. There is evidence that "future shock" can result in illness and death.

The following quote from Toffler is worth considering:

> The move from manufacturing to service production, the psychologization of both goods and services, and ultimately the shift toward experiential production all tie the economic sector much more tightly to non-economic forces. Consumer preferences turn over in accordance with rapid life style changes, so that the coming and going of sub-cultures is mirrored in economic turmoil. Super industrial production requires workers skilled in symbol manipulation so that what goes on in their heads becomes much more important than in the past, and much more dependent upon cultural factors. (page 401)

Still another aspect of change that is often overlooked is the amount of change that has taken place over time and the way this has affected users, sellers, and makers of goods and services. This change has also influenced the government's role.

If asked to describe the changes that have taken place in the history of this country, one might say that we were originally an agricultural society rather than an industrial-manufacturing society. Later we became a marketing society, and it would appear that now we have become a service-leisure society. In this respect even our existing economic indicators may be false measures of prosperity; what was good yesterday may not be good—or even applicable—tomorrow.

It is important to note that consumer issues are primarily an outgrowth of a service society. When people do not consider serving others to be part of their job—whether they are professors serving students, salesclerks serving customers, bus drivers serving riders, or waiters serving hungry customers—then it is obvious that incongruence and dissatisfaction must exist. It would seem that there is a need for individuals to recognize that serving others is an important part of any job. For example, the repair of a broken appliance or automobile could be considered a service. Too often the sour taste engendered by poor service and delay obviate the satisfaction that might otherwise be gained from the repair. Greater emphasis on service may well lead to a reduction in conflict, which is the essence of consumer complaints. In this instance the *change*—that is, more and better service—may go a long way toward resolving many consumer problems.

To summarize, whether our concern is society, groups within society, or individuals, we must recognize that tradition and change are at loggerheads. Traditionally, business has tended to do its own thing. Years ago the suggestion that laws might govern working conditions, hours of work, and even the minimum wage was an unheard-of heresy and quite "unamerican." It was predicted that minimum wages would virtually end our economic system. We hear this each time a proposal is made to increase the minimum wage.

On the other hand, there are times when business believes that government should pass laws to protect it. Tariffs and other financial privileges for certain industries, according to business, improve the economy.

Change must and will take place. It will be healthier to learn to cope with change rather than resisting it. Any change that takes place should be considered in terms of rights, justice, and even freedom for those who have not had their share but need and want it just as much as those who already have a considerable share.

BIBLIOGRAPHY

1. TOFFLER, A., *Future Shock* (New York: Random House, 1970).
2. BRYAN, W. L., and N. HARTER, "Studies in the Telegraphic Language," *Psychological Review*, 6 (1899): 346–376.

14

Socialization and the family life cycle

The preceding chapter indicated the importance of recognizing the phenomenon of change and its consequences as they relate to buyer-seller-maker transactions. This chapter will point out that the maker and seller have advantages over the buyer, especially when it comes to change.

Makers decide what products to make and how to modify those products on the basis of experience. The maker, with the benefit of experience, knows the appearance and characteristics the product should have and can usually predict with reasonable accuracy how many units to make.

There are those with a strongly market-oriented point of view who insist that the maker makes what the buyers want and that market research proves it. This, at best, is only a partial truth. The inputs of market research come from within the company; the only thing the consumer can decide in such studies is which of the alternatives offered he/she prefers. A case in point, and one that has serious consequences, is the disappearance of automobile bumpers. Do consumers, with life and limb at stake as well as the cost of repair, really want no bumper protection because it "looks pretty"? Do they really want nonnutritious foods? Do they really want to pay higher prices for shoddy merchandise?

The seller can and does influence the buyer's decision. The experiences of the seller in the aggregate are far greater than the experience of a single buyer. This is so because in the course of a year a consumer-buyer's experience is much more generalized and covers a wide range of products and services. The seller and maker, on the other hand, have more specific and continuous experience with their products and services. In other words, on both an actual and a relative basis the makers have more experience with the products they make and the sellers have more experience with the products they sell than the buyer has with any particular product.

The point that the consumer-buyer must understand is that in the purchase of practically any product or service he/she does not have the experience to match that of the maker or seller. In short, the consumer is at a disadvantage compared to the other two parties. The sooner the consumer learns this, the better.

Every individual is involved in a continuous process of change that takes place throughout lifetime. However, the maker and seller of cradles has more experience with cradles than the consumer. There is likely to be a lot of emotion involved in the purchase of a cradle, especially for the firstborn in the family. Likewise, the seller of coffins has more experience with coffins than the consumer who buys one for a beloved deceased. Again the consumer will mix emotion into the purchase decision, and again the seller will have a distinct advantage. Extending the example to all purchases between the cradle and the coffin, in each case the buyer has less experience and is subject to greater change. The maker and seller have more experience and consequently less change to contend with.

To illustrate, let us imagine a consumer who does most shopping at one supermarket, one department store, and one auto dealer. The supermarket is visited once a week, the department store once a month, and the auto dealer maybe once in three years. The seller in all three instances is open about six days a week and sees many, many customers. As a result the seller has experience. Further, he can change prices and lines of merchandise with or without the knowledge of the buyer, and the same goes for the maker.

It does not much matter whether one is 3, 19, or 64. Each age group has the experience of having been younger but not older. Getting older requires adjusting and coping with various changes that take place either subtly or drastically. An infant becomes a child, who then becomes a teenager, a young adult, an adult, and finally a senior citizen. Under conditions of constant change, the individual is better prepared to relive yesterday than to face tomorrow.

The consumer makes buying decisions commensurate with

perceived needs or goals. Sometimes the decision is made for a child; at other times the child influences purchase behavior. Marriage often means compromises in the consumer's needs and goals: Purchase decisions become subject to the mutual agreement of husband and wife. In some cases there is an agreement that one or the other will make the decision unilaterally. Add to this the socialization process and the consumer needs help— more help than he/she generally is willing to admit.

A way out of this morass is for the individual to become part of the "society of consumers" and recognize that such a subculture can be effective.

A person can benefit from social learning, or socialization. The term *socialization* describes the process of learning to fit into society—if one chooses to be part of it. The socialization process includes language, gestures, dress, and behavior patterns. It also includes "food styles" like chow mein, pizza, wines, and even caviar.

One should not infer that the hereditary influences do not have any effect on consumer behavior; they do. To illustrate, a society may accept certain body types as attractive and others as unattractive. The heredity influences that to a large extent determine body size, bone structure, and eye and hair coloring are predetermined. To be sure, one can gain or lose weight or dye one's hair and thereby change one's appearance. However, an individual's facial or physical characteristics are often predetermined by genes, which are the carriers of heredity. The acceptance or rejection of such physical characteristics on the part of individuals is often a sign of prejudice. People who do not like long noses, slanted eyes, or a skin color different from their own are revealing prejudice rather than judging standards of beauty. In short, biological, chemical, and physical characteristics, as well as societal influences, shape the individual, his/her life style and are keys to different varieties of consumer behavior.

The question is, What relation do social, psychological, and sociological concepts have to consumer psychology? The answer is that the relationship begins at the very roots of consumer psychology. For example, the family is the basic unit of society. For most people, most of their lives, it is the basic group they belong to and are accepted by. Consider the following somewhat arbitrary stages or phases of family life:

1. newly married
2. married without children
3. married with children up to 3 years old

4. married with children 3 to 6 years old
5. married with children 6 to 12 years old
6. married with children 12 to 15 years old
7. married with children over 18 at home or away from home
8. married with married children
9. survivor
10. any combination of the preceding

In addition to the family unit, there are households in which single or divorced individuals live alone or with others.

These classifications represent several different types of consumers with different patterns of buyer-user behavior. The relationship between phase of life cycle and life style strongly influences these patterns. We go through the cycle with no experience of each new phase. Tales, advice, hopes and conjectures, yes—but experience, no.

This is the problem of being a consumer. The sad part is that few consumers realize their lack of preparation. In the case of the newly married couple, an important psychological change is the requirement that both parties learn to live together. This learning experience requires adjustment, which may or may not require changes in personality in addition to the sharing of time, money, and interests. Doing this together and learning to be involved in mutual decisions creates a modified life style.

From the point of view of consumer psychology, newly married couples are in a highly creative phase. They are setting up a household, buying or replacing furniture, and decorating. There are also considerable adjustments to be made in buying patterns related to clothes, food, and life style. For example, people tend to buy more ground beef during this phase. Apparently there is not much that can go wrong with hamburger. Newly married couples also spend quite heavily on home furnishings and, as a result, find that they have to reduce their spending on entertainment.

The second phase of married life is often a money-saving period prior to the arrival of children. It is also a period of weekends, vacations, and adjusting to the in-laws.

Not all married couples can have children. For some this results in adoption. Others attach themselves excessively to pets, while still others demonstrate an excessive fondness for nieces or nephews. The expenditures of childless marriages are based primarily on the needs of the couple. Hobbies are pursued with more freedom and intensity than they would be if young children were present.

Children up to three years of age are very dependent and

require quite a lot of time. They also contribute to purchase patterns—now the family needs nursery furniture, clothes, and toys. The babysitter appears on the scene, and going out is a planned occasion rather than an impulse. Food consumption and buying patterns change. The once-a-week supermarket shopping pattern appears. Hamburgers give way to chicken and simple meat dishes.

Three- to six-year-old children attend nursery school and begin to put financial pressure on middle-income families. Toys, growing up, and family togetherness are dominant interests. By this time bowling teams, home entertainment and the occasional movie appear, and the need for a more varied life style begins to be expressed.

The family with children ready for school experiences both relief and trauma. The child is now subjected to additional discipline and learns that there are other ways of life besides what he/she has known up to now. Depending on the ages of other children in the family (if there are any), he/she learns to play differently and without the interference of older or younger brothers and sisters. Problems related to the neighborhood where one lives become quite prominent. By the time this phase in the life cycle is reached, the family has probably moved at least once, usually into an area where educational facilities are "good" for the children.

The junior and senior high school phase involves more socialization and visiting. Quite frequently adult friendships are formed because the children are friends. Home entertainment, especially for the children, becomes a major expenditure. Not to be overlooked is the role of transportation; at this point, if not before, the two-car family appears.

In the next phase, whether off to college or off to work, the children are likely to begin to live away from home. It is at this time that the husband and wife reevaluate where and how they live and begin to consider other value systems. If not already employed, the wife is likely to find full- or part-time employment.

People with married children now become very lonely as well as very happy. Their housing needs are likely to change; less space and fewer material things are needed.

All this finally leads to the drastic family change of the survivor, who in our society is most often the wife. The adjustment depends on how long the survivor lives. As they get older, senior citizens need more help, and their consumer pattern revolves around services rather than products.

As for the single and divorced groups, the consumer pattern

varies according to the life style the individual prefers and can afford.

Running through the life cycle in such a rapid fashion should serve to illustrate the theme of this chapter. Each day brings new changes to the consumer, who benefits little from previous experience. The consumer must continually learn, adjust, and cope with varied needs as a function of the passage of time as well as individual differences.

15
Ghetto dwellers— the limited consumers

Certain subgroups within the population present very special problems as consumers. This chapter and the following one will concentrate on consumers who, for a number of reasons, are not typical because they consume less rather than more. These groups include ghetto dwellers, the young, and the old.

The ghetto dweller's problems are severe. They go to the very roots of personality and family structure. It is within this context that consumer psychologists must study and understand the ghetto dweller—as a "limited" consumer as well as one who is disadvantaged.

In former times, a *ghetto* was a section of a city where Jews were required to live. Ghettos were found in most European countries. In recent years, however, this definition has been extended so that today it means a section of a city, especially a thickly populated slum area, inhabited predominantly by blacks, Puerto Ricans, or other minority groups. Today ghettos often result from social and ethnic restrictions.

Nowadays there are ghettos for blacks, Chicanos, Puerto Ricans, Cubans, Indians—any disadvantaged group. Another example is the "ghetto" of elderly Jewish people living in South Beach, the area south of the hotels and motels of Miami Beach. Different ghettos may exist side by side; thus in New York City there are neighboring black and Puerto Rican ghettos, while in Miami there are neighboring Cuban and black ghettos.

The underlying cause of ghettos is prejudice. The intensely negative attitude of some individuals or groups toward other individuals or groups is at the root of the problem. Probably prejudice itself is the strongest factor producing the social and ethnic restrictions that result in a ghetto and operate to create or continue poverty.

Realistically, a strong majority group cannot be threatened by a minority group. Nevertheless, most prejudice is found among majority groups that feel threatened by minority groups. However, possibly even more damaging is the prejudice of one minority group toward another. In such instances the displays of prejudice are more obvious; worse, the forms they take are quite cruel—not the subtle, sophisticated techniques used by majority groups. They are accompanied by feelings of fear, hatred, anxiety, and insecurity.

Knowing the dictionary definition of a ghetto and the forces that produce it is not enough, however. A clear understanding of the ghetto is impossible without understanding the common denominator of ghettos: poverty. Probably the most outstanding characteristic of any ghetto is the fact that those who live there are *poor*.

Rev. Martin Luther King was correct when he emphasized the plight of the poor. His approach was simple and direct, but many people, blinded by prejudice, refused to recognize his appeal. He revealed who the poor people were and how they lived. He clearly identified with them.

What does all this have to do with consumer psychology? It is basic. The problem is not whether one happens to be black or speaks a different language or comes from a different part of the world or belongs to a different religion. One can be a member of any of these subgroups and not live in a ghetto. When one is a member of such a group *and* poor, it is then that one is likely to live in a ghetto.

In other words, people with similar characteristics may want to live in close proximity. But as long as they are not poor, the areas they live in are not ghettos. A ghetto per se is where poor people live together. This contributes to their helplessness.

An area that needs further study is the consumer behavior of the poor. The problem of the ghetto dweller is the way of life that poverty generates. This way of life has at least four clearly discernible factors: deprivation, the feeling of powerlessness, restricted movement, and insecurity.

By deprivation we mean something broader than deprivation of money. It is a restricted pattern of living.

Powerlessness is the inability to exert any influence on the institutions that exercise power in society. In the main, contacts with such institutions just do not exist.

Except for the occasional promise from a candidate for office or a group of social scientists who want to "do good," even if it is only to conduct research, little really happens to benefit the ghetto. A more virile approach is summed up in the slogan "power to the people," which means getting rid of the feeling of powerlessness. Realistically, this does not mean becoming all-powerful; rather, it means building contacts with the institutions where power resides.

Restricted movement means living and dying within a small geographic area. Even when the poor migrate from one city to another, the only thing that changes is the city. The poor still live in ghettos.

The fourth characteristic of ghetto living is the insecurity it generates. This insecurity may well be the core of a personality that, instead of being developed, has been trampled upon and warped. It arises because the poor are forced to simply exist, without the meaning, hopes, and aspirations that make life worth living for those who are not poor.

The typical person is likely to strive, to have goals and values. The poor are so restricted and deprived that dealing with normal, attainable goals is almost beyond their reason and ability. They spend their days in misery and timelessness. Many no longer even hope. An occasional flurry of activity only results in greater deprivation, and the unfulfilled promises of "do-gooders" make things worse.

The problem, then, is poverty. Many attempts to solve this problem have failed miserably. An outstanding example is the concept of public housing. It seems to have had a long enough chance to work, but it probably never will. Most public housing simply redevelops the slum characteristics of the ghetto. Changing the housing without changing the individual by creating incentives that will increase the chances of success does nothing.

Consumer psychologists generally find that the poor pay more for their basic needs. But even if the poor paid less it would not solve the problems of misery, hopelessness, and futility.

There are many factors that affect pricing. Supermarket pilferage, insurance rates, the inefficiencies of smaller stores all contribute to price variation. Studies show clearly that within the same supermarket chain in the same city the same product may vary in price even in nonghetto areas. Some chains as a matter of policy have less uniform pricing than other chains.

However, it is also true that unscrupulous businessmen take advantage of the poor and uneducated consumer. Add to this credit charges and shoddy merchandise, and one can easily see that the answer to the question "Do the poor pay more?" makes little real difference in solving the ghetto problem.

Of course the poor pay more. They pay more in so many different ways that whether they pay more for food or furniture is academic. Prices in the ghetto are higher. But even if the poor paid less for food or furniture, this would not solve the ghetto problem. The difference in dollars and cents would be meaningless. The ghetto poor pay more because of the life style the ghetto promotes.

Material like that published in the *Ghetto Market Place* (1) is likely to have little effect. The information contained in that collection of readings is already familiar to the ghetto dweller, though it may be new to scholars who mean well. The ghetto needs more than descriptive studies by scholars. The point of including a chapter on the ghetto in this book is to encourage a change in the ghetto dweller.

A positive approach is suggested by Ross and Glaser (2). Their study, published in *Professional Psychology,* is probably one of the most informative and important publications about the ghetto to appear in many years. The article points to the role of the family influence in making it out of the ghetto. It is obvious, in this context, that it is a waste of time to talk about the pricing in ghetto stores. It seems more relevant to study the role of the father and whether he abdicates this role in a poverty situation.

Ross and Glaser studied reasonably comparable groups of blacks and Mexican-Americans who had made it out of the ghetto, as well as similar groups that had remained behind. An impressive finding of this study is that in adolescence the self-esteem of successful individuals is related to their notions about achievement, while that of unsuccessful individuals is maintained by a high reputation among peers on the street. The successful ones are not involved in gang activities. In other words, the gang is not a necessary part of the ghetto. In fact it may be a self-perpetuating institution. The gang exists, but the individual either joins it or avoids it. Those who join accept the values of the gang, want the approval of their peers, and conform in behavior to the lowest common denominator, which is often exemplified by the severest forms of antisocial behavior.

This study indicates clear-cut differences between the groups of blacks and Mexicans who made it out of the ghetto and those who did not. The specific items differentiating successful from unsuccessful subjects in both ethnic groups are presented in Table 15.1.

TABLE 15.1   Items differentiating successful from nonsuccessful subjects in both ethnic groups

Successful Group	*Nonsuccessful Group*
1. There was at least one strong parent (or parent surrogate, such as a grandmother) who had high expectations of the child as well as giving sustained love.	There was no manifestly caring person in the family who presented clear standards for the child or indicated high expectations in terms of behavior or achievement.
2. Home atmosphere was described as warm.	Home atmosphere was described as neutral or hostile.
3. Now contacts parental family frequently or occasionally.	Now contacts parental family rarely or never.
4. Now is most alienated from father.	Now is most alienated from mother or siblings.
5. Participated in school activities.	Did not participate in school activities.
6. Parental discipline consistent.	Parental discipline inconsistent.
7. Never received failing grades.	Occasionally or frequently received failing grades.
8. Up until 16 was confident about the future.	Up until 16 was pessimistic about the future.
9. Expressed positive attitude toward himself.	Expressed negative attitude toward himself.
10. Feels more successful than youthful peers.	Feels equally or less successful than youthful peers.
11. Has sometimes or often felt pride in accomplishment or workmanship.	Has rarely or never felt pride in accomplishment or workmanship.
12. Feels more successful than family (siblings).	Feels equally or less successful than family (siblings).
13. Mentioned gaining some recognition in school, either academically or in sports, or in his family by being responsible in some special way.	Never seemed to feel successful at anything he tried.
14. Fully supporting present marital family (if married).	Partially or not supporting present marital family (if married).
15. Current marriage cohesive.	Current marriage uninvolved or estranged.
16. Positive feeling toward present wife.	Negative feeling toward present wife.
17. Present marriage intact (or never married).	Separated or divorced.
18. Remembers his parents as encouraging him to speak good English.	Parents seem not to have been concerned with the way he expressed himself.
19. Now speaks English well.	Now does not speak English well.

TABLE 15.1 (*Continued*)

Successful Group	Nonsuccessful Group
20. Remembers that his parents went to church frequently and religious values were important in their home.	Remembers that his parents went to church occasionally and did not stress religious values, or religion seemed unimportant in parents' home.
26. Appears outwardly as if he likes himself, is a "good" person, feels liked by others, is self-confident, has self-esteem (any or all).	Appears outwardly as if he is not a "good" person, feels disliked and rejected, doubts himself, has low self-esteem (any or all).
27. Sense of self-esteem seems to come from some achievement, either educational or occupational.	Sense of self-esteem seems to come from knowing or in being friendly with some set of people or in belonging to some group.
28. Seems to think that hard work and education are the best means for getting ahead.	Talks about hustling as a good means for getting ahead, or seems concerned about getting ahead but is somewhat confused about how to do it.
29. Feels at home in the ghetto but has an interest in moving out.	Feels completely at home among his peers in the ghetto.
30. Was not charged with delinquency as a juvenile.	Was charged with delinquency as a juvenile.
31. Was not charged with a criminal offense as an adult.	Was charged with a criminal offense as an adult.
32. Feels he has never been jailed unjustly.	Feels he has been jailed unjustly.
33. Has never had trouble with the law.	Has had trouble with the law both as a juvenile and as an adult.
34. His legal record isn't seen as interfering with either getting or holding a job, or hasn't any legal record.	His legal record is seen as a factor which deters him from getting or keeping a job.

SOURCE: H. L. Ross and E. M. Glaser, "Making It Out of the Ghetto," *Professional Psychology*, 1973, 347–356.

It is important to recognize the need for factual information that produces change in ghetto dwellers. Knowing more about the characteristics of people who get out of the ghetto as well as what they did to get out can lead to change. The need is to be able to transmit such information in a believable and acceptable fashion so that successful behavior modification can get people out of the ghettos.

Point by point, the items found by Ross and Glaser are significant. For example, risk-taking capacity means being willing and able to endure the anxiety, suspense, disappointment, and humiliation of experimenting with new behavior. There are also degrees of risk taking. As in betting, the larger the odds, the greater the risk and the greater the gains. The smaller the odds, the less the risk and the fewer the gains. An advantage of research is the fact that, when successful, it furnishes information that reduces the risks and at the same time allows greater gains.

Another point made by the article is the importance of channeling rage. Rage may have grown out of a feeling of helplessness but can be funneled into strategic action.

In summary, the article has social meaning. It implies that one climbs out of the ghetto. This can result in reducing the size of the ghetto. Social reforms merely change superficial characteristics of the ghetto while leaving the people who live there exactly the same—as badly off as they were before. The point is that ghetto dwellers are minimal consumers with probably a minimum of consumer satisfaction. Changes that get people out of the ghetto can increase varieties of consumer satisfaction for such people. Consumer psychologists, then, must examine the characteristics of ghetto dwellers and discover how the more successful ones make it out of the ghetto. The information would then be transmitted to the peers of ghetto dwellers. They, in turn, could possibly be more effective teachers in behavior modification of ghetto dwellers. It would be delightful to rid society of prejudice. The solution to the ghetto problem, though, can be more direct. It can be achieved by enabling the poor to acquire the wherewithal to climb up and out.

Words of caution must be added before leaving this chapter, which itself is likely to arouse prejudice and protest. Not everyone can climb out of the ghetto. Some people are too restricted, feel powerless beyond despair, need help in many forms. They have no background or training to obtain a job or keep it if given the opportunity. This is most disconcerting. For them, regardless of age, "handouts" are needed. Years ago handouts took the form of charity meted out by benevolent groups. Now, more often, this is a function of government. Welfare, social security, and food stamps are simply subsidies to the poor, not unlike tariffs that raise the prices of imported goods or the tax incentives that are supposed to encourage oil companies to find new reserves of oil. A subsidy is a subsidy.

A point about all government aid, once started, is that it tends to perpetuate itself primarily because the government people involved benefit. They have the advantage of employment, whereas the poor obtain only the limited benefits that are handed out. Soon the system expands and perpetuates itself like any bureaucracy. About the only difference is in the terminology: commercial transactions involve buyers and sellers, whereas in the "do-gooder" world they involve givers and receivers—the government is the giver and the poor (or the oil company or the farmer—anyone who is subsidized) are the receivers.

Some people are concerned with the by-products of welfare. For example, does welfare dull the senses and decrease motivation? Accurate data are not available, but it would appear that the condition of poverty itself is what has dulled the senses, decreased motivation, and created a restricted life style without much room for aspirations.

What needs to take place, it would appear, is further research along the lines of Ross and Glaser and then application of the findings to the existing scene—which means turn them over to the poor so they can help themselves.

The ghetto dweller who is in greatest need of a better way of life is least likely to obtain it under the present system of handouts. The need for change must be suggested in such a fashion that the ghetto dweller is able to perceive a benefit if he/she successfully completes the change.

Every now and then a writer or reporter nails the truth in a way that accomplishes what social scientists have been groping for for years. A column by W. Raspberry of the *Washington Post* is worthy of reflection (3). It is reproduced here in its entirety as an appropriate ending for a chapter on consumer psychology and the ghetto dweller.

HELPING HAND POLICY DOOMED
BY A SENSE OF UNDESERVEDNESS
By William Raspberry

If what I'm trying to say comes out confused and inconclusive, it's because the subject is one on which my thoughts are confused and inconclusive.

I thought I'd just start writing and see where it leads. I know where it starts. It starts with the conflict between the notion of human equality and basic human rights on the one hand and the concept of individual deservedness on the other.

No, that's too confusing. Let me try it this way: There are some things that we consider to be the "natural" rights of people because they are people, or more specifically, of Americans because they are Americans . . .

And yet, conscientious efforts to implement these rights so often turn out badly.

Example. Decent housing and recreation are things that, in a country as rich and (theoretically) democratic as America ought to be available to people whether they have the money to purchase them or not.

But efforts to make them available—public housing projects and inner city playgrounds for instance—are repeatedly vandalized, often beyond repair, by the people they were built to serve.

Example. Good schools, adequate public transportation and reasonably convenient shopping facilities ought to be available as a matter of right to all Americans. But disorder, vandalism and pilferage continually weaken the quality of public institutions designed to implement these rights and drive the private ones out of business.

Obviously, there is no single, simple explanation of why these things happen. But a part of the answer seems to lie in what might be called deservedness.

People tend to value those things that they think they deserve to have, whether because they have earned them through some personal exertion or because they consider themselves innately special and therefore deserving.

People tend not to value things that have come to them in ways they consider illegitimate. Housing, food, training, recreation or jobs that are distributed on the basis of some negative attribute—poverty or criminality, for instance—are frequently treated with contempt.

It isn't just the intrinsic worth of the goods or services that determines whether they will be valued or not; it is also whether the recipients consider that they are deserved.

The critical sense of deservedness is in their minds, not ours. You and I may believe that we are distributing things that people deserve simply because they are people. Many of the programs that supply these things are conceived and supported by people who take deservedness for granted.

No matter. If the recipients feel otherwise, the programs are likely to fail.

We see public housing projects savaged by residents to the point where they have to be demolished—as is happening right now in St. Louis' huge Pruitt-Igoe project—and we tell ourselves that what is wrong is that there is too little play space, too great a concentration of people, too few social services and not enough johns.

All these things are true, but not necessarily crucial. What strikes me as crucial is that the families who occupy the projects know that they have been set apart on the basis of their economic failure. The public housing that was designed to meet a basic human need thus has a dehumanizing side effect of reaffirming the residents' sense of undeservedness.

If you don't think you deserve it, you tend not to value it. Nor is this exclusively a poor people's syndrome. I suspect that one of the reasons so many sons and daughters of the rich are turning away from money and prestige and position is that they think themselves unworthy. Their riches are unearned, the result of no effort or intrinsic worthiness on their part and, therefore, illegitimate and unvalued.

Legitimacy in this sense has nothing to do with how a thing is actually acquired but with the recipient's sense of deservedness. For one man, goods acquired through thievery, sharp dealing or inheritance may be altogether legitmate because he considers himself innately deserving. For another, the winnings of a lucky lottery ticket may be unvalued and squandered because the winner considers the windfall undeserved.

I don't know what any of this means for rich people, but it does seem to suggest some changes in the way we design public programs for the poor. For instance, guaranteed income programs may have to be redrafted in a way to avoid a feeling of undeservedness on the part of the recipients. We may want to try to build into all our public welfare programs some way for recipients to "earn" what they receive—no matter whether you and I think they have earned it just by being alive. We may have to devise some way for even the poorest of the poor to set themselves apart on the basis of something considered positive.

I don't know what the specific techniques might be. But I do know that the present programs mostly aren't working, and I suspect we've misjudged the reasons why.

Miami Herald, June 7, 1975

BIBLIOGRAPHY

1. STURDIVANT, F. D., *The Ghetto Market Place* (New York: Free Press, 1969).
2. ROSS, H. L., and E. M. GLASER, "Making It out of the Ghetto," *Professional Psychology* (1973): 347–356.
3. RASPBERRY, W., "Helping Hand Policy Doomed by a Sense of Undeservedness," *Miami Herald,* June 7, 1975.

16

The young and the old as consumers

The young and the old are special types of consumers with characteristics quite different from those of most consumers in the middle age brackets. The needs of the latter are more prolific; they purchase many more items such as cars, appliances, and fashion clothes. Probably because the two extreme age groups purchase fewer products and services, they are too often overlooked and underappreciated.

When one looks at each of these groups separately and makes comparisons, the importance of the socialization process is emphasized. The lack of regard on the part of sellers, makers, and even other consumers for the young and the old is due to the fact that as consumers of products and services they are a minority. All this brings clearly into focus the special problems of younger and older consumers.

Aging is the process of becoming old. The phenomena of aging and change are so highly correlated that the relationship is taken for granted.

The phenomenon of change varies in speed and direction, but probably the subtlest manifestation of change is aging. The changes involved in the aging process take place day by day. They often go unrecognized until suddenly one is aware that an irrevocable change has taken place.

The earlier years are characterized by the development of coordination, growth, and increased activity. The older years are characterized by a decrease in coordination and activity; slowly but surely one recognizes that one's physical capacities are declining.

Just as aging and change are correlated, the behavioral patterns and interests of the young change day by day as they become older. Accordingly, the special problems of the two extreme age groups present a panoramic view of the life of a consumer.

For the purposes of this chapter, the young are defined as children from birth to 6 years of age, while the old are people 65 years of age and older. These two groups have been chosen to illustrate the role of the individual rather than the family in the unfolding of the life of the consumer. Researchers and writers pay surprisingly little attention to consumers in these extreme age groups. Consumers in these groups tend to have less influence than consumers in the middle group, which covers the period from first grade through adulthood. The young buy practically nothing and exert relatively little influence on what is bought for them. The old are faced with a host of new problems very different from those they experienced in their earlier adult years. This is not to suggest that the old are not adults but, rather, that they are older adults. The old should be recognized as consumers if they are to be understood, helped, and encouraged to help themselves.

Both the young and the old require a much narrower spectrum of products and services. The major big-ticket items—houses, appliances, furnishings, cars—are of little concern to either group. Neither the young nor the old are heavy buyers of any product or service. Accordingly, market research pays little attention to them except in the case of certain special interests. As far as consumer research is concerned, for all practical purposes the work done to date has not even scratched the surface. Despite pediatrics and geriatrics, child psychology and the psychology of the aging, the young and the old need more attention as consumers. It is hoped that this chapter will serve as a goad.

By arbitrarily defining the young as those from birth to six years of age we automatically link the socialization and developmental process to the family. The family life style sets the stage for growing up in a particular culture or subculture. At first the child needs the care, attention, acceptance, and love of his/her parents. Following in rapid succession are the siblings and other relatives, but the child's relationships are mainly with family members. The family generally provides for the child's simple wants and needs.

The developmental process includes such forms of communication as locomotion, talking, limited reading capacity, and very often an abundance of television. But what about the child as a consumer or user of products and services? To begin with, there are baby foods, rash resistant powders, diapers and disposable diapers. Furniture, even "hand-me-downs," plays a role. Next come cereals, snacks, clothes, and a wide variety of playthings ranging from rattles and mobiles to trucks and dolls. It is in this setting that the young are considered as consumers. Although they are not direct buyers, to the degree that their parents are permissive they may be more or less influential in the purchase decision.

Among the earliest items purchased are playthings. The popular ones are brightly colored, make sounds, are pleasant to the touch, and are easily moved or manipulated. By the time the child is three or four years old, parent-child differences in toy preferences are clear and are subjects of controversy. Parents prefer safe, durable items that are not battery operated. Children quite often prefer items advertised on television. Sometimes the parent decides in the child's favor and sometimes not. The point is that at a rather early age differences in toy preferences create problems for the young and their parents. Some parents, for example, prefer toys that encourage the child to use imagination. They may believe that a plain, ordinary doll does more for the child than one that walks or dances or defecates.

Playthings are bought primarily at Christmas or birthday time. The influences beyond the parent-child relationship include other children and advertising. Many parents do not like television advertising directed at their children, but a great many indicate that they feel powerless to prevent some toys from being acquired as gifts. Others just cave in under the pressure.

A consumer trap that should be avoided is any item that is proportionately low in cost but requires accessories that are proportionately higher in cost. For adults this might be a camera or razor that needs special film or blades. As applied to children, it might be a low-priced doll for which the clothes and accessories are sold at proportionately higher prices.

Children play alone or with others, including brothers and sisters, and this encourages socialization, particularly when older children determine the play activity. Toys, however, afford the child many opportunities to grow, learn, empathize, project, love, fight, and relate. They help him/her gain experience, fill time, grow up, and become independent. They are the focal point of the earliest phase of learning to be a consumer.

Play is generally a happy activity. When it is not, the problem may be a seller or maker that has greedily misrepresented a product or made an unsafe toy or one that breaks easily.

Turning now to the old as consumers, a difference is that one can define "old" in legal terms, such as the age of retirement or the age at which a person is eligible for social security or medicare. Defining "old" in terms of age alone is not so easy. For example, teenagers don't trust people over 35. A book written some years ago was entitled *Life Begins at Forty*. Few people in their fifties regard themselves as old; they think "old" is the sixties. Those in their sixties think "old" is the seventies, and so on.

A salient feature of the aging process is the denial that "old" is the age you happen to be. "Old" is a term for someone older. Hence, in this chapter we recognize that age is a sliding scale of reference.

As consumers, the old manifest a limited need for products, especially as advertised on television, with one or two exceptions. (How old are the models on television who need iron or laxatives or relief from arthritis?) The old buy fewer clothes and, for that matter, less of everything. Their needs revert heavily to the first two steps in the Maslow hierarchy—physiological needs and safety. They seem to give up on the two highest steps—self-esteem and self-actualization. When they are concerned with self-actualization at all, this concern is likely to be revealed in stories that retell the past. Of course this is far from true self-actualization.

Just as food stamps and public housing do not really solve ghetto problems, so, with the old, what is needed is activities that can create a feeling of self-esteem and even self-actualization. This is what will do the old some good.

For a variety of reasons, the older one becomes, the less it is possible to continue the patterns of independence that existed previously. Changes of a narrowing and confining nature take place socially and economically as well as physically. With fewer social involvements and diminishing physical capacities, and finding themselves out of the mainstream of life that formerly involved them, the old lead more restricted and lonesome lives. In other words, the "golden age" is a euphemistic travesty. Many elders find themselves dependent on family, social security, food stamps, or other types of handouts, and for quite a few this change results in a feeling of powerlessness, bewilderment, and even shame. They did not have to resort to handouts when they were younger. In fact, when they were younger they were the providers. The greatest problems of the old person are to maintain his/her health and not to fall victim to fraud or criminal attacks. Overlapping these problems are the consequences of inflation, which for this group can actually mean less to eat. And this, in turn, often results in malnutrition.

An article by E. Waddell (1) summarizes the limited research that has been done in this area and introduces a valuable concept in understanding the lives of older consumers: "poverty of meaning." This phrase is used to indicate that the elderly are suffering, in addition to economic poverty, a form of poverty that results from being out of the mainstream of meaningful living.

Waddell indicates that older people are the most frequent victims of criminal fraud and that such fraud is so commonplace that it has become institutionalized among con artists as "getting granny."

According to testimony at Senate hearings on the elderly, old people are particularly susceptible to fraud and deception because of a combination of characteristics not usually found in younger people. Such characteristics as low income, limited education, and feelings of helplessness, loneliness, and grief make the elderly highly susceptible. Further, the elderly have fewer opportunities for legitimate feedback because of their relative isolation. Their concern and desire for health—and freedom from pain—make them prime targets for quackery.

Unfortunately, the elderly and the ghetto dweller have much in common. A minor difference is that the elderly voluntarily form their own ghettos. This appears to them to be a means of survival since they are with peer groups with similar problems which need to be understood.

The elderly have surely had the benefit of the experience of aging. However, one of the major contentions of this book is that experience per se prepares one more for the past than for the future. Two things are needed. The first is more research on the elderly by subgroups (65–70, 70–75, etc.). The second is a special form of consumer education geared to the group's special problems. To put it more succinctly, the elderly deserve a better reward for having lived and contributed to society.

The excessive prices of food and utilities have hit the elderly worst of all. Since their limited and fixed incomes are just enough to cover the basic costs of continuing to exist in the first place, they do not, like other consumers, have the option of cutting down on such items as entertainment, clothes, or luxuries. An overlooked consequence of rising prices is the damage being done to the elderly as consumers.

Tussing (2) writes of the "absolute poverty" found in the

less developed countries and the "relative poverty" found in affluent societies. The latter, he contends, is worse because the poor feel poorer. This form of poverty also applies to the elderly who, when younger, were "making it." A considerable number of elderly people can no longer support themselves. The sad fact is that many have simply outlived their economic resources, and they know it.

Research and resources to get a man on the moon—yes. Research and resources to better understand the needs of the elderly —no. Why is so little money available to research the needs, attitudes, and behavior of the elderly as consumers?

As a poor substitute for research, especially when issues have political implications, there is often a White House conference. A conference on the elderly was held in 1971. As in most such conferences, involving too many important people in too short a time in a much too structured situation, there was little time to listen, let alone actually do anything of consequence. Most conferences end up with a statement about the seriousness of the problem and a long list of recommendations, very few of which are ever carried out.

White House conferences are prestigious. They flatter the egos of the select few invited, who rarely, if ever, are the ones who have the problems the conference is talking about. But surely the White House has more to do than run conferences. Further, it should recognize that, generally speaking, such conferences raise false hopes and in some respects are as ineffective as study commissions—both achieve nothing but delay.

An example of research on the aged is offered by Waddell, who interviewed 287 members of the National Retired Teachers Association/American Association of Retired Persons in a study similar to a survey conducted by *Changing Times* (3). Comparing results, Waddell reports that inflation forces older people to cut back on an already limited life style. The elderly can cut back in areas of discretionary spending, if any, but have little margin for cutting back in such areas as food and utilities.

Beyond the problems of balancing an impossible budget are the varieties of professional help that the elderly need. They need counsel from physicians, psychologists, and lawyers, and they need it on a personal basis. They don't need long lines and perfunctory care.

A way out of this dilemma is to encourage professionals who are themselves elderly to concentrate on research about the elderly and establish face-to-face communication with them. Through empathy as well as ability, the elderly physician, lawyer, psychologist, dietician, or nurse can start building a subculture that could achieve results as well as solve individual problems.

Just as more research must be conducted to advance the knowledge and status of the consumer, so there must be a specialty within this field that will comprehensively study the aged as consumers.

By way of example, such research might lead to new kinds of products and services. These products should enable the elderly, with their more limited capacities, to cope better with everyday life. Traffic lights may be poorly timed for an older person trying to cross the street safely. Jumbo-size cans or boxes of food are inappropriate for people who need smaller quantities, and smaller sizes are proportionately too expensive. Telephones may need a different bell pitch in order to be heard more clearly by the elderly. Different delivery systems and more conveniently located stores may also be needed.

From the standpoint of products and services, the prevailing distributive aspects of business, which include retailing, selling, and advertising, may need modification if the elderly are to be served adequately. The shopping needs of the aged are different, and because of physical characteristics their shopping behavior is also different. Accordingly, zoning laws that separate retail facilities from living facilities may need change. Just as hospitals have general stores that sell gifts and miscellany, so maybe multiple dwellings where the aged live should have general stores that can supply them with their limited needs, provided that price is not made a function of convenience—the prices in such stores should be lower rather than higher.

What the elderly want most is the opportunity to be active, to continue the socialization process and be accepted in society. In short, they want, within limits, to live as they have in the past. Most of all, they should not be approached with "golden age" nonsense. They see the "golden age" as tarnished—and so will the reader when he/she gets there. Unless there is, first, research, and second, a drastic change in attitudes and behavior toward the aged, their problems will continue to go unsolved.

Just one more example from the field of psychology should suffice. It is known that isolation and sensory deprivation, when combined, tend to increase irritability as well as other forms of emotional lability or instability. Since aging leads to isolation and limited physical capacities, the aged should be able to live in an environment that compensates for their special limitations. We would then see the "golden age" of consumer psychology.

BIBLIOGRAPHY

1. WADDELL, FREDRICH E., "Consumer Research and Programs for the Elderly—The Forgotten Dimensions," *Journal of Consumer Affairs,* winter 1975.9, no. 2: 164–175.
2. TUSSING, D., "Poverty and Education and the Dual Economy," *Journal of Consumer Affairs,* 4, no. 2 (winter 1970): 93–102.
3. "Here's What's Been Happening to Your Living Costs," *Changing Times* (April 1971): 13–19.

4

THE
PARTICIPANTS
IN CONSUMER
AFFAIRS

This section is concerned primarily with the purchase process, some of the things that happen after it occurs, and a psychological appraisal of the various parties involved—consumers, business, labor, and government.

17

The consumer in a buyer-seller-maker transaction

The buyer-seller-maker transaction is a process that consists of a number of steps both before and after the purchase has been made. Regardless of whether the purchase is a high-priced item ($100, $1,000, or more) or a low-priced item ($5 or $10), there are two sets of common denominators involved. The first is the purchase process itself, which generally includes seven steps. The second is the psychological framework. With reference to the first, the steps in the purchase process are as follows:

1. initiation of the idea of a possible purchase
2. exploration and investigation
3. general shopping
4. decision to buy
5. specific shopping
6. purchase
7. post mortems

(Step 4 sometimes follows or is combined with step 5, but usually it precedes the specific shopping.)

A wide variety of stimuli can trigger step 1, the idea to purchase a product or service. The stimulus may be a person, an advertisement, or any form of communication that tells you that a particular item is something you should own, rent, or have. It should be noted that the initiator stimulates awareness of a need or want that probably already existed in a dormant state.

A "best buy," or at least a "good buy," is considered a neces- sary part of the purchase process by most consumers because they perceive themselves as sharp, frugal, or competent. Because of this, a series of explorations or investigations (step 2) take place—reading, looking at ads and displays, consulting friends and relatives, talking to salespeople. All this serves the purpose of providing information about the product or service. This step is generally followed by a period of general shopping (step 3), which may involve merely looking at competitive products on a shelf or visiting several different stores.

After gathering what is regarded as an adequate amount of information, the consumer reaches a decision to buy or not to buy (step 4). If he/she decides to make the purchase, then the question is where. The place of purchase often is not the first place shopped; this is why some ads suggest that you "shop the competition and then shop us" (step 5). Finally the purchase is made, and it results in varying degrees of satisfaction or dis- satisfaction (step 6). The latter results in the need for service, exchange, and so on (step 7).

The psychological framework of the purchase process in- volves a number of phenomena. Once the purchase process starts, there are psychological manifestations in addition to needs and wants. Learning may accompany the purchase process, or at least it should. The knowledge to be gained includes the charac- teristics of the product or service considered for purchase in re- lation to the competition.

The stronger the real or imagined need, the more it is likely that the consumer will rationalize his/her purchase, tending to exaggerate rather than deprecate its characteristics. This is un- fortunate and is a big factor in making the consumer the disad- vantaged party in the buyer-seller-maker transaction. Considering product characteristics often invokes additional judgments. These are more complicated than judgments of product attributes per se. They include ratios, such as the ratio of price to value and that of product performance to consumer needs.

In short, the consumer can create a predisposition for in- correct evaluations. To make matters worse, this is quite often not even recognized. Further, if an error of judgment is called to the buyer's attention by a friend or relative, its existence is often denied. In other words, the buyer feels more secure as the degree of risks taken are relegated to the unconscious. Front and center is the shiny gadget that is not only needed but the best thing that could ever be bought. Thus the consumer sometimes attributes to a product characteristics that do not really exist.

Imagination and fantasy build up the ego, but this benefit can be short-lived when the product does not work well or last very long.

There is some question as to whether all or most of the steps just mentioned are involved in the typical purchase pattern. The answer is that most often they are, but exceptions do exist. For example, no mention has been made of "impulse" buying— the so-called spontaneous or unplanned purchase that results from seeing something while shopping for another item. It may be that "impulse" purchases are less frequent than is generally believed. The point is that the impulse purchase is often a compressed version of the steps involved in the typical purchase process. It is either a rationalization or a self-justification to which the word *impulse* is assigned. After all, few people will admit to buying a totally useless product when they knew its lack of utility in advance. So those products are said to be bought on impulse. This makes the purchase a magical or mystical act.

In reality, all purchase have behind them a predisposition to buy, or what might be called a "buying set." Although no attempt will be made to insist that every purchase involves all the steps we have described, it is also true that there are not as many exceptions as one might believe. To substantiate this, the reader is asked to analyze his/her most recent purchase. Further substantiation of a qualitative sort can be obtained not only by talking to friends, relatives, or neighbors about their recent purchases but also by observing shoppers in retail establishments. A consumer may make an unwise purchase because of a variety of stimuli. These include advertisements, new fads, ambiguous appeals and so forth. They can result in a drive toward a particular behavior—in other words, a purchase.

Thus the two common denominators in the purchase process are closely intertwined. The steps in the process not only result in the purchase of a product or service but also satisfy a need or motive, thus enabling the consumer to regain the equilibrium that existed before the purchase process was initiated. Another way of stating this is that when *congruence* exists for the individual, the chances are that satisfaction also exists. Factors contributing to incongruence produce imbalance and, hence, the need to restore equilibrium.

Among the factors that influence the purchase process are the following:

1. predisposing product characteristics (ideal)
2. actual product characteristics (real)
3. personalization

4. relative roles of husband, wife, others
5. retail outlet

A purchase is satisfactory when the individual matches the characteristics of a product with his/her own needs. A mismatch results in dissatisfaction. In this connection it is important to recognize that some product characteristics do not exist in the product but do exist in the mind of the purchaser. Under these conditions dissatisfaction is very likely.

Sometimes the "ideal" product is elevated to unattainable heights. The ideal characteristics often bear no resemblance to the actual product characteristics.

For example, no matter how many times a person has bought a particular item, such as a car, or been dissatisfied, one day they might see the same item displayed in an idealistic light and ascribe to it characteristics that do not exist in reality. But soon after the purchase has been made, the ideal and reality may diverge.

Another example might be the anticipated appeal of electrical home appliances that either roasts, blends, or toasts. When the anticipation of better prepared food is balanced with the cost of electrical operation, once again the expectation and reality may diverge. The trade-off is between the food preparation and the increased electrical bill. The former is an expectation but the latter is the reality that may make the original decision an unhappy one. Of course, according to the buyer this is the fault of the product, the seller, or the maker. Blaming someone else for one's own poor decision can preserve some people's egos but for others it can produce ulcers.

Among the characteristics that can lead to disparity between the ideal and the actual are quality, features, availability, service, and price (not necessarily in that order of importance). For different individuals, at different times, and for different products, the importance of these characteristics varies.

The quality of a product or service relates to intrinsic features of that product or service. A product has quality when it is durable and appeals to the senses. The consumer somehow relates quality and price and makes a judgment about that relationship. Quality includes good workmanship and durability. Its opposite is shoddiness. It is erroneous, however, to assume that price and quality are correlated—that as one increases the other does too.

"Features" include automobile windows that are operated by pressing a button, ice cubes that automatically drop out of a refrigerator, food that is already mixed and prepared, and the like. Very often features are what differentiate the bottom of the line from the top of the line. The more features are offered, the greater the satisfaction expected. Often hidden or overlooked is the fact that there will be more dissatisfaction when such things go wrong. Features and add-ons have negative as well as positive qualities. Too often the negative qualities are given less thought and the positive ones overrated.

Availability is another important factor. When the decision has been made to actually purchase a particular item, then incongruence is at its height. Having the product immediately is the only thing that can produce congruence.

A characteristic of our changing economy is the fact that we are learning to live with shortages instead of plenty—and we have a hard time learning who created the shortage. We are also made aware that there is frequently a discrepancy between promised and actual delivery dates. This applies to services as well as products. Probably lack of service creates as much if not more dissatisfaction than the product itself.

At the time of purchase the seller and buyer have the potential for optimal congruence. The seller assures the buyer that if service is necessary it will be handled with dispatch. The buyer, despite previous experience with poor service but possibly out of desire for the product, expects things to be different this time. The problem occurs when the buyer discovers the difference between expectation and reality, promise and performance.

A large amount of product dissatisfaction relates to service dissatisfaction. Manufacturers and retailers frequently blame each other for the lack of service. Probably both are right. However, the user either forgets or overlooks the fact that servicing a product is as important as selling it. Business, to be successful, must make a profit, and servicing a product costs money. The consumer should know whether he/she pays for service in advance, that is, whether it is included in the purchase price. Otherwise he/she pays for it later, when the guarantee or warranty has run out. The consumer must learn that very little if anything is free. There are always strings attached.

If more consumers would sincerely believe that "you get what you pay for" and you never get a "steal" or a "big bargain," then there might be fewer problems. Most consumers believe that this applies to other consumers but not to themselves. The reason is that one thinks of oneself as a "sharp," informed person who surely is more than a match for the salesperson. The consumer has a great deal to learn.

One of the most obvious product attributes is price. Most stores clearly mark the price by tagging or stamping the item. When the retailer raises the price, the lower price is obliterated in one way or another. Variations in price on the same product exist from outlet to outlet. On the other hand, there are items that sell at the manufacturer's "suggested" price. There are retailers who sell the product only at the price marked. Others have perpetual "sales" with at least two or three prices on the tag as "evidence" of the markdown, and still others have more than one price—the final selling price is a result of "negotiation." In such instances the "sharp" consumer is left to torment himself with "Did I really get the lowest price?"

It would be well for the consumer to assimilate and integrate the predisposing product characteristics (ideal) and the actual product characteristics (real). This can be accomplished not only by becoming more aware of the steps involved in the purchase process but also by objectively reviewing previous experiences. However, as we have emphasized, experience alone is not necessarily the best teacher. In fact, it can result in no learning at all.

For self-protection the consumer must learn to probe for the real product attributes and not project ideal characteristics. One must understand and adjust to needs, evaluate wants, and most important, have expectations of product performance that are related to the product itself.

Consumers tend to exaggerate their desire for a particular product beyond any need that may exist in reality. Purchasing a product may not be the answer to a need or, for that matter, a mood—as, for example, when you feel depressed and buy an item of clothing in order to feel better. The acquisition of the hat or shoes may give you a bit of fleeting happiness, but when the depression returns you have both the same old depression and the new item of clothing—which may not even be paid for.

It is quite probable that a more realistic appraisal of a product need results in less personalization or too closely associating the product with the self. When this is clearly understood, fewer useless purchases will be made.

Another factor related to personalization is the "I need it *now*" theme. Very often such a need is exaggerated. To be sure, if one suddenly has to travel, does not have a valise, and does not like to carry one's belongings in shopping bags, then the valise has to be purchased *now*. However, either better planning for the trip or a better shopping schedule would probably result in a better purchase. The point is that "I need it *now*" is more often a rationalization than a reality.

The price-value ratio is significant. Studies have indicated that when people are asked to estimate the price of a product they generally do so in relation to their perceptions of the product rather than the product itself.

Most individuals do not live alone and totally independently of others, and so quite frequently a person's behavior as a consumer is related to the cultural or social class within which he/she seeks acceptance. To a great extent this determines not only life style but purchase style as well. Running the gamut from furniture to clothes and food, life style also determines the individual's social behavior. In other words, one chooses products and services in accordance with a preferred style of living.

In the purchase process the buyer's perception of the needs of others is of value. This applies especially when one is purchasing an item for someone else. At this point there is a need to balance the buyer's perception of the recipient's need with the actual need of the recipient. For example, in buying birthday or Christmas gifts does one buy an item that is the purchaser's desired need or something that the recipient will actually need—which makes the better gift?

Even the parent-child relationship is reflected in the purchase process. Do parents buy lots of toys for their children because they had lots of toys when they were little? Or do parents overindulge their children because they themselves were deprived?

Games and toys are for children, but similar items for adults are known as hobbies. This makes them more expensive. Are golfing, fishing, tennis, and sailing athletic activities, social activities, or simply toys? And how do they fit in with the needs of other members of the family or the social group one belongs to? The point is that products and services are bought in response to individual needs related to survival at one extreme and sophisticated social behavior at the other.

As mentioned earlier, considerable spending takes place when a couple gets married. The creation of the first household, as well as replacements and additions, amounts to a very high percentage of consumer expenditure over many years. The roles of the husband and wife in making these purchases may vary considerably. If the husband perceives himself as the family's accountant and controller, the wife may be reduced to the role of errand runner. On the other hand, sometimes the wife controls the family budget. These extremes may be rare, but the attitudes and decisions related to expenditures vary nonetheless. Wives do more than 80 percent of the supermarket shopping, and while they like their husbands to come along, they are also aware that the husband's suggestions may disrupt the food budget.

It is also true that both husband and wife are involved in

more expensive purchases. This gives rise to a surprising amount of nonsense. For example, a chain selling appliances decided that sales would be made only when both husband and wife were present. What is overlooked is the fact that the wife is frequently doing exploratory shopping. When she is treated curtly, she is not likely to consider making a purchase at that particular store.

Not to be overlooked as part of the purchase process is the "fighting it out" that occurs on the family scene. It is normal to expect that husbands and wives will have different orders of priority as regards expenditures and, as a result, perceive their relative importance differently. The opportunities to agree in advance are not as great as the opportunities to eventually agree, that is, compromise. Sometimes it is the husband who is doubtful of the wisdom of the purchase; sometimes it is the wife. However, one or the other has already reached a decision.

A most interesting exploratory study with respect to the influence of spouses on purchase decisions is reported by Sheth and Cosmas (1). The actual study was limited to reports of automobile and furniture purchases.

The research illustrates the greater scope, concern, and implications of consumer research as compared to market research. The authors investigated the factors that determine whether a purchase decision is made by one spouse or both and whether certain sociometric factors are conducive to one or the other type of decision. Further, they explored the incidence of disagreement in the buying behavior of spouses and how such conflicts are resolved. The most fascinating question they raised was whether life style has any effect on conflict resolution.

Essentially, this study investigates the prevalence of conflict in household decision making and the tactics employed by spouses to resolve such conflict. It hypothesizes that "conflict in purchase behavior may provide more subtle insights into the causes for divorce: it is often the little things which are marginally more critical in sustaining a marriage." How true!

Conflict arises when there is a felt need to decide jointly while, at the same time, there are differences between the spouses in goals or perceptions. Depending on whether the spouses have such differences, Sheth and Cosmas' model specifies four distinct types of conflict resolution: problem solving, persuasion, bargaining, and politicking.

Using this model, almost two-thirds of the respondents claimed that they made major purchase decisions together with their spouse. Among the most frequently mentioned reasons for joint decisions were the nature of the product (requiring joint consumption), the perceived risk involved in the purchase decision, the importance of the product class to the family, and the family life style itself, which encourages joint decision making. The remaining third of the respondents claimed that decisions were made by one of the spouses. They frequently mentioned greater competence on the part of one partner, a preference for dividing the responsibilities of household management, the greater importance of the decision to one of the spouses, the feeling that they were too busy to decide together, and peer group norms as responsible for autonomous decision making in regard to purchases of furniture and automobiles. The decisions tend to be more autonomous in households with no children or with grown-up children, in the low or middle socioeconomic classes, and in cases in which the wife has a blue-collar occupation, as well as among older women. With reference to the correlation between tactics of conflict resolution and individual life style, Sheth and Cosmas found that:

> People who are self-confident, optimistic about present and future life ambitions, liberal in their values, as well as opinion leaders and adventurous tend to be problem solvers. On the other hand, people who are not self-confident, pessimistic about present or future life, highly traditional or homebodies, secure and contented who live a sedate life and seek advice from others generally tend to be users of persuasion tactics in conflict resolution. The bargainers tend to have less self-respect and self-confidence, frustrated with their present life, and lack security of mind. They seek no outside advice and tend to be nonconformist and liberal in their attitudes toward law and order. Also they tend to be night people rather than day people. (page 18)

The purchase process also involves the place where the item is bought—the retail outlet. There must eventually be congruence between the retailer's positioning of the product's characteristics and the personalization on the part of the consumer that results in a decision on where to purchase the item. Some retailers sell primarily, if not solely, their own brand. Others sell only a nationally advertised brand, and still others sell a number of competitive brands.

Obviously, the consumer is involved in the decision as to which type of outlet is "best." A related variable is the type of store —department store, discount store, chain store, independent store, supermarket, and so on. These classifications overlap, however; some discount stores prefer to be known as department stores, and vice versa. Consumers are generally in agreement as to what type of store a particular outlet is, regardless of the image the store tries to convey. They also recognize that department stores offer service and even sales help to a greater degree than most discount stores do.

A related factor is the policy toward sales personnel, that is, whether salespeople are on a commission, a bonus system, or a fixed salary. Many people believe different pay systems result in different degrees of aggression toward the potential customer.

There is also the judgment of the salesperson that results from "looking at" a potential customer. Sometimes this is erroneously called "psychology." Salespeople do make judgments, however. They either consistently use a "tested" technique or base their strategy on their own insights. Among their options are selling what is asked for, offering advice, refusing to offer any advice, or saying "this is not my department."

Even though there is a trend toward self-service and a desire on the part of the customer to "just look," from time to time potential customers do want to talk to someone who knows something about the product being purchased. This includes the consumer who wants to talk to the butcher in the supermarket (who seems to be permanently encased behind large glass windows). By contrast, a salesperson may use a "sales pitch" that is highly technical and act as if the customer knows and understands the supposed advantages that are being expounded. In such a situation the buyer may be too embarrassed to admit a lack of this technical knowledge. Tires, automobiles, air conditioners, and television sets, among other items are often advertised as having "manufacturer's exclusive features" or technical improvements over competition. Quite often these technical features make little difference in performance. The buyer should get the salesperson to talk in plain language and to explain all technical or engineering features. When the salesperson talks technically to the average consumer, the buyer should say "I don't understand, please explain what you are saying."

The purpose of this chapter is not only to set the stage but also to review the process consumers go through as they purchase products and services. This is the base from which consumer psychology stems.

A better understanding of the purchase process may be obtained by considering some of the possibilities that exist when the purchase process is in operation.

1. Complete congruence between ideal product characteristics, actual product characteristics, the product image, the retail outlet, the personalization attributed to the product, and the

relative roles of husband and wife results in a purchase in the shortest possible time.

2. Some time may elapse between the initiation of the idea and the purchase itself. This happens when the existence of incongruence creates tension and anxiety. To resolve the incongruence and restore stability, the consumer must make a decision to purchase or not purchase.

3. When the product is purchased, then the degree of congruence between the product and the buyer's expectations results in varying degrees of satisfaction or dissatisfaction. The greater the satisfaction, the more the purchaser is predisposed toward similar preferences in the future. The greater the dissatisfaction, the more the purchaser is predisposed to switch brands.

4. When the decision not to purchase or to postpone purchase has been made, it is likely that any change in the individual's equilibrium will start the purchase process over again.

A most important point to recognize is that the consumer as a buyer is neither effective or efficient. This statement is both sad and true. To be sure, when one purchases an automobile one purchases not only make, model, features, and accessories but also faith. One has no way of knowing whether the car will turn out to be a "lemon."

On items that are replaced only after a number of years, such as furniture and major appliances, the shopping process is probably too short in relation not only to the investment of money but also to the length of time the item will be used. It is as if the customer wants to believe he/she can make the "best deal" in the shortest possible time.

Hundreds of interviews with consumers have revealed that they offer strong rationalizations and "evidence" to prove that they did make the best deal. However, the definition of the "best deal" varies with price, convenience, features, and sometimes characteristics that exist only in fantasy or are believed as a result of false advertising claims or an overenthusiastic salesperson.

When an item is replaced continually, as in the case of food items, then habit can play a strong role. By habit we mean the repetition of a behavior without deliberate or involved decision making. Lighting another cigarette or repeatedly buying the same brand are examples of habit.

In an unpublished study, people about to enter a supermarket were asked what brand of ketchup they used. They were then told to purchase some ketchup; the only thing they could *not* do was to buy the brand they ordinarily used. They were told that they would be reimbursed when they came back. Some bought higher-priced brands and some bought lower-priced brands. This procedure created a situation known as "forced brand switch." When contacted again at a later date, quite a few indicated that they did not repurchase the brand they had been using for years. Instead, they repurchased the new brand. Others, having made a switch, decided to switch to still another brand. Thus while habit is a factor in purchase decisions, it is also a weak link in the purchase chain. Purchase by habit is a form of an addiction.

In summary, buyer-seller-maker transactions involve both the purchase process itself and the psychological framework. The consumer can be helped to the degree that he/she understands the motives, perceptions, and attitudes of buyers, sellers, and makers that encourage the decision to purchase. All three are hardly ever in complete congruence. From the point of view of the user, he/she should buy only when whatever congruence there may be is in his/her best interest.

Another aspect of purchase behavior is the difference between potential and actual satisfaction as a result of the purchase. The potential dissatisfaction in the purchase of a tennis racket, a backgammon set, or a bicycle will be considerably higher than the expected satisfaction if the person does not learn to play a good game of tennis, continues to lose at backgammon, or does not ride the bike.

BIBLIOGRAPHY

1. SHETH, J. N., and S. COSMAS, "Tactics of Conflict Resolution in Family Buying Behavior," paper delivered to the American Psychological Association, Chicago, 1975.

18

Issues
and complaints

Consumer complaints are the symptoms of buyer-seller-maker transactions that have gone wrong. They require much time and result in adjustments more often than solutions. The consumer with a product or service that does not conform to expectations is likely to blame anyone or anything. Anxiety, conflict, and irrational behavior on the part of the consumer are matched by the overly defensive seller or maker, who often does not even empathize with the consumer. The labels "irate" and "unfair" are now attached to the person who only a short time ago was being congratulated on a "wise purchase decision."

Consumer complaints are caused largely by incongruence in the goals of business and consumers as well as by differences in their perceptions of the characteristics of products as they relate to the user's health, safety, and satisfaction. In addition, each side perceives quite differently its own rights and freedom and is quick to observe the excesses indulged in by the other. Accordingly, sometimes one side and sometimes the other expects government to preserve or extend its rights and freedom.

A basic assumption should be that a consumer has the right to be correctly and completely informed about any product or service. It follows that if the consumer has been presented with the full truth rather than half-truths, deceits, or fraud, then he/she has a right to expect that the products and services available are healthy and safe.

To the extent that this occurs, many of the issues related to consumer affairs can be resolved. Issues and conflicts relate to or are caused by product expectations that do not match reality. The belief that business is bound by legal and ethical considerations to offer products and services that promote the health and safety of their users apparently is naive. The weekly Federal Trade Commission reports add much credibility to this statement as it lists claims of misrepresentation.

From a product's conception in terms of design through the manufacturing process to the advertising and marketing stage, there are many pressures to cut corners in order to cut costs. As a result the product that enters the marketplace may be less durable, perform less adequately, and be less safe and healthy than it was designed to be—but look "great." These factors contribute to differences in expectations and performance and give rise to complaints.

Consumer psychology enables one to understand the incongruence of goals and the conflicts that result as groups move in different directions and adopt different points of view. Not only the products and services one buys but also the servicing of those purchases involves issues and complaints. For example, the granting of credit often is not in the best interest of the consumer. *Credit* is a euphonious word for *debt*. Whereas governments and large corporations can indulge in deficit spending, such practices do not apply to individuals. Low- and middle-income consumers can easily get into trouble when they play the deficit-spending game. Under adverse conditions they lose not only the money they have paid for houses, cars, television sets, furniture, and so forth but also the items themselves.

The promotion of "free and easy credit" has encouraged some misinformed or uninformed consumers to get into debt beyond their ability to repay. When things go wrong, then and only then comes the sad realization that credit did nothing but put them into hopeless debt, which can have a terrible effect on their lives for many years.

Negative feelings are coped with in various ways; some individuals cannot handle them at all. Of course debts should be paid, but lending money involves risk. Both parties have the best of intentions—a congruence of goals and perceived mutual benefits—at the start. When things go wrong, then goal incongruence emerges.

Possibly business should offer "credit," but the consumer should clearly understand that he/she is a *debtor* and be clearly informed of the consequences if the debt is not repaid according to the agreed-upon terms and conditions, which involve more than added interest charges. Truth in lending is only part of the story. The greater part that should be told relates to the consequences of not repaying. Try to imagine the way you would feel and what you would do if, despite all your efforts, your car or television set were repossessed before your eyes.

There are many other psychological problems related to consumer issues. Among the by-products of consumer dissatisfaction are various emotional reactions—anger, rage, misplaced aggression. Dissatisfaction may also result in a negative, passive, dejected feeling of powerlessness. As a result varied forms of rationalization develop. All this is negative and keeps the consumer from coping adequately. Moreover, it decreases the consumer's trust in business.

Another fundamental aspect of consumer issues is the freedom concept. If business can do anything it wants, then consumers will be handicapped. So when the issues finally surface an additional conflict arises. This relates to whether business or government can best act to "protect" the consumer. While this goes on, each side acts independently to preserve its rights and powers by flexing its muscles. This can be illustrated by the solutions of "volunteerism," proposed by business, and legislation, proposed by government.

Not to be overlooked is the fact that the various issues of consumer affairs tend to have low saliency among consumers. Other interests, preoccupations, causes, and movements tend to gain more supporters more easily.

Consumer issues are reflected in proposed national legislation that is intended to protect the consumer. The index of the Consumer Legislative Monthly Report, issued by the Office of Consumer Affairs (1), is included here to show the areas in which various congressmen believe new laws are needed. Such laws would change the "balance of power" in matters directly related to consumer protection by guaranteeing greater honesty in the advertising and marketing of products and services and greater health or safety for consumers as they use those products and services.

    Advertising
    Agriculture
    Automobiles
      Insurance
      Mechanics Licensing
    Class Actions
    Complaint Resolution Mechanisms

Consumer Protection Agency
Consumer Agencies, Councils, etc.—Other
Consumer Education
Cosmetics
Credit and Finance
   Billing/Collection
   Disclosure of Terms
   Discrimination
   Financial Institutions
   Money Orders
   Mortgages
   Reporting
   Other
Drugs
Energy
Food
   Additives
   Imports
   Ingredient Standards
   Labeling
   Registration of Processors
   Supplements
   Surveillance and Inspection
      State Inspection
   Other
Franchising
Fraud
Health
Housing
Packaging and Labeling
   Alcoholic Beverages
   Appliances
   Fabrics
   Foreign-Made Products
   Manufacturer
   Point of Sale
   Pricing
   Throw-Aways
Privacy
   Census
   Disclosure
   Mailing Lists
   Records—Credit, Insurance, Employment
   Records—Criminal
   Records—Federal Income Tax
   Records—Financial Transactions
   Records—Freedom of Information Act Amendments
   Surveillance

Universal Identifier
Other
Regulatory Reform
Safety
  Medical Devices
  Motor Vehicles
  Products
  Other
Standards
  Hobby
  International Voluntary Product
  Metric
  Testing
Toxic Substances
Transportation
Warranties
Consumer-Related Public Laws

Since health is so closely related to and dependent on food and drugs, this was the first area in which laws were passed to protect the consumer. However, issues related to food are still with us. The index makes this amply clear: Note the presence of date labeling, unit pricing, warranties, food stamps, and nutritional labeling, for example. In the case of drugs, clearly established standards of purity and uniform prescription pricing are necessary.

Advertising and its exaggerations, misrepresentations, and deceptions can affect all consumers, including children and their toys as well as senior citizens and their health insurance.

Invasion of privacy is another consumer concern related to the granting of credit and the accompanying investigative process. Here again incongruent goals are both in focus and in dispute. Does a company considering lending you money have a right to know if you drink, live beyond your means, and so forth? There are some who say yes—like loan companies and banks. There are some who say no—like the debtors who think they are getting "credit." Considerable evidence exists that caprice and arbitrariness characterize banks and insurance companies as well as manufacturers and retailers who operate their own loan companies. On the other hand, those institutions consider such investigations to be sound business practice. However, at times this results in unfair and unexpected consequences for people who are otherwise judged to be honest. If false information is obtained or information is falsely evaluated and the person investigated does not even know of its existence, then the applicant cannot even defend himself. What are the consequences? One is that we may well be on our way to building a commercial world with paranoid tendencies. Such a trend, if continued, could result in a psychotic society.

Warranties and guarantees also foment issues. Many consumers do not know the difference, and many do not know what either one means because it has been misrepresented. The small print and legal language confuse the buyer. Only when the item needs service does the buyer discover the escape clause. The fact that he/she has misinterpreted the guarantee holds little comfort for the user whose purchase is no longer usable.

Once again it is necessary to return to the principle that fewer issues would occur if complete and clear information were exchanged at the time of the transaction. Equally important, the buyer should read every word before signing and ask questions if anything is unclear.

The preceding discussion of issues and complaints was not intended to be complete. It has attempted to indicate the wide range of issues that involve the incongruent goals of labor, business, consumers, and government not only in matters of health and safety but also as regards who shall get what share of freedom.

What is needed is greater consciousness and concern on the part of everyone involved in consumer affairs. This includes *labor,* which makes the things that *business* decides to make so that the *seller* can get the *consumer* to buy and use those products and services. When the goals of these parties do not coincide, then we have consumer issues. If such consciousness can be achieved, then much fraud and deceit will "go away" and people will be psychologically and physically safer, healthier, and happier.

Regardless of the industry, it might be assumed that there would be very few arguments advanced against the consumer's right to be treated honestly and to be sure the products or services he/she uses are healthy and safe. Right? *Wrong.* Face-to-face dealings sealed with a handshake may sometimes exist among businessmen, but it would appear that such agreements, real or implied, do not exist between business and the consumer. Even when contracts exist, despair and frustration can result—especially because of the small print, often on the reverse side of the card, which turns out to be a contract that the courts will recognize and enforce.

Buyers must learn to avoid the *consumer's illusion.* Beyond the efforts of makers and sellers, buyers too willingly create a set that predisposes them to false perceptions about a product. The chapter on perception pointed out that illusions are misinterpretations of reality or false perceptions. Buyers create the consumer's illusion when they attribute to a product qualities that it does not really have. The consumer must establish whether he/she is participating in the false world of illusions.

Issues are manifestations of broad, comprehensive principles related to the need to establish justice. Complaints, on the other hand, are specific manifestations of dissatisfaction. For example, the question of whether the purchase of a product or service shall be accompanied by some form of guarantee or warranty is an issue. A complaint occurs when the consumer finds that the product's performance is not as was presented or expected.

Either the consumer is finally beginning to be heard or more companies are recognizing a responsibility for product performance after sale. In any case, more guarantees and warranties are being written in simple English. There is even progress in the direction of allowing the buyer to unilaterally abrogate the "contract" when there was not a meeting of minds between the buyer and seller in the first place.

Consumer complaints are much more specific than issues, but complaints are at the root of a wide variety of issues. Complaints are clear indicators that the buyer is not satisfied. They reveal that product performance is not as expected or represented. By the time a consumer registers a complaint, disappointment and possibly frustration have occurred. Few people are willing to contain themselves at such a time. As a result rationality and composure go by the board. Instead, accusations and recriminations are triggered.

There is an urgent need to study consumer complaints scientifically. To do so one would have to know a great deal about a product's performance (or lack of it) on a purely objective basis. Beyond this, one should know the factors and forces that led to the consumer's false expectations, if any. It is not enough to know the nature of the complaint and the characteristics of the complainer; it is equally important to know the policy and characteristics of the retailer and its sales personnel as well as those of the manufacturer. In this relatively early stage the work that has been done has consisted primarily of classifying the complaints.

Before discussing such classifications, however, a few questions must be raised. The first is, What does it mean if complaints increase or decrease? The assumptions involved here could fill another book, but a complete answer is not available. For example, complaint counts may increase because channels are more available or the economy is getting worse or more people believe complaining will result in satisfaction. On the other hand, complaints may decrease because things are getting better, it does no good to complain, or the obstacles in the path of the complainer are worse than the frustration of living with an inadequate product.

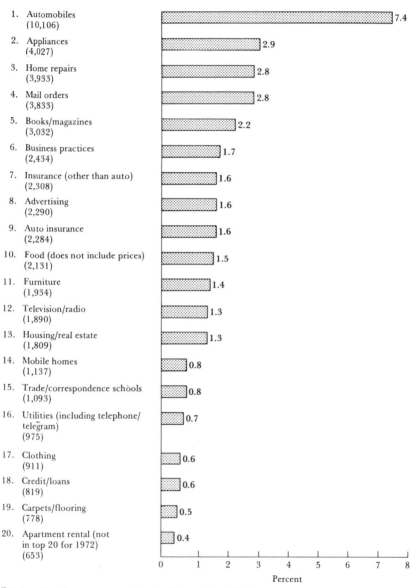

1. Automobiles (10,106) — 7.4
2. Appliances (4,027) — 2.9
3. Home repairs (3,933) — 2.8
4. Mail orders (3,833) — 2.8
5. Books/magazines (3,032) — 2.2
6. Business practices (2,434) — 1.7
7. Insurance (other than auto) (2,308) — 1.6
8. Advertising (2,290) — 1.6
9. Auto insurance (2,284) — 1.6
10. Food (does not include prices) (2,131) — 1.5
11. Furniture (1,934) — 1.4
12. Television/radio (1,890) — 1.3
13. Housing/real estate (1,809) — 1.3
14. Mobile homes (1,137) — 0.8
15. Trade/correspondence schools (1,093) — 0.8
16. Utilities (including telephone/telegram) (975) — 0.7
17. Clothing (911) — 0.6
18. Credit/loans (819) — 0.6
19. Carpets/flooring (778) — 0.5
20. Apartment rental (not in top 20 for 1972) (653) — 0.4

Percent

Total number of consumer complaints in all categories: 136,181
Number of offices reporting: 47

FIGURE 18.1   Top 20 Consumer Complaints, 1971

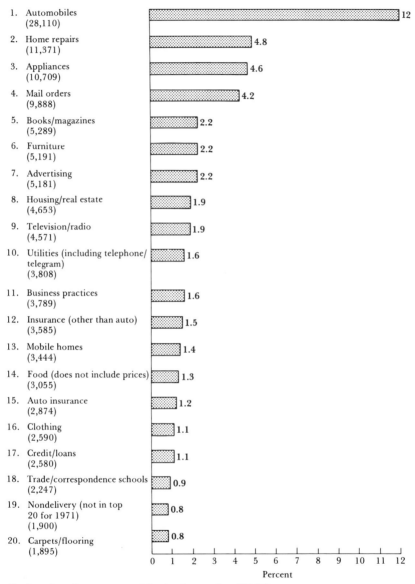

1. Automobiles (28,110) — 12
2. Home repairs (11,371) — 4.8
3. Appliances (10,709) — 4.6
4. Mail orders (9,888) — 4.2
5. Books/magazines (5,289) — 2.2
6. Furniture (5,191) — 2.2
7. Advertising (5,181) — 2.2
8. Housing/real estate (4,653) — 1.9
9. Television/radio (4,571) — 1.9
10. Utilities (including telephone/telegram) (3,808) — 1.6
11. Business practices (3,789) — 1.6
12. Insurance (other than auto) (3,585) — 1.5
13. Mobile homes (3,444) — 1.4
14. Food (does not include prices) (3,055) — 1.3
15. Auto insurance (2,874) — 1.2
16. Clothing (2,590) — 1.1
17. Credit/loans (2,580) — 1.1
18. Trade/correspondence schools (2,247) — 0.9
19. Nondelivery (not in top 20 for 1971) (1,900) — 0.8
20. Carpets/flooring (1,895) — 0.8

Percent

Total number of consumer complaints in all categories: 232,723
Number of offices reporting: 81

Source: Figures 18.1 and 18.2 are from Department of Health, Education, and Welfare, *State Consumer Actions Summary '73*, Office of Consumer Affairs, DHEW Publications, no. (05)–74-116.

FIGURE 18.2   Top 20 Consumer Complaints, 1972

Another problem is the establishment of a uniform data-gathering system to record the details and objective facts. In addition, a system for making important judgments regarding the rights of both sides must be developed. Finally, who is to decide whether the complaint was resolved in a satisfactory fashion? A scale measuring degree of satisfaction must be developed, since satisfaction is invariably a matter of degree.

It is necessary to determine not only the satisfaction of the complainer, who is generally the buyer, but also that of the seller and the maker. This would lead to a total satisfaction score encompassing all the components of the complaint.

To obtain an idea of what complaints occur with what frequency, the reader may refer to Figures 18.1 and 18.2, which were compiled by the Office of Consumer Affairs on the basis of a sampling of responses from state, county, and city consumer offices for two successive years. Automobile complaints form the single largest category, with the second echelon consisting of complaints about appliances, home repairs, mail orders, and books and magazines.

The twenty most frequent complaints are presented in the

TABLE 18.1   Relative ranking of complaints

	Rank 1971	Rank 1972	
Automobiles	1	1	0
Appliances	2	3	+1
Home repairs	3	2	−1
Mail orders	4	4	0
Books/magazines	5	5	0
Business practices	6	11	+5
Insurance (other than auto)	7	12	+5
Advertising	8	7	−1
Auto insurance	9	15	+6
Food (not pricing)	10	14	+4
Furniture	11	6	−5
Television/radio	12	9	−3
Housing/real estate	13	8	−5
Mobile homes	14	13	−1
Trade/correspondence schools	15	18	+3
Utilities (including telephone)	16	10	−6
Clothing	17	16	−1
Credit/loans	18	17	+1
Carpets/flooring	19	20	+1
Apartment rental	20	x	
Nondelivery	x	20	

SOURCE: A comparison of rankings as established in Tables 18.1 and 18.2.

tables on pages 186–187. The average number of complaints per office for the years 1971 and 1972 remained constant at slightly less than 3000 complaints per office. However, 37 percent of the complaints were registered in 1971 and 63 percent in 1972. This change was due to the increase in the number of local offices.

If one merely considers the ranking and assumes that all reporting was consistent and uniform, Table 18.1 indicates a rela-

TABLE 18.2   Ranking of products, services, and/or methods of sale generating most complaints

State Agencies' Responses	Voluntary Organizations' Responses
1. New automobiles—sales and servicing	1. New automobiles—sales and servicing
2. Home improvements	2. Appliance repair service
3. Used automobiles—sales and repairs	3. Books, magazines and/or newspapers—subscriptions
4. Door-to-door sales	4. Mail orders
5. Mail orders	5. Home improvements
6. Appliance repair service	6. Used automobiles—sales and repairs
7. Mobile homes	7. Credit and/or loans
8. Credit and/or loans	8. Mobile homes

SOURCE: R. M. Gaedeke, "Filing and Disposition of Consumer Complaints: Some Empirical Evidences," *Journal of Consumer Affairs,* Summer 1972, 6:1, 45–46.

TABLE 18.3   Ranking of products accounting for most warranty and/or guarantee complaints

State Agencies' Responses	Voluntary Organizations' Responses
1. Automobiles	1. Automobiles
2. Appliances*	2. Appliances*
3. Television sets	3. Television sets
4. House siding	4. Mobile homes
5. Mobile homes	5. Boat motors

* Refrigerators, washing machines, air conditioners, water heaters, and automatic dishwashers.

SOURCE: R. M. Gaedeke, "Filing and Disposition of Consumer Complaints: Some Empirical Evidences," *Journal of Consumer Affairs,* Summer 1972, 6:1, 45–46.

TABLE 18.4   Top ten categories of complaints—1972

Vehicles		Finance	
New car dealers	335	Credit	47
Used car dealers	144	Insurance	30
Auto repairs (garages, etc.)	347	Small loan companies	26
Auto accessories	87	Banks	20
Boats	33	Collection agencies	19
Cycles	30	Misc.	32
Misc.	119		**174**
	1,095		
		Weights and Measures	
Commercial Services		Net content food	122
Mail order business	304	Net content non-food	18
Home solicitations	119	Scales	15
Health and beauty salons	121	Liquid petroleum gas	13
Hotels and restaurants	21	Taxi meters	11
Upholsterers	49	Misc.	71
Dry cleaners	38		**250**
Misc.	167		
	819	*Appliances*	
		Television	300
Home Furnishings		Hi-fi, stereos, tape recorders	109
Furniture	172	Air conditioners	90
Carpets	114	Refrigerators	76
Drapes	41	Stoves	29
Interior decorators	24	Washer-dryer	29
Misc.	18	Misc.	98
	369		**731**
Retail Merchandise		*Real Property*	
Clothing	119		
Jewelry	57	Housing	35
Animals	44	Land promotions	29
Drugs and cosmetics	35	Real estate	16
Sport equipment and toys	27	Misc.	8
Photography	22		**138**
Going-out-of-business sales	22		
Medical devices	22	*Home Improvements*	
Misc.	135	Roofing	181
	483	Swimming pools	36
		Windows	31
Recreation		Building additions	27
Travel (boat, air, others)	79	Plumbing	24
Sport events	10	Doors	23
Theater	7	Flooring	21
Misc.	13	Misc.	121
	109		**464**

Referred to other agencies   243

Unusual Complaints: 791 complaints received against one Health Salon which brought about 252 charges filed against same company, case to be tried next Fiscal Year.

Source: Dade County, Fla., Consumer Protection Div., annual report, 1971–1972.

TABLE 18.5   Top ten categories of complaints—1974

Commercial Services		Retail Merchandise	
Mail order business	474	Clothing	134
Health and beauty salons	110	Jewelry	86
Van hauling and storage	101	Photography	62
Dry cleaners	64	Sports equipment and toys	45
Hospitals and clinics	56	Personal accessories	45
Home solicitations	36	Animals	44
Exterminators	33	Drugs and cosmetics	42
Hotel, restaurants and bars	33	Office equipment	27
Upholstery	28	Medical devices	23
Laundries	18	Building supplies	18
Doctors	15	Musical instruments	10
Employment agencies	14	Misc.	106
Franchise and distributorship	10		**642**
Misc.	198		
	1,187	*Appliances*	
		Television	256
Home Improvements		Air conditioner	123
Roofing	265	Refrigerator	113
Painting	59	Washer-dryer	42
Plumbing	52	Hi-fi, stereos, tape rec.	41
Building addition	51	Stoves	28
Swimming pools	38	Radios	26
Kitchen cabinets	35	Sewing machines	17
Windows	32	Vacuum cleaners	7
Doors	27	Misc.	56
Flooring	22		**709**
Fences	21		
Landscaping	18	*Home Furnishings*	
Misc.	111	Furniture	349
	731	Carpets	122
		Drapes	72
Weights and Measures		Household accessories	30
Food	181	Interior decorators	26
Liquid petroleum gas (LPG)	65	Blinds and shades	6
Scales	31	Misc.	19
Non-food	23		**620**
Water meters	12		
Taxi meters	6	*Real Property*	
Misc.	35	Housing	167
	353	Land promotions	69
		Real estate	45
Recreation		Cemetery	7
Travel agency	37	Misc.	6
Boats	19		**294**
Airplanes	19		
Theaters	5	*Vehicles*	
Misc.	135	Auto repairs (garage, etc.)	509
	215	New car dealers	494
		Used car dealers	162
Finance		Auto accessories	78
Credit	74	Mobile homes	68
Insurance	48	Boats	42
Banks	21	Cycles	29
Small loan companies	20	Car rentals and shippers	23
Collection agencies	16	Tractors	4
Misc.	34	Misc.	23
	213		**1,432**

SOURCE: Dade County, Fla., Consumer Protection Div., annual report, 1973–1974.

tive improvement or deterioration in each category. When a plus sign appears before the number in column 3, it indicates the degree to which that category improved in rank. A minus sign indicates a decline in rank.

As can be seen, the rank of 11 of the 21 items remained almost the same. Among the items showing relative improvement are business practices, insurance (other than auto), auto insurance, and food (not including pricing). Among the items relatively worse were utilities, furniture, and housing and real estate.

An interesting attempt to better understand consumer complaints is offered by Gaedeke (2). His view is that consumer discontent is intensifying. Responses to a questionnaire he mailed to both state agencies and voluntary organizations handling consumer complaints led to the ranking of complaints reported in Table 18.2. Although the terminology and classification system are somewhat different, the topics and areas of complaint are highly similar to those just reported.

Gaedeke also investigated the issue of product guarantees and warranties. He states that "issues dealing with product guarantees and warranties involve the failure or refusal to honor them, receiving unsatisfactory warranty repair service, failure to honor within a reasonable time period, receiving less than the customer expected and ambiguity in warranty or guarantee specification." The products that account for most of these complaints are reported in Table 18.3.

TABLE 18.6   Relative rank and percent increase (decrease) in number of complaints (base 1972)

Complaint	Rank 1972	1974	Percent Increase or Decrease Since 1972 in Number of Complaints
Vehicles	1	1	31%
Commercial services	2	2	45
Appliances	3	4	(3)
Retail merchandise	4	5	33
Home improvements	5	3	58
Home furnishings	6	6	68
Weights and measures	7	7	41
Finance	8	10	22
Real property	9	8	115
Recreation	19	9	97

SOURCE: Comparison of Tables 18.5 and 18.6.

In its report for the fiscal year ending in 1972 (3), the consumer protection division of Dade County, Florida, reported the top ten categories of complaints received. (See Table 18.4.) A similar tally for the following fiscal year is presented in Table 18.5. The changes in rank, as well as the percent increase or decrease in each category, using 1972 as a base, are presented in Table 18.6.

Table 18.6 indicates a drop in rank for such categories as appliances, retail merchandise, and finance. Increases, or higher relative rank (which means a worsening condition), are found in home improvements, real property, and recreation. The remaining four categories maintained the same rank.

However, there was an increase of 38 percent in the total number of complaints. As can be seen in column 3, the percentage increase was greatest in the real property and recreation categories. Only one area, appliances, showed a decrease.

The percentage contributed by each category to the total number of complaints received is presented in Table 18.7. Here rather consistent results were obtained. The one area in which improvement occurred was appliances.

The Council of Better Business Bureaus occasionally compiles the various complaints handled by its 139 local Better Business Bureau offices (4). A report for the nine months ending in September 1974 includes the finding that 15 out of 88 types of business account for over 55 percent of the complaints processed. These business categories are reported in Table 18.8.

Further insights are offered by the reports of complaint settlements. As Table 18.9 shows, department stores have the highest

TABLE 18.7   Percent of complaints received, by category

	1972	1974
Vehicles	24%	22%
Commercial services	18	19
Appliances	16	11
Retail merchandise	10	10
Home improvements	10	12
Home furnishings	8	10
Weights and measures	5	6
Finance	4	3
Real property	3	5
Recreation	2	2

SOURCE: Table comparison.

TABLE 18.8   Compilation of complaints handled by various better business bureaus

	Rank	Percent
Mail order companies	1	15.5%
Auto dealers—car/truck	2	5.1
Home furnishing stores	3	4.2
Misc. retail stores/shops	4	3.9
Misc. service establishments	5	3.9
Department stores	6	3.1
Magazines, ordered by mail	7	2.9
Misc. home remodeling	8	2.9
Appliance stores	9	2.5
Apparel and accessory shops	10	2.0
Television servicing estab.	11	2.0
Real estate sales/rentals	12	1.9
Auto repair (independent, ex. trans.)	13	1.9
Home remodeling contractors	14	1.8
Mobile/modular home dealers	15	1.8

SOURCE: Statistical summary of BBB system activity, January–September, 1974, Council of Better Business Bureaus, Washington, D.C.

TABLE 18.9   Settlement rates by business categories

Highest Settlement Category	Percent	Lowest Settlement Category	Percent
Department stores	90.4	Market research co.'s	27.6
Magazines, ordered by mail	88.2	Legal services	39.5
Music/record stores	88.1	Vacation certificate co.'s	57.0
Manufacturers/producers	86.5	Dry cleaning/laundry co.'s	57.3
Savings and loan co.'s	85.1	Paving contractors	59.5
Mail order companies	84.3	Reupholstering shops	60.5
Banks	84.3	Traveling agencies	60.9
Telephone companies	84.0	Funeral and related service	
Credit card co.'s	83.9	co.'s	61.0
Chain food stores	83.7	Misc. home remodeling	
Insurance companies	83.4	co.'s	61.8
Hospitals/clinics	82.8	Homework companies	63.3
Utility companies	82.8	Roofing contractors	65.2
Direct selling co.'s—		Floor covering stores	65.9
encyc.	81.4	Business opportunity co.'s	66.1
Consumer finance and		Home remodeling	
loan co.'s	81.1	contractors	66.7
		Mobile/modular home	
		dealers	66.9

SOURCE: See source for Table 18.8.

TABLE 18.10   Type of complaint

	Percent
Delay in service	25.2%
Unsatisfactory service (unrelated to repair)	14.6
Product quality/performance	13.7
Repair	10.0
Credit/billing	9.2
References not provided	7.4
Guarantees	6.7
Selling practices	6.7
Advertising practices	6.4

SOURCE: See source for Table 18.8.

percentage of settlements and market research companies the lowest percentage. Of the 30 business categories in the highest and lowest settlement ranges, 5 also appear in Table 18.8, which lists those with the highest complaint rates. Note that home re- modeling contractors and mobile-modular home dealers, in addi- tion to attracting a large number of complaints, are among those that tend not to cooperate in settlements. The reader should be doubly alert when dealing with these businesses.

Another matter of interest is the array of complaints by type. The nine most frequent types of complaints are listed in Table 18.10.

It is obvious from the assorted data presented that despite the lack of standard ways of judging complaint recording, han- dling, and disposition, some businesses and products are more culpable than others. The consumer should be offered the oppor- tunity for redress. This would go a long way toward resolving many complaints. The various compilations indicate that there is too much evidence for the culprits, notably the automobile, to go unregulated.

This series of tables was presented in order to reveal the areas where complaints are frequent. Effective redress systems need to be developed. The more effective the system, the more likely it is that complaints will be based on product inadequacy, lack of safety, or threats to personal health. Until that time, the watchword is *caveat emptor,* or consumer beware!

BIBLIOGRAPHY

1. U.S., Dept. of Health, Education and Welfare, office of Consumer Affairs, *Consumer Legislative Monthly Report, 93rd Congress,* Oct. 18, 1972 (Washington, D.C.: GPO).
2. GAEDEKE, R. M., "Filing and Disposition of Consumer Complaints: Some Empirical Evidences," *Journal of Consumer Affairs,* 6, no. 1 (Summer 1972): 45–46.
3. Dade County, Florida, Consumer Protection Division, Annual Report, 1971–1972.
4. Council of Better Business Bureaus, *Statistical Summary of BBB System Activity,* January–September 1974 (Washington, D.C.).

19

Consumer organizations

Organizations create the structures that determine the effectiveness of their programs, goals, and performance. Such structures also reveal the strength and weakness of the institutions or establishments they represent, be they business, labor, government, or consumer groups.

A study of the varieties of consumer organizations reveals patent weaknesses. In general, they do not seem to be well structured. Organizationally, they surely are no match for the Better Business Bureaus, chambers of commerce, and other types of organizations that represent business.

With reference to the future of the consumer movement, a supportable inference is that it will not make any noticeable progress until the existing organizations change in a number of ways. For example, many of these organizations are dedicated to the "consumer movement," but there is no unified consumer movement. If such unity is to be achieved, it is necessary to establish an order of priority for the various consumer issues. After this has been done, the organizations should go to work in a concerted fashion. A problem is that while there are a multitude of national organizations, none has achieved strong leadership. The various organizations exist in an atmosphere of friendly distance. They do not really communicate.

In general, national organizations tend to be successful when they have active local chapters and when communications flow in both directions. Within the total consumer organization structure there are local organizations with no ties to national groups and national groups with no local chapters. A strong local-national network does not exist. This must be achieved if the movement is to succeed.

Another problem confronting consumer organizations is that some emphasize many issues and overlap with others, while others select a single issue and concentrate on it to the total exclusion of everything else.

Even the age of various organizations gives few clues as to the future of the consumer movement. For example, two groups have reached their fortieth and seventy-fifth anniversaries, respectively. On the other hand, too many consumer groups appear one day and disappear the next.

What is indicated is that growth can take place by doing things differently, from an organizational point of view, than in the past. Stronger and more effective organizations with programs that do things for the average consumer will have to evolve. It is not enough to appeal to the beleaguered citizen to join still another organization for what is supposed to be his/her own good.

More meaningful activities should be the theme if greater effectiveness is to be achieved. The change will have to be in the direction of doing things for the consumer, things that the consumer can perceive as beneficial. To be successful, consumer organizations must represent consumers better than the other groups claiming to represent them. It is no wonder that both business and government attempt to "protect" the consumer.

In the future, consumer organizations will have to either combine or coordinate with groups that prefer to start afresh rather than join an existing group. More unity, vitality, and benevolence must be generated.

To offer greater insight into consumer organizations in general, we will describe three different organizations in the remainder of this chapter. A good place to begin is Consumers Union (CU). Among all the consumer membership organizations it may well have made the most significant contribution. It meets such criteria as age (1936), size, and membership (over 2,250,000)—members who pay dues and receive the monthly magazine *Consumer Reports*. CU's major activity is the testing and evaluation of a wide variety of products, all in the public interest and without one dollar from advertising revenue or corporate funds.

CU's product testing and evaluation service marks it off quite distinctly from commercial testing companies that will, for a fee, independently (?) test a product for a client. It is also different from magazines that grant "seals of approval" for products that, more often than not, are advertised in the magazine. The point is that CU cannot be accused of any possible conflict of interest through the influence of an advertising or research expenditure.

The major role of *Consumer Reports* is to provide information about products and brands in a simple, straightforward, and uncontaminated fashion. This it does, to the best of its ability, within the framework of budget and time requirements. To do this it devises ingenious, unbiased tests. A visitor to its headquarters in Mt. Vernon, New York, would be impressed by the methods, "props," and machinery that have been devised for this purpose. They are a most amusing reflection of a combination of necessity and imagination.

Historically, CU had a predecessor, but it broke away in the 1930s. The person most deserving of credit for the success, progress, and stability of this organization is the man who has been its president since 1936. Professor Emeritus Colston E. Warne has been a giant among giants in handling with tact and dexterity every attack on the organization and, incidentally, on his own character. Few could have survived those attacks, which called him everything from a communist to the devil himself.

Dr. Warne's philosophy may be seen in this excerpt from a speech he delivered in 1974 (1):

> The conditioning of the youth of America was increasingly being left to the unfettered institution of advertising which, in the 'Twenties, was coming into its own with the emergence of giant corporations which sought to counter inhibitions and to condition people to accept the good life of Camel cigarettes, Chevrolets and Alka Seltzer. Indeed, embodied in brand name advertising we had a most potent private agency of consumer education—an agency of immense potential which was to shatter conventional buying patterns and ultimately virtually to recast the social values of a nation by reaching into the most remote village to put Post Toasties in every kitchen and to add chewing gum into the life pattern of every child.
>
> Fortifying this siren force came the potent influence of radio, and later television, both of which added an extra dimension to product acceptability. The dramatized human voice penetrated through the walls of the household to alter the way of life of Middletown in astounding ways. (Middletown was the "Middle America" of Robert Lynd, Muncie, Indiana.)
>
> Consumption patterns as catalogued by the Lynds were to be dynamited by yet another potent influence—the advent of the

automobile and of a nation on wheels. In large market areas, the auto created the phenomenon of suburbia. It developed massive shopping centers and eradicated much of the central city. As a nation we became dependent upon the internal combustion engine. Detroit became a symbol of our new-found affluence.

Fortifying this optimistic thrust of the 'Twenties was the advent of consumer credit which tore the nation away from its puritanic conviction that debt was sinful—at least an object of scorn. Our mounting GNP became dependent upon going in debt; credit suddenly became acceptable. The cash customer became an eccentric. Debt was a way of life.

Another force which dynamited traditional consumption patterns was the advent of synthetics. Our "chemical revolution" brought us a cellophane civilization with additives and preservatives in foods, with invention running wild, creating a host of new products, most of them of scant social consequence. (pages 2, 3)

Consumers Union has provided the data for some interesting research. Based on an analysis of findings and recommendations published in *Consumer Reports*, Morris and Bronson (2) raise some very basic questions about the effectiveness of competition within the American market. A comparison of the quality ratings of various products and their prices reveals that price and quality are not necessarily correlated. In fact, the average correlation reported is +.29. This measure is, for all practical purposes, too low for individual product predictions. In other words, the consumer has little reason to believe that higher price necessarily means higher quality when a wide variety of products are considered. For zoom motion picture cameras and upright vacuum cleaners, the correlation between price and quality were highest; for nylon cord tubeless tires and lightweight vacuum cleaners they were lowest. In fact, some correlations were actually negative, which suggests that higher price and lower quality tend to go together. These findings are based on research and statistical analysis; they are not the ravings of antibusiness prejudice.

To make matters worse, the relative quality of a particular brand compared to other brands does not stay the same over time. In other words, a brand's price-quality ratio is not necessarily the same over successive model changes. The study suggests that price and quality shifts are chaotic and unpredictable. Quality may go up or down for a brand and so may its price, but there is no reason to believe that price increases reflect quality improvements.

Obviously, each consumer must obtain adequate, unbiased

information when making a purchase decision. The inference is that experience with a brand may not be enough to form a basis for a purchase decision.

In fact, a study by Engeldow (3) changes this statement from an inference to a fact. Engeldow finds that subscribers to *Consumer Reports* are better educated, have higher incomes, and show all the other favorable qualities that a typical market research study manages to find. But from here on the Engeldow study is different, *quite different.*

The subscribers, when compared with two other populations, a random sample, and a matched sample, were decidedly more favorable toward business and, at the same time, more critical of advertising. *Consumer Reports* subscribers were likely to be more liberal on the question of the individual in society but negative toward measures involving increased governmental activity in business-related areas. Subscribers manifested interest in all consumer- and product-related reading materials. They were more concerned with performance, durability, and service. Their neighbors (the matched sample) were more concerned with credit, styling, and availability.

Users of the product ratings, whether subscribers or not, reported more product satisfaction. Nonusers, whether subscribers or not, reported less product satisfaction.

Engeldow concludes that the *Consumer Reports* subscriber is information sensitive in general, a curious blend of liberal and conservative, and a "rational" buyer. The subscriber relies more on outside information sources and is less likely to rely on personal judgment in the form of either past experience or personal observation of products. Once again we see the recurring theme that experience may not be the best teacher. Too heavy a reliance on experience may make you, as a consumer, your own worst enemy.

Before leaving Consumers Union, a pamphlet by R. T. Morris (4) should be mentioned. It is a critique of the testing methods and sampling techniques used by CU. It is a rigorous work and raises questions that are not likely to be answered within the practical aspects of limited staff, budget, and time.

Insofar as it desires CU to improve, it is most laudable. Insofar as its negative criticism occupies more space than its positive statements, it may be damning with faint praise. However, Morris states that "Consumers Union is one of the most valuable private social institutions in the United States, a blessing to those sufficiently well informed to employ it."

The testing done by CU is quite different from the market research of products and media, which somehow tends to reach conclusions that favor the client. CU's solid approach should be known and used by more consumers.

Shifting to a more typical type of consumer organization, the National Consumers League (NCL) is notable for its longevity and perseverance. Founded in 1899, it is the oldest national consumer membership organization. It is one of a number of national organizations headquartered in Washington, D.C. Others include the Consumer Federation of America and the National Consumers Congress.

The NCL and the Congress have sparse membership lists, and their revenue sources present a perennial problem. It appears that membership in a national consumer organization is not important to most consumers. There are some well-meaning, spirited individuals who, to the extent that they pay their dues, receive the occasional bulletins and wish for better days.

Visits to national consumer headquarters in Washington leave much to be desired. The visitor gets a "poor as a church mouse" impression. By contrast, the marble edifices of trade associations look more like Taj Mahals. It is also quite apparent that another difference is in the salaries the executives receive. For budgetary reasons consumer organization executives are rather poorly paid and have shorter tenures than their counterparts in trade associations.

On the Washington scene consumer groups are usually regarded as powerless and given only lip service by politicians. Because of the sheer dollar advantage that business and trade associations have over the consumer movement and its leaders, "David" looks much too small compared to "Goliath."

Claims that the consumer movement is already too strong and has too many laws to protect it must be recognized as either utter propaganda or blatant lies. They are calculated to prevent further growth in the movement. In fact, no organization in the consumer movement has come close to winning the battle for freedom and power. Only one individual seems to approach success in this respect, and that is Ralph Nader.

The typical format of the *National Consumers League Bulletin* is to report the activities of the League. For example, the September 1974 issue reported that the League would join with other national consumer groups to provide a consumer voice at (still another) White House summit conference. One of NCL's continuing themes is that conferences and hearings in general have a distorted makeup and are dominated by producers and corporate representatives.

The issue also reports on a Food and Agriculture Conference and offers an update on proposed legislation as well as a plan to train consumer survey teams to evaluate medicare nursing homes in the Washington area. It goes on to refer to three new government publications on consumer matters and a commemorative biography of Judge Felix Frankfurter, and includes an application blank for new members. This kind of information does not create interest at the grass-roots level.

In 1974, to commemorate its seventy-fifth anniversary, the NCL published the *Consumers Almanac* (5), which essentially reviews the history of the NCL and of the consumer movement as a whole.

The Almanac contains some interesting information on the evolution of the consumer movement. For example, it traces the history of the consumer movement to the early Mosaic and Egyptian laws governing the handling of meat. In 1202, King John of England proclaimed a law to punish those guilty of short weight and adulteration of bread. In early 1900, the NCL and the American Medical Association joined forces in uncovering ineffective or dangerous medicines, generally known as home remedies, which often contained morphine and opium.

The Almanac points out that four companies—Kelloggs, General Foods, Quaker Oats, and General Mills—control 83 percent of the breakfast food market. It claims that such tight control leads to such monopolistic practices as higher prices and control over the allocation of supermarket shelf space. Further, the Almanac reports that all is not well with American nutrition. Since World War II soft drink consumption has gone up 300 percent and snack consumption has gone up 85 percent; at the same time, consumption of dairy products, vegetables, and fruits has gone down between 21 percent and 25 percent. Think of the implications of these figures for nutrition and health!

Here is another important point: In 1972 Hamburger Helper cost 57¢. If consumers bought the noodles separately and prepared their own sauce, the same meal would cost 26¢. The tragedy is that people who stretch hamburger because they need to in order to fill their stomachs are being misled, "ripped off," or both. The problem is, Are people who buy Hamburger Helper willing to pay 31¢ more (1972 prices) for the convenience, or do poor people think they are really stretching their dollar and being economical?

A page from the Almanac is worth reproducing. Written by Adam Smith in 1784, it is another example of the timeless nature of some topics.

> Consumption is the sole end and purpose of all production; and the interest of the producer ought to be attended to, only so far as it may be necessary for promoting that of the consumer. The maxim is so perfectly self-evident, that it would be absurd to attempt to prove it. But in the mercantile system, the interest of the consumer is almost constantly sacrificed to that of the producer; and it seems to consider production, and not consumption, as the ultimate end and object of all industry and commerce . . . .
>
> It cannot be very difficult to determine who have been the contrivers of this whole mercantile system; not the consumers, we may believe, whose interest has been entirely neglected; but the producers, whose interest has been so carefully attended to; and among this latter class our merchants and manufacturers have been by far the principal architects. (page 21)

Another excerpt from the Almanac worth perusing is the following, which illustrates the job exchange market and the closeness of business and government.

MUSICAL CHAIRS

> Top-level executives are always coming and going between positions in regulatory agencies and in the industries regulated. A sample:

Dr. Virgil Wodicka Director of Bureau of Foods FDA	came from:	Ralston Purina, Manager, Cereal Research Lab; Libby McNeill, Libby, Manager, Nutrition Research
Peter Hutt FDA General Counsel		Covington & Burling, Washington law firm counsel for Institute of Shortening & Edible Oils
William Goodrich Former FDA General Counsel	went to:	President Institute of Shortening & Edible Oils

Stuart Tipton CAB staff lawyer	came from:	Air Transport Association, President
Charles Denny FCC Commissioner		National Broadcasting Corp., Vice President
Owen Clarke ICC Commissioner		C & O—B & O Railroad, Vice President
Lawrence J. O'Connor, Jr. FPC Commissioner		Standard Oil of Indiana, Vice President
Earl Butz Secretary of Agriculture		Ralston Purina
Clifford Hardin Secretary of Agriculture		Ralston Purina
Clarence Palmby Assistant Secretary of Agriculture		Continental Grain Co.
Clifford Pulvermacher General Sales Mgr. USDA Export Marketing Service		Bunge Corp.
Carroll G. Brunthaver Associate Administrator Dept. of Agriculture		Cook Industries

Business experience is generally considered as a qualification for the next job up the ladder to success. When executives come and go from business to government and vice versa—and the preceding list contains only a few of the possible examples—it makes one think more seriously about the relationship between business and government.

The Almanac's historical review of the NCL clearly reveals the organization's roots in the labor movement. Its earliest activities were concerned with curtailing sweatshops, fighting for a minimum wage, protecting women and children from exploitation, and similar causes. Now the consumer issues in which the NCL is involved include the energy shortage, adequate medical coverage, corrective advertising, auto safety and repairs, installment financing, and other unfair and illegal trade practices.

As a source of little known or long forgotten information, the *Consumers Almanac* is recommended.

Another important consumer organization is the American Council on Consumer Interests (ACCI), which held its first annual conference in the mid-1920s and has continued on a professional level ever since. Its participants come from a wide variety of academic backgrounds, including economics, family economics, home economics, agricultural economics, electrical engineering, engineering, journalism, marketing, psychology, and law. Also included are government personnel and people working in various capacities on the community level.

The ACCI also publishes a newsletter. It is factual and well written and briefly reports such activities as council business, news of other consumer-oriented organizations, and government activities related to consumer affairs, as well as brief annotated summaries of relevant literature. There is nothing "puffy" about it.

The annual conferences are also oases of sanity. Speeches and workshops at these conferences cover such areas as methods of consumer education, analyses of government positions, family economics, consumer responsibilities, and consumer reaction to products. In the 1973 conference a paper worthy of attention was presented by D. R. Pittle (6). Pittle recognizes that few consumers take advantage of available materials on product safety and that they buy items on the basis of criteria unrelated to safety. He proposes the establishment of "modules" of safety that could be applied to a series of product categories. This approach would set standards for such safety features as electrical insulation, bonding characteristics (glues or welds), design of corners, toxicity, and radiation.

A paper with quite a few implications for the consumer movement was delivered by R. O. Herrmann at the 1972 conference. It was entitled "The Roots of Support for Consumerism" (7). Using a telephone survey with slightly more than 900 respondents, Herrmann attempted to determine the willingness of individuals to support Ralph Nader. As can be seen from Table 19.1, which has been modified from the original, whereas almost half of the population were either uninformed or unaware of Nader at the time of the survey, almost four out of ten were either sympathizers or supporters. About 16 percent were opposed to "Naderism." The beliefs of these five groups about a variety of items are reported in the table.

The ACCI also publishes *The Journal of Consumer Affairs,* which has appeared semiannually since 1967. Its format includes articles, viewpoints and communication, and book reviews. The material is relevant to consumer affairs and in an unimpassioned way presents information based on research or observation on such issues as nutritional labeling, the warranty problem, truth in insurance, consumer credit, private labels, imitation foods, consumer education, consumer purchasing patterns, and consumer complaints.

There are, of course, many other organizations whose sole or primary purpose is to identify with or raise the consciousness of the consumer. Those we have selected should illustrate that the consumer movement has existed for many years, that it does not consist of wild-eyed radicals, and that most are not "wet behind the ears."

Media, lobbyists, and propaganda sources sometimes tend to accentuate the oddities and the rarities. They do this in all fields that are considered in the "public interest"—thus the consumer movement is not left out.

TABLE 19.1   Consumer attitudes based on awareness and beliefs about Nader (modified)

Consumer Concerns	Un- awares	Unin- formed	Re- jecters	Sym- pathizers	Sup- porters
Number of respondents	172	249	149	191	147
Percentage of respondents	18.9%	27.4%	16.4%	21%	16.2%
Present financial situation "fair" or "not too good" (%)	70	62	49	51	50
High concern about product safety and reliability (%)	36	47	50	62	67
Felt strong need for more product information on expensive items (%)	27	37	38	41	48
Concern that laws and regulations favor business at expense of consumer (%)	19	25	35	40	46
Political orientation "liberal" (%)	12	16	24	37	47
Strongly favor having government requiring proof of advertising (%)	69	82	80	84	88
Nader is for free enterprise but with changes (%)	—	—	76	95	96

SOURCE: Modified from R. O. Herrmann, The Roots of Support for Consumerism. Proceedings, 18th Annual Conference, American Council on Consumer Interests, 1972.

The consumer must seek out the information that is available and then decide on the truth. Consumer organizations can help in this respect. But they need to become more effective and stronger. It would also help if the consumer recognized that the claim that consumer organizations are already too strong is false. The sad fact is that they are much weaker than business and labor organizations and no match for government. There must be more unity and effectiveness if consumer organizations are are to become competitive.

The consumer movement, if it is to grow, needs to agree on its goals, coalesce, and act in a mature fashion. Sensationalism may attract attention, but it can also detract from the movement's progress by encouraging the opposition to accuse consumer organizations of being irresponsible or irrational. A case in point is the "Food Day" sponsored by the Center for Science in the Public Interest with the support of thirty-five organizations and individuals. The purpose was to focus attention on three themes: the severity of the world food shortage, rising food prices, and the decline in the quality of the average diet, with its effect on public health.

As part of Food Day, the following list of "The Terrible Ten Foods" (8) was compiled. The list seems somewhat incoherent, as if the criteria for selecting the items were not clear. Some of the items in the list are nonnutritious foods, but one must wonder whether there is any scientific evidence that the items selected really are the ten "worst" foods. It may well be that the items on the list are serious offenders, but it is not easy to understand exactly why.

The Terrible Ten Foods

Food Day coordinators have compiled the following list of the ten worst foods:

WONDER BREAD   Plain ordinary enriched white bread, made by Continental Baking, a division of ITT (which also owns Sheraton Hotels and makes military supplies). Wonder bread costs up to thirty percent more than other white breads. The Federal Trade Commission recently accused ITT-Continental of using unfair marketing practices to try to monopolize the baking industry.

BACON   Perhaps the most dangerous food in the supermarket. Bacon contains nitrosamines, which the government admits "are a family of chemicals, some of which have been shown to cause cancer in test animals." These fatty strips of porkbelly cost as much as $1.59 per pound—a good investment for masochists.

SUGAR   The Justice Department recently indicted six big sugar refiners for alleged price fixing and conspiracy to reduce competition. The Health Department should indict sugar for contributing to obesity, tooth decay, diabetes, and heart disease.

GERBER BABY FOOD DESSERTS   The major ingredient of this baby food is water, which cost 40 cents per pint. All the desserts contain added sugar, which helps foster a child's sweet tooth. Eating junk baby foods may lead a baby down a lifetime path of junk foods and ill health. Gerber controls 60% of the baby food market.

FRUTE BRUTE   This breakfast cereal-candy contains about 40% sugar and costs about $1.40 per pound. The cost does not include dental bills, but does include the cost of TV advertising aimed at children. General Mills, symbolized by Betty Crocker, has been the junk breakfast cereal leader for years. Four companies control 90% of the cereal industry.

BREAKFAST SQUARES   Another marvel from Betty Crocker's chemical kitchen. The two main ingredients of this "Gainesburger for people" are sugar and fat. The undesirable effects of these ingredients are not canceled out by the added vitamins and minerals. The acronym for Breakfast Squares is uniquely appropriate.

PRIME GRADE BEEF   High in fat, high in cost, high in cholesterol. The beef is fattened up in feedlots on grain that could otherwise be consumed by hungry people. The food shortage has contributed to millions of deaths in the last several years; an estimated 400,000,000 more are at risk.

TABLE GRAPES   The United Farm Workers are conducting a nationwide boycott because growers refuse to sign UFW contracts. It is easy to forget that the people who harvest much of our food are hungry, ill-housed, and in great need of schools and health care.

PRINGLES   The ultimate insult to the potato, a terrific vegetable. This reconstituted, preserved chip is one-third more expensive than regular chips and at least thirteen times more expensive than real potatoes. Pringles' long shelf life permits nationwide distribution and may enable Procter & Gamble to monopolize the potato chip market.

COCA COLA   Contains no nutrients; costs more than milk. The Coca-Cola Co. peddles its wares in underdeveloped countries, where the beverage is a cause of economic hardship and nutritional harm. If you want the "real thing," get something real, like milk or fruit juice or water.

This attack, it would seem, is as emotional and biased as the statement by the National Association of Manufacturers cited in Chapter 1. The point is that solutions emerge when conflicts are reduced. Statements that tend to intensify conflicts make understanding and communication less possible.

BIBLIOGRAPHY

1. WARNE, C. E., "The Need for and Pathways to Consumer Education," *Consumer Education Conference*, Indianapolis, April, 1974.
2. MORRIS, R. T., and C. S. BRONSON, "The Chaos of Competition Indicated by *Consumer Reports*," *Journal of Marketing*, 33 (1969): 26–34.
3. ENGELDOW, J., "The *Consumer Reports* Subscriber: Portrait of an Intense Consumer," *Indiana Business Review*, July–August, 1972.
4. MORRIS, R. T., *Consumer Union—Methods, Implications, Weaknesses and Strengths* (New London, Conn.: Litfield Publications, 1971).
5. SHABECOFF, A., *Consumers Almanac* (New York: Universe Books, 1974).
6. PITTLE, D. R., "Reducing Consumer Products Related Injuries via Mass Technical Education," *Proceedings*, 19th Annual Conference, American Council on Consumer Interests, 1973.
7. HERRMANN, R. O., "The Roots of Support for Consumerism," *Proceedings*, 18th Annual Conference, American Council on Consumer Interests, 1972.
8. "The Terrible Ten Foods," *California Citizen Sun*, March 19, 1975.

20

Consumer leadership as illustrated by an interactional workshop

The preceding chapter described three types of consumer organizations and their programs. In addition, it suggested that the total organizational structure as well as the interrelationships among consumer organizations is rather weak compared with the organizational structures of business, labor, and government. If the organizational structures are lacking, then a further question arises: Who are the leaders of these organizations and what are their attitudes? Most important, how effective are they?

To answer these questions, eleven people who qualify as consumer leaders by virtue of their roles in consumer organizations were convened for an interactional workshop. These individuals represented different national and local organizations from different parts of the country, but no attempt was made to select "one of each." The group's membership was set at eleven to allow for reasonably effective interaction. The members were chosen by first meeting with four consumer leaders, who, in turn, suggested well over forty people as candidates. The group of four also considered the discussion areas to be included and finally recommended the following areas to be covered in the interactional workshop: *

1. Today's goals
2. The unfulfilled needs of the consumer movement

* See Chapter 9 for an explanation of this research technique.

3. Practical steps to achieve those needs
4. The how and where of funding
5. Next steps
6. Summary statements by participants and observers

What follows is a summary as well as a commentary. *It is not intended to be projected to all consumer leaders.* It is merely intended to convey the hopes, fears, and attitudes of eleven well-meaning men and women who are serving in leadership roles in the consumer movement.

Accordingly, the first item of information that can be gleaned as a result of the workshop is not whether it accomplished what previous meetings have attempted. Rather, it is clear that until either the leadership of the consumer movement changes or the characteristics of the current leaders change, existing problems will continue to go unsolved. It is clear that the leaders participating in the workshop perceive a need to work together. The difficulty is that perception may not lead to behavior.

The patterns and themes of discussion were often quite similar, regardless of the question being discussed. In quite a few instances the comments revealed consistency of personality and mode of expression rather than offering an answer that might lead to a solution.

Over and over again it appeared that the speaker believed he/she had a secret key to the solution of a problem. The difficulty was that there seemed to be a number of secret keys. No one was interested in finding out which secret key would really do the necessary unlocking, especially if it turned out not to be one's own particular key.

To be sure, sometimes personal doubts were expressed, but for the most part others were asked to remove the doubt. This never happened. This led to continued consistency in the expression of the person's viewpoint as well as the doubts.

The findings may be summarized by stating that the participants agreed on the need for unity but not on the what, how, or when. There was agreement on the need to unify—or at least coordinate and thereby make stronger—national, state, and local groups, as well as service systems among the groups. There was also agreement on the need to clarify themes, concepts, and actions.

While all the participants were polite and most, if not all, were cautious and reserved in their statements, the criticisms expressed reflected the feeling that "we have been here before" or "it is those others" (the ones not at the workshop) who create obstacles.

An interactional workshop deliberately avoids forcing either an artificial consensus or a vote. Rather, it seeks individual expressions of opinion with the hope that others, united by a common bond (i.e., the importance of consumer issues), will listen to different theories and approaches. However, there is little evidence that people are willing to give primary credit to someone else's point of view. For example, even when a person was asked if his/her organization should be abandoned, there was a lot of pleasant talk but no direct answer.

Sometimes a particular question may have been too challenging to the individual's ego and personality; instead of answering the question some would criticize it. It may well be that the question was challenging, but the refusal or inability to answer is significant.

Another surmise that suggests a "holding back" pattern may be seen in the queries concerning the nature and form of the report, which occurred even before the group discussion started. At least one person inferred that the discussion might be less than candid unless there was some assurance that the participants could see a draft of the report. There was no pressure, but there was parrying. There was no agreement to show the participants a draft since this might lead to attempts at censorship. It seems as if quite a few were looking for reassurance that the other participants, including the workshop leader, would not abuse their frankness.

It was both sad and amusing to hear some participants accusing those not in the group of not representing consumers and not being open and aboveboard, without recognizing that from time to time these criticisms might be applicable to themselves.

In the following report by the interactional workshop leader names and organizations are omitted, but the material in the report is based on analysis of tapes of the workshop, the themes expressed, and experience in interpreting their meaning and content.

The fact that eleven consumer leaders participated and presented different views is most healthy. It would have been a pity if the group had presented a facade of total agreement. However, many of those present were singularly unyielding in their belief that while others could coexist, those others did not seem to recognize the importance of their point of view. For example, do we need a service, a national body with a larger membership, a campaign against utilities, or a strong local organization? Of course all these suggestions are valid. But no one asked why they have never been packaged together and what it is that is preventing the package, regardless of its form and shape, from being put together at this time.

The workshop deliberately included only six questions to be covered in an entire day. Interestingly, it did not matter what the question was; the answers always dealt with the same theme: "It would be nice if we could get together, but don't overlook my way when we decide to do it together."

Frankly, there was not a complete, full, fair exchange of information, and while one should not impute motives, it did seem as if there was not going to be a real sharing of secrets—at least not for a while. The excessive politeness and lack of criticism were signs of holding back rather than indicators of true feelings.

Among the talents of consumer leaders, the "know-how" of funding is not a strong one. It may also be that past efforts accompanied by lack of success have left doubts in the minds of some leaders as to what is really "best." When one repeatedly does not achieve success, then defense mechanisms must be built to preserve one's ego. The alternate is the inability to cope with the situation and a neurosis is likely to form. Since consumer leaders have no fund-raising talents or abilities, they must demonstrate other ways to develop the consumer movement and feel that they are making a meaningful contribution. In such circumstances one needs to preserve one's ego by using whatever psychological dynamism one believes will be helpful. When one really cannot cope, then a neurosis can form. Accordingly, consumer leaders may look for other ways of demonstrating their success in the consumer movement.

New channels should be pursued. A first step would be to study the techniques used by other groups in different movements or institutions. This might offer a series of alternates from which a new approach could evolve.

TABLE 20.1   Participants' listing of major goal of meeting

Coordination or unification of local and national groups for more effective consumer action	5
How to raise funds	1
How to increase membership	1
Need to develop a program	1
Have participants achieve a better understanding of the movement	1

At three points in the workshop the participants were asked to write their answers to certain questions on a questionnaire. This was done before the question was discussed by the group, so it can be assumed that the answers were not influenced by the views of others.

The three questions referred to the major goals of the workshop, the three greatest unfulfilled needs of the movement, and the method of fund raising most likely to be successful. Although eleven people attended the group session, two did not arrive until the third question was being discussed. Accordingly, they did not complete the questionnaire.

Table 20.1 lists the perceived major goals of the meeting. It is clear from the goals listed that a majority of the participants want some form of improved coordination and a unification of organizations and efforts. It would appear that this is the first step. If the desire is strong enough, then the methods can be developed. The next step might be to consider a wide variety of alternatives, and a third step might be to evolve a plan that would be acceptable to the many local and national groups that already exist.

Of less concern to the individual, but still important, is the "how to," that is, how to improve fund-raising methods and, as a result, have money available to do certain necessary things. Another "how to" is to discover methods that would result in increased membership.

The participants were also asked to list what they considered to be the three greatest unfulfilled needs of the consumer movement. A tally of the responses is presented in Table 20.2. In

TABLE 20.2   Mention of unfulfilled needs (N = 9 participants)

	Number of Mentions	Intensity Score
Funding needs	6	22
Coordination and organization among groups	7	21
Define and clarify consumer movement	3	15
More/better communication	3	9
More members	3	9
Improve leadership	2	4
Improve effectiveness	1	3
Research	1	1
Improve relations with government and business	1	1

addition, an arbitrary scoring system was used. A 5 was assigned each time an item was listed as first, a 3 each time an item was listed as second, and a 1 each time an item was listed as third. This scoring system indicates intensity as opposed to frequency.

Only nine different unfulfilled needs were mentioned, which would imply overlapping of the participants' perceptions of the needs of the consumer movement. Heading the list in terms of both frequency of mention and intensity score are funding needs and the need for coordination and organization among groups. Distinctly in third place is the need to clarify and define the consumer movement. Tied for fourth and fifth place are the need for more and better communication and the need for more members.

It is clear that this group of leaders regards funding, coordination, and clarification of purpose as the most important needs to be fulfilled.

The participants were also asked to name the one method of funding likely to have the greatest success. Table 20.3 lists the various items mentioned. Some participants listed more than one, but in those cases only the first one listed was tallied.

It would appear that there is less agreement about the "best" funding method than there is about such things as goals and unfulfilled needs.

The group's discussion of the question of goals supported the major finding obtained from the frame-of-reference questionnaire: that efforts should be made in the direction of unification and coordination of regional and national groups. The group also agreed that there is a need for better information leading to a better understanding of the consumer movement. Another concern was know-how about raising money.

In the remainder of this chapter, virtually unedited quotes are used to illustrate the points of view expressed. The following quotes refer to the discussion of goals.

> I'd like to see people discuss possible directions toward unification of both objectives and organizations within the national consumer movement.

TABLE 20.3   One method of funding likely to be most successful

Variation on check-off theme	2
Variation on direct mail request	2
Fee for service	2
Membership dues	1
Foundation grants	1
No answer	1

Coordination of the local, regional, and national groups. Make them more viable.

The discussion of unfulfilled needs resulted in responses somewhat different from those on the questionnaire. The discussion consisted of a series of comments related to matters of personal concern rather than direct answers to the question. This type of response is significant because of its latent, as opposed to manifest, content. It is a bonus that an interactional workshop often provides.

Although the discussion was polite and moderate, it indicated that the participants were not in agreement as to whether there is a consumer movement and whether that is the right way to describe it. The point is that these people, who are sufficiently informed to know that there is a movement, recognize that it is far from unified. As a result it is perceived so differently that some even deny its existence.

Sometimes people try to clear up problems by using another word. But this is merely an exercise in semantics. For example, there were fewer objections when the word *movement* was changed to *thing*. Greater acceptance occurred when *thing* became *shtick*.

The discussion of unfulfilled needs was sometimes discordant and at other times rambling. It also served to reveal the participants' personal projections. Sometimes the needs of the movement were stated directly, candidly, and even simplisticly, especially as those needs were related to the participants' own activities in the consumer movement. However, most of the participants wandered from the topic and anchored themselves to the presentation of a particular point of view.

There was a noticeable lack of reference to consumers as individuals—their needs, their wants, and ways to get them to join. Those who favored the grass-roots movement talked about the importance of having an organization on the local scene rather than about the potential membership of such an organization.

The quotes that follow are intended to illustrate the discussion that occurred at this point. However, they also illustrate that sometimes experts do not express themselves very clearly.

As a concept I think that we do not have adequate organizational clout either as individual organizations or as a movement politically. I'm not just talking about legislation; I'm talking about the administration as well.

It's been charged a lot of times that there is no philosophy, no common purpose, no common goals to the consumer [movement]. I don't think that's a problem and I don't believe that. I personally believe that a group working on one subject under any organizational framework is part and parcel of this whole thing. The greatest need of the movement is to be able to structure something that will allow a strength in numbers. Somehow we have to take what's out there and put some cement in between so that it can be more effective in things other than legislation.

The interactional workshop allows the participants to discuss areas perceived as important, so when the discussion ranges far afield from the question asked it is important that as content it be considered as an indicator of the participants' interests and concerns.

As in many other instances throughout the workshop, there was little discussion of the needs themselves. Rather, the discussion centered on issues and conflicts. Examples are the relative importance of national vs. local organizations, or whether there is a need for a communication system between local and national organizations—which, incidentally, is different from the need for an information clearinghouse.

In addition, there was disagreement over whether programs come before money or money comes first. In this connection there was disagreement as to whether a paid staff and unpaid volunteers can coexist. A few felt that paid staff meant the eventual demise of volunteers and, hence, of the organization itself. At least one person held this view with considerable intensity. Others did not feel that way at all. There was also disagreement over the importance of concentrating on national legislation, and in this connection there did not seem to be very enthusiastic support for the proposed new consumer protection agency. This feeling, or the lack of it, should be probed in depth.

> In the last five or six years there have been tremendous gains on the state and local level in every respect; there have been tremendous changes. This kind of change has not happened in Washington.
>
> You always worry about money and I think it's significant that most of the activity that's going on in the consumer movement in the country is going on with groups that are 100 percent voluntary. All the staff-oriented organizations are ineffective as far as I can tell.

Concern about the "Washington syndrome" was expressed but not clearly defined or explained as far as consumer affairs is concerned. In this connection the need for a national organization, not necessarily located in Washington, was differentiated from the need for a centralization of functions that would be located in Washington.

> I call this the Washington syndrome. I don't think people in Washington understand what's going on in the United States. It's the most parochial town in the world. People have a lot of speculative ideas about what's happening out in the states and they really have no information about what's happening. They don't even have enough information to be able to ask questions.

> There is no organization that's visible enough nationally that a group popping up in a local area would automatically say, "Hey, we've got to get in touch with these people."

There was general agreement on the need for a legal advisory group and for a clearinghouse to disseminate information. In addition, the participants considered it important to concentrate on future issues by looking for early signs. Here it was recognized that local groups could most effectively do battle with the public utilities in their areas. Such groups would also be better equipped to discover evidence of price fixing on milk or meat, among other things.

> There is very little effective intercommunication and exchange of information among people in the consumer movement. We went through a rate case recently, for example. Let me tell you that if any of the groups get into utility rate cases we've got one of the best men in the country to handle a utility rate case.

> One of the things that we should find a great help would be to have some sort of legal advisory council or something to help us.

An interactional workshop differs from a meeting governed by parliamentary procedure in that the participants make suggestions regarding proposed actions but the group leader does not call for votes. Action results when most of the members support a proposal and the objections stated by the others are considered unimportant or invalid. This workshop suggested several potential actions that did not take place. It was suggested that a single newsletter be issued rather than each organization having one of its own. Such an effort would combine talents and result in savings in both money and time. These savings could then be allocated to areas of greater need. It was agreed that the single newsletter would not necessarily mean a merger of organizations or even a step in that direction. But somehow the matter was never settled.

> I think we need a coordinated umbrella.
>
> What do you want, a coalition of national organizations?
>
> An organization has to come from the bottom up, and that's supposedly what our organization is about. I think we've missed the boat 90 percent of the time. There's a real problem in communication and I'm not sure I understand what it is. In some ways we're trying to find what local people need, but I think we're still coming on with a top-down approach.

Another suggestion was made by the leader of a national organization in the form of a question as to whether the organization should continue or fold. Here the comments reflected vague support for continuation, but the reasons were never discussed and in reality the question was not clearly answered. In this situation the decision to continue was made by omission rather than commission.

Most important, the suggestion that related to forming a coalition of groups—possibly called the United Consumer Front —also had no dissent but no affirmation either.

> It seems we are working at cross purposes because we don't work more closely together. I think we have to start dividing up some of the efforts. I think much of the efforts that all of us are into are overlapping. Maybe what we have to do is allocate. We get organizationally bound. Maybe what we have to start talking about is, let's take our personal agendas and say, "Yes, we all have the truth in a particular way, and we've all done something of value." However, I think you have to examine some of the ego and self-protectiveness in all of this and see if we can overcome some of that here. Never mind going out there and talking about all of the other organizations that have their own agendas; can we sit around and talk about sharing that effort and that acclaim?

An interesting suggestion related to the building of a firmer and more broadly based consumer movement was that study be made of other types of organizations. Among those considered were trade associations, the American Association of University Women, the League of Women Voters, and the Council of Jewish Women. Such a study could lead to a better understanding of organizational structure and membership recruiting and maintenance. However, some participants were skeptical because they felt that the analogy might be inappropriate for the particular problems faced by consumer organizations.

> Are there some parallels that we ought to look at more in some of the women's organizations, those voluntary organizations where you pay a certain minimum amount and then the state

organization can elect to have certain services from the national office for a fee? Is there any university who has done a study of how these organizations are financed so that we could really see what the structures are and in what the experience has been? The example that is more meaningful for us is the example of some of the voluntary organizations such as the League of Women Voters, the National Council of Jewish Women, the AAUW General Federation, even. It just seems to me a good study could be made very simply of looking at their constitutions, what services they get, what they pay for it, and how.

Insight into the problems of the consumer movement as well as the variety of organization it encompasses can be obtained by becoming aware that there are many concurrent issues. Some organizations select a specific issue and pursue it. This awareness led to an important suggestion: that consumer organizations become aware that there are specialists who have faced and fought the problems that someone else may be working on for the first time. Here it was recognized that a clearinghouse could be most helpful.

I think one of the key things said in terms of resource is there's a guy in one area who has worked for 14 years on rate cases. Now there must be people around who've done things for 30 years and stayed with them. One thing I'd like to see as part of any national service organization would be a talent search section.

One of the reasons they [new groups] die is the ego of [members of] the existing group who feel that somebody is trampling on their territory and taking some of their shining glory, and another is that the groups flare up and die frequently because of an anomie that sets in with a sense of helplessness; a lot of them just scream.

Again, almost by default, the participants agreed that there was room for more than one national organization, each working in a different area and yet cooperating.

It seems to me that what we've got to do is identify the functions that need to be performed and then relate those to groups that can perform them, which may be two groups or it may be twenty groups, and then coordinate the efforts. I'd be interested in the performance. Let's find people who can do jobs and then work with them on doing those jobs.

In addition, there was an expressed need for the vitality of groups involved on the local scene with problems that may or may not be different from national problems. Quite important is the need for a system of communication between national and local organizations, and this must be developed with an equal two-way flow.

> I think we have to sit back and look at our resources and look at relationships to one another. I believe the people are there and I believe the capacity is there. I don't think the challenge has ever been there to work in a cohesive framework before. The challenge to work in a cohesive framework has been philosophical; it has not been a practical application because of the problems of powerlessness and authority that have compounded every one of the discussions we've had in the past.

An undercurrent running through the entire meeting was, as one of the observers stated, the middle-class syndrome of not honestly expressing one's feelings. In addition, there was awareness of the need for change, but most of the people present were unwilling to consider any change that would modify their activities or their organization. At the same time, they were not overtly critical of any of the organizations represented at the workshop. However, they were critical of those that were not represented.

A potentially valuable result of this meeting would be recognition by the participants that unless they encourage change they themselves will create the "déjà vu" they complain about. Existing groups recognize that local groups start on their own, without the benefit of help from experienced consumer leaders. These new groups vigorously fight a particular issue and then disband. Most of the time the leaders of the existing movement neither offer help nor recognize the potential for increasing their membership by working with these new but transient groups. Instead, the ongoing organizations surround themselves with caution and concern, almost secrecy.

With reference to national vs. local organizations, there was a discussion as to whether the tree had to be planted or was already grown. "Planting the tree" refers to the grass-roots movement. The "grown tree" refers to the belief that the movement already exists.

It is obvious from the fact that the discussion centered on organizations rather than membership that this is where the leaders' interests lie. There was little discussion of the consumer who belongs to these organizations. Further, the leaders do not seem to recognize either the need for or the importance of research. They seem to be organizationally minded, issue oriented, or activists to the extent that they see that there is a need for action and that they must act.

There was polite and neutral tolerance of what others were saying. Comments and criticisms of what others around the table were doing were lacking or deficient in content. Guardedness and minimal personal disclosure characterized most of the meeting.

Toward the end of the workshop at least two people were aware that unless the discussion pattern changed, the results would be similar to those of other meetings in the past: "nothing new." At this point there was some opening up on the part of a few, but at the same time some members felt threatened. While no positive actions were taken, it at least became clear to some of the participants that they would have to change in order for the consumer movement to change. The implication was that some form of coalition or at least a mechanism for coordinating the efforts of various groups should be established. However, rather than taking action, the group decided to wait until the draft of the report was available.

> I personally don't think there's enough confidence at this point in everything that I've heard. Everyone said a lot of nice things but nobody really cares who's running the show as long as we set something up and nobody gets a leg up on anybody else— but my whole experience in ten years of this thing has been that everybody has always first looked at how it came out for them, and I'm not including the people that are out there doing the work. I'm talking about whenever you move it into a concentrated effort and try to take what A's doing or B's doing or C's doing and saying, "Aha, isn't that great, now let's form a national or regional organization." That's exactly where the problem lies because somehow there's a transformation when that happens of taking away the power and putting it into the new organization.
>
> I'd like to say that I'd like to see it happen. I'd like to see it brought together.

The afternoon session started with a question from a participant on whether the group felt that a certain national organization should continue. Members of another national organization volunteered that they cooperate and work in different areas so that there would be a minimum of friction between the two organizations. The constructive aspect of this discussion was that instead of talking about eliminating organizations the particpants discussed how to get organizations to work together and how to obtain larger membership lists.

> I think if we could go through the various groups that are here and get an idea of what resources there are—that's part of it. If XYZ* can provide arbitration training, that's something that groups should know about. If ZYX* can provide expertise

* Letters changed so as to not reveal identity.

in a specific issue area and they're offering that kind of training, people should know about it—we should all know about it, what resources there are in each one of the groups, so we get an idea of how these three or four national groups are interreacting right now rather than perhaps committing ourselves to one new national network. That at least is a beginning for then deciding, Do we need a specific organization to provide the services we have been mentioning here today, or can they be parceled out among existing organizations.

Even though many of the people had known each other for many years, they were not fully informed on the activities and involvements of the various organizations represented. This further reinforced the view that the consumer movement faces many problems and that no one organization can be everything to everybody. The greatest consensus was that there is a need for the continued existence of the various organizations, but with the addition of a network that would provide for better coordination and information sharing. It was not considered necessary to combine these functions. Under present circumstances it probably would be best to have the coordinating function separate from the information-providing function.

I'm concerned about dissipation of effort. I'm concerned about the groups competing with each other, vying with each other over things they all agree about. That doesn't make any sense to me. That's why I wonder when the question was asked, "Should XYZ* collapse?" Well, should QRS collapse or should MNO collapse, should ZQR collapse or should they all collapse? Is there something here that we're all talking about that we're afraid to say? Should we try to find a way to get together? Divide responsibilities, but in [such] a way that we're together rather than in a way that will create dissipation. Everybody agreed that servicing should be separate from the policy and advocacy—there's no doubt about it, but does that mean we need five groups or three groups or can that happen in one group but split so that there is clear delineation as to who's doing what, when, where, and why?

I think there is a needless friction between us. Maybe we all ought to get together.

More than any other, the discussion on funding stayed on target. Although it was not openly discussed, the limited funding of various organizations creates serious problems. It places major

* Letters changed to conceal identity.

obstacles in the way of the future of the consumer movement. Some participants were reconciled to a continuation of voluntary rather than paid work, which is in fact a substitute for funding. At a time when charities, hospitals, and colleges are hiring professional fund raisers, it would seem that the consumer leaders are rather complacent; they create the impression that their efforts might be somehow tainted by the availability of funds, whatever the source.

A suggestion worthy of consideration is that new and different funding methods, such as a check-off system, should receive top priority. Considerable encouragement should be given to those who will pursue such possibilities. Much study is required as a prelude. The questions of who will actually contribute the money —the consumer, the manufacturer, or the retailer—and who will receive the funds are going to take some serious thought.

More mundane suggestions dealt with membership dues and direct mailings for contributions. These are the most commonly used methods, and their limitations should be obvious.

Another suggestion was to use the Nader technique, whereby liberal-minded businessmen make direct contributions. Grants and awards from foundations and government funding via revenue sharing were also mentioned.

Two rather novel ideas were presented. One was that in the future the consumer movement will raise funds by sitting at the bargaining table and bargaining for rights the way labor does. Another novel suggestion was based on an inquiry by an automobile manufacturer about whether consumer groups could participate in compulsory arbitration with reference to warranties and guarantees, for which they would receive funding.

Considering another aspect of funding, there were some who viewed the problem as both immediate and long term. Immediate funding might best be promoted on a project-by-project basis, but the continuity and perpetuation of the consumer movement requires long-term financing.

> I think that we have to look at ways of tapping industry money in some way that is not directed from any single industry. It's got to be some kind of check-off system 'cause that's where the money's at. If that's the group we're fighting we'd better be able to gather the kinds of sources and funds that they have. I don't know how we do that, but somewhere I feel we've got to be able to get our finger in that pot.

> Why not 50¢ on the purchase of every car? That's $3,500,000 a year.

Foundation grants for research, and not to be ignored in foundation grants are revenue-sharing funds.

What I'm looking for is a mechanism to allow those enlightened people* to make their contributions while insulating the consumer people from being controlled by those people.

The biggest problem we have is that we think small. Maybe if the people sitting around this table and the rest of the people in the consumer movement could begin to understand what a large ballpark we're playing in, an awful lot of the contentiousness that goes on between consumer groups and the little pickiness we have about problems would suddenly disappear— because they would become very inconsequential compared to what the real problem is in getting this thing going.

One of the discussion areas was "next steps to be taken." At this point quite a few participants expressed their true feelings. In some instances they rather candidly stated what the next steps should be. The majority either said or implied that there was a need to get going—even though they disagreed on the numbers involved and the when, where, and how of getting on with it. By this time fewer participants were expressing feelings of futility and powerlessness and more were aware that the consumer movement could become a major force in the economy.

At this point very few were willing to remain in a status quo situation. Most wanted to set up an umbrella that would provide the opportunity to work together. They also wanted to avoid duplication by establishing a division of labor. There was even some recognition of the need for research.

In many ways these action recommendations exceeded the workshop's goals. One should not be overly optimistic or unrealistic, however. If the group disbands and is content to search for inadequacies and untruths in the report, then little can be expected. If some participants assume the initiative, design the umbrella, and agree on the need for change as well as the specific kind of change, then something will have been accomplished.

I have felt all day this politeness and hesitation and saying the right things, but also I have felt in nearly every seat in this room a feeling of fear. A fear of opening up and a fear of allowing these ideas to happen. We are all sitting here holding on to our little package and so frightened that if somebody sees what's inside it they're going to grab it away from us. I really do feel that we need an umbrella type of organization.

* Names deleted for purposes of anonymity.

I think there's a heck of a lot more agreement around this table about next steps than I hear being said about.

We need a coordinating council.

I don't think we can solely be a service organization. I don't think we can only be a national voice organization, nor do I think that we can ignore the need for research and development and experimentation. I am for a merger, whether formal or informal, today—or at least an agreement to study that. I would say that we have to immediately talk about how to start the lines of communication.

Two observers were present at the interactional workshop. They were informed in advance that they would be asked to be frank and candid in offering their views. This they did. Their reactions represent their own independent thinking. Nevertheless, they are considered as important as the report itself.

After the observers made their comments each participant was asked to be candid and reflect, via a summary statement, his/her true feelings regarding the day's happenings. The comments made by the participants were in many instances models of ambivalence. Individual satisfaction or dissatisfaction seemed to be related to expectations of what the meeting should accomplish rather than an evaluation of what actually was accomplished. Among the comments were the following:

In favor of joint action but disappointed that there was not more openness.

Have come farther than we realize at this time. Lurking behind is a united consumer effort.

Felt the candidness and tempo picked up the last hour and a half of the meeting.

Potential to put it together.

Gone a long way in one day.

There was more agreement on the negatives than the positives.

The need to work together is more basic than a report suggesting this.

We are not used to being in contact with each other.

Possible to resolve issues and proceed at an accelerated pace and accomplish things.

The comments of one observer were as follows:

My general impression of the group and the discussion is that this is a remarkably middle-class group. It suffers from most of the ills of middle classness, that is, politeness and a covering up of feelings. It is also a group of people that like each other a good deal, so that there is a certain willingness to stick the neck out a little bit but there are real trust problems that are unresolved. I'll give my final conclusion first: I do not sense that any consensus has been reached about cooperative action. The reason for saying that is that you don't reach a consensus until you've laid your feelings out on the table, and since feelings have not been laid out on the table you've got a lot of hard work to do before you're ready to do anything cooperative, except in the most tentative sort of way.

Conflicts emerge early in the discussion, with a conflict between an emphasis on the federal vs. local level, between money vs. people. Both of these are versions of a kind of provincialism.

I detected a considerable feeling of powerlessness which I have trouble rationalizing with the real world. I'm not sure what criteria you use for power, but I think perhaps you need some self-reexamination on that.

X and Y were early established as the enemy. Their elements were left out of the group, so clearly that kind of controversy was not desired as part of the interchange that took place here. Certainly the two might have been a reasonable element to have been represented in some form and would have represented some kind of technical expertise—but, for whatever reasons, they were not here.

Some real issues emerged. I think one of the basic issues that emerged is that of dealing not with a movement but with a kaleidoscope. You're dealing with an ever-changing shift of actors that appear on the scene, disappear from the scene, a total spectrum from great organizational stability to great instability. How these can be merged and orchestrated in any kind of meaningful way is really an extremely difficult problem, and I think that's one of the basic issues that ultimately has to be dealt with.

A number of practical suggestions were raised, and I think they're things that merit further investigation, such as looking at industry models and industry association models.

The closest thing we saw to a consensus was the need for a clearinghouse whereby information and expertise can be shared, but there's no consensus on what or how. But I think, if there's anything that comes out of this it is the seed of cooperative action . . . .

The kind of thing that has to be resolved before you can move ahead on that is either, as someone suggests, you lay out the turf so there is no turf problem and everybody has a piece of it or, alternately, there is some willingness to subjugate one's own glory and authority to that of someone else, and that's an issue that has to be resolved yet.

Another one of the real issues that arises, mentioned this morning but not really followed up on, is the fact that the movement is complaint driven. Complaints are ephemeral; they often represent levels of aggravation rather than identify true issues or true problems—but your priorities are driven by these. This means, then, that you're going to blow this way and that way with the wind.

This has led to an increasing concern with legislation, which is a more stable base on which to generate priorities for action. Action becomes most feasible and most productive when there's a focusing in on very specific issues, particularly at the local level. We saw here a division into two groups with a kind of third group in between them. One is a sort of pragmatic, very local, very issue-oriented kind of organization. The second might be called theoreticians—but that's not really correct—they are the global, national thinkers. There's some tension between these two points of view. The third group kind of goes in one way or the other way on a particular issue.

There were some useful suggestions about funding, but one of the things that kind of came through to me on the funding issue was what I call "the morality of righteousness." That is, you appear to feel that you deserve to be funded because you have the power of the right, or whatever, where, in reality, we deal with a society that's based on an adversary system. If you want to get a piece of the pie, you've got to give something. So there's a kind of unreality in some of the thinking about funding. There was also a paucity of discussion about how policy works, how you deal with policy, and of course the real power payoff is when you begin to pull the policy levers.

The policy dimension is extremely germane to what you're going to do as a movement and, particularly, how you're going to do it.

The defensiveness of the group was particularly characterized when a real question was asked, "Should Y go out of business?" No one wanted to answer it. Two or three people rose to defend its continued existence, but no one wanted to address the real question raised. Everybody wanted to stay away from it; nobody wants to deal with a messy issue like that. I think you have to deal with those messy issues before you're going to make real progress.

I guess I gave my punch line at the beginning, that is, that there's much work to be done yet. A coalition or joint action is possible, and some of that work is letting each other know more about what you really feel about things, and that means you've got to fight a little bit, because without fighting you're not going to get together. I don't mean to say that I think this has been a negative effort. I think it's been an illuminating one and I think all of you have some suggestions to think about that you haven't thought about before.

The comments of the other observer were as follows:

My most basic observation is the utter amazement I felt all during the day at the fact that the discussants did not tackle the perhaps key issue of how to stimulate greater public involvement.

The issue of consumer identity, or how to make people out there think of themselves as consumers as they think of themselves as women, blacks, and auto workers, and then how to meld this consumer consciousness into a vigorous force—these are the issues which were never touched upon during the meeting.

The meeting was characterized by a curiously restrained atmosphere, in which there was less dialogue among the participants than I could have hoped for, given the urgency of the economic situation we are trying to address.

Participants were, to all intents, involved in trying to protect their own images—their egos as individuals as well as their group's ego. An emphasis on how well "I'm doing" and "my group" belied the basic fact that everyone was there because they know darned well the consumer movement *isn't* doing all that beautifully.

In talking about working together, either the general notion thereof or the specifics about which group would take care of which needed function, there was a lot of turf protecting, obstructing practical remedies.

A consensus seemed to emerge that local groups were more effective than national groups (although I wonder if the national group leaders present were simply being more honest than the local leaders—I can't tell). It was thus agreed that the structure of consumer organizations should reflect that the movement's strength is local.

Consensus also seemed to be reached that the most pressing need immediately was for a network that would provide (1) information exchange, (2) action coordination, and (3) a talent bank.

Not discussed, however, in that network were two other very important needs outlined by two national leaders: (1) the need for a structure with enough visibility to make its presence known to budding groups who might want some help and (2) a mechanism into which groups with a single interest, such as toy safety, can fit and still become part of the overall consumer movement.

Everyone agreed that they as individuals and as groups were dissipating their energies. Yet throughout the day's discussion ran comments such as "I'm bored with this, all I want to do is go back home and fight utilities" and "Essentially I'm an anarchist. All I need is time." (Both remarks, interestingly, came from local group leaders.)

Concrete suggestions I would hope someone can follow through on were to analyze the good points in other structured groups, such as trade associations, women's groups, unions, to learn from them what might be incorporated in a consumer movement structure.

And now my gut reaction: I was not overwhelmed by the day's content nor outcome.

21
Labor

Labor's role in consumer issues is generally overlooked. By contrast, the interaction among consumers and business and, to a degree, government is quite apparent.

Labor often acts as if it were neither a participant in nor a contributor to consumer affairs. It may well be, however, that labor is much more involved in many consumer problems than is generally acknowledged. Labor's role in consumer affairs is mostly indirect, that is, through affiliation with certain consumer-oriented organizations. Like business, labor plays the game of "lobby," which means it pressures government for its own special causes.

Comparing the four institutions, labor's goals are much clearer than those of the other three groups. The roles its leaders play are rarely disputed. Labor protects and enhances the welfare of its members. It apparently clearly recognizes Maslow's theory that the individual, "becoming restless and discontented again [seeks] for more." Labor is quite effective in the areas it chooses to involve itself in. It has fought very hard for its rights and still does. In fact the balance of power between labor and business is so equal that much strife may be avoided because each recognizes the damage they can cause each other.

Quite clearly, consumer groups are in no such situation. They do not have money, power, a large membership, a strong organizational structure, or specific issues that are forcefully presented.

Labor has the power to protect its members, but like business, it has generally limited its social consciousness. This means that both give only lip service to consumer affairs.

Labor organizations could increase the power of the consumer if they became more active in consumer affairs. For example, environmentalists and consumer activists have much in common in terms of social awareness, but the two groups seem to go separate ways. A similar parallel exists between labor and consumers. The point is that both environmentalists and consumer groups could be helped if labor recognized that it has a responsibility to society in general. The point is that environmentalists are active in those consumer issues that protect the environment. Consumer activists are involved with those issues that command attention from mass media. Labor takes a stand when consumer issues do not interfere with the primary advancement of labor issues. The possibility of combining all these forces into a more involved consumer movement is remote since those who take primary and general interests in representing the consumer seem to have interests that are too general for the three types of specialists, namely environmentalists, activists, and labor.

Organized labor has directed only minimal efforts toward enhancing the consumer movement or aiding or educating union members as consumers. Such activities seem to be quite peripheral to labor's major interests and concerns. Its obvious main role is to organize workers and bargain for higher wages, better working conditions, and a variety of fringe benefits. A secondary role is concern for the general welfare of union members. It is from the latter perspective that consumer affairs are sometimes considered.

The role of unions in consumer affairs is clearly illustrated by the activities of two major—and quite different—union organizations: the AFL-CIO and the UAW. The American Federation of Labor and Congress of Industrial Organizations has no formal department or committee that coordinates activities related to consumer affairs. Instead, matters involving legislation, publications, education, and research are handled by the Legislative Committee, the Department of Social Security, the Department of Urban Affairs, the Community Services Department, and the Research Department. In other words, it would appear that the AFL-CIO, like the federal government, has not as yet brought under a single jurisdiction the increasingly important area of consumer affairs.

When consumer affairs are handled in a decentralized fashion this often implies that the issues are considered unimportant and are being kept on the back burner. When a series of issues with a common core is divided into small parts, then no one has the authority to combine them or even to recognize that the issues could or should be considered as a unit. But the whole is often greater than the sum of its parts. Decentralization often results in the parts being much less significant than they would be if taken as a whole. Assigning different issues to various departments can lead to much confusion. Effective handling of consumer affairs requires a department or division equal to other departments in status and responsibility.

When one reads the report of the Executive Council of the AFL-CIO (1), one gets a kaleidoscopic view of the issues confronting the world as well as the United States. The report is a position paper on almost any issue from Watergate to vocational education. Its 500 or so pages read like a compendium of facts supported by reasons for the position taken. One gets the impression that the AFL-CIO regards everything in the world as within its scope. For example, in the mid-1970s there was a controversy as to whether wheat shipped to Russia would raise bread prices in this country. The AFL-CIO took a strong stand against loading Russian ships with wheat—until it was agreed that the workers who did the loading would be paid more money.

Consumer affairs is apparently one of the less important issues confronting the AFL-CIO. At least it would appear so from an analysis of the space devoted to consumer issues in the Executive Council report, as well as from the fact that consumer affairs are not handled in a coordinated or unified manner. If one considers such issues as civil rights, urban affairs, housing, and community services as being within the realm of consumer affairs, then the coverage is greater.

The AFL-CIO strongly supported the National Consumer Products Safety Act. It has also favored legislation related to national no-fault insurance, as well as the establishment of a consumer protection agency. Other labor-supported legislative proposals, many of long standing, include enactment of a comprehensive fish inspection program and improved inspection procedures for food in general; consumer credit and credit insurance reform; legislation on guarantees and warranties; consumer class action suits; requirements for more informative labeling on consumer products; inclusion of cosmetics and medical devices under federal safety testing requirements; and continued improvement in safety programs for automobiles and drugs. Labor also favors enlarged powers for the FTC.

The AFL-CIO lobbies with great effectiveness and is surely

a match for the strong lobby groups that represent business. It successfully lobbies in behalf of laws that favor the consumer, as long as they do not conflict with its own priorities. It also informs and educates its members on consumer issues through its various publications.

Many of the AFL-CIO's international unions support legislation favored by the Consumer Federation of America. These unions include the Amalgamated Meat Cutters and Butcher Workmen, the Retail Clerks International Association, and the International Union of Operating Engineers.

Most unions have their own publications for the purpose of educating the members. Some include a syndicated column by Sidney Margolius, a consumer writer.

The large unions within the AFL-CIO do very little, at least as far as this author was able to establish from correspondence with more than a dozen of the larger unions. Only five responses were received, and none was written by the president of the union. One letter referred to a consumer page in the union's monthly newspaper. A second indicated that the union is a member of the Consumer Federation of America and also mentioned that it has a staff member permanently assigned to directing its consumer activities. The third letter referred to active sponsorship of poultry inspection and membership in the Consumer Federation of America.

The fourth letter listed membership in the Consumer Federation of America, encouraging rank-and-file members to organize committees to deal with consumer complaints, and occasionally publishing articles pertaining to consumers in the union's monthly publication. The union also communicates with retirees to help prevent them from making mistakes in poor land investments. The fifth letter referred to activity in the National Consumer League and the Consumer Federation of America. It said, "We have supported practically all of the consumer legislation in the U.S. Congress."

To summarize, it would appear that the AFL-CIO does not actively concern itself with consumer affairs and that as a result members are on their own and have little direction from their leaders. In other words, union members would benefit if unions supplied more consumer information.

The International Union, United Automobile, Aerospace and Agricultural Implement Workers of America (UAW) takes a somewhat different organizational approach from that of the AFL-CIO. The UAW has a Consumer Affairs Department headed by a vice president. Olga Madar pulls few, if any, punches. In her report at the union's 24th Constitutional Convention in 1974 (2) she covered quite a few items. No-fault automobile insurance is strongly favored, and eight states are criticized for "enacting laws that give the illusion of no fault but are totally inadequate." Also strongly favored are the consumer protection act and truth in housing.

In addition, the UAW takes a clear stand on discrimination against women in the granting of credit. It is also concerned about the plight of more than 3 million families who live in mobile homes. It believes the rapid increase in mobile homeownership illustrates the desperate plight of people seeking housing across the nation. The UAW is committed to defending the rights of mobile homeowners by securing legislation establishing standards covering the safety and construction of mobile homes.

The UAW also forcefully favors abolition of the "holder in due course" doctrine. It claims that such action will eliminate 90 percent of the abuses that the present doctrine permits. The doctrine allows retailers to sell certain installment contracts to banks and allows the latter to demand payment even if the product was never delivered or was delivered in a defective condition.

Probably the most important contribution of the UAW is in the promotion of its Consumer Affairs Committee (CAP) councils.

The following is an excerpt from Vice President Madar's report on CAP.

> We have been greatly heartened with the increased number of local unions and CAP Councils that have set up Consumer Affairs Committees since the last Convention. One of the most successful is the Cuyahoga and Medina CAP Council Consumer Protection Committee which, according to a recent story in *Solidarity*, since its inception, has saved UAW members and their families more than $100,000. The Consumer Protection Committee handles a wide variety of complaints including auto warranties, car repairs, shoddy merchandise, failure to fulfill a contract, defective appliances such as refrigerators with cracked door seals or faulty workmanship or materials in a home improvement job. At the Caterpillar Tractor Local 215 in Davenport, Iowa, the Consumer Protection Committee has won more than 80 percent of its consumer complaint cases and that's the batting average of almost every local union Consumer Affairs Committee. Merchants, car dealers and businessmen respond when UAW represents an aggrieved member.
>
> Consumer conferences have been held in California, Missouri, Ohio, Indiana and Michigan and consumerism has been on the agenda of summer schools, winter institutes and the Walter and May Reuther Family Education Center Scholarship Programs.

Assistance provided by a local union or a CAP Council to a frustrated member to correct an unresolved consumer problem carries enormous potential for building the Union and bringing the member and his family closer to the Union.

Through pre-purchase counseling, local union committees are providing information to their members that assists them greatly in making major purchases or substantial investments including the purchase of a home. Having comparative price, quality and performance information can save the purchaser many dollars and can result in the purchase of a product, appliance or service which will meet the actual needs of the purchaser. Locals, too, are beginning to provide information on how to avoid the pitfalls of supermarket traps. As food prices mount, UAW members can literally save 10 to 20 percent of their food budget by wise buying, learning to resist impulse shopping and tricky promotions of high profit items.

We are deeply grateful for the splendid cooperation of the CAP Department and CAP Councils, *Solidarity* and the Public Relations staff, the Education and Legal Departments and Retirees Department whose deep involvement and commitment to advancing the consumer interests of the members and the Union have made possible the significant gains in extending consumer protection to our members during the past two years.

The International Union will continue to give increased attention to developing and strengthening local union and CAP Council consumer activities. Special attention should also be given to the special consumer needs of retirees, while at the same time the retirees will continue to provide invaluable assistance toward the UAW's legislative lobbying efforts. (pages 57–58)

An important value of the CAP is its grass-roots base, which involves people in a determined effort to solve their own problems. It may well be that the UAW, to a greater extent than any other group, including consumer groups, is right on target by getting people to "do their own thing" rather than seek protection from others.

The consumer movement will grow to the extent that local groups take care of their own affairs. The CAP program deserves much credit because it is developing activities at the local union level. It is evident that labor and consumers may have more in common than has been demonstrated to date.

Obviously, raising consumer consciousness among labor union members is a way to achieve better representation for consumers in many varieties of activities related to consumer affairs. The more information that people have, the more likely they are to make rational decisions. The more people know and understand who is for and who is against almost any consumer issue, be it no-fault insurance, automobile safety, flammable fabrics, or unsafe toys, the more likely it is that the consumer will reach decisions appropriate to his/her own welfare.

A full evaluation of the actual and potential contribution unions can make toward the solution of consumer affairs is difficult. Much is left unanswered. A major problem for labor is to educate its members and thereby make them more aware not only of consumer affairs but also of the ways they contribute to consumer issues.

A concern of considerable consequence with reference to issues related to defective products and the resulting need for service is the degree to which business or labor is at fault. Unbiased research leading to an answer to this problem seems to be shirked equally by labor and management. Each is willing to blame the other. Less blame and more facts are needed.

The critical question is when and whether product defects are caused by business or labor. Business contributes to this by cutting corners to make extra profits or failing to concern itself with the durability and safety of its products, thereby creating trouble for unsuspecting consumers. On the other hand, when are product defects caused by the worker who knows what to do and just doesn't do it?

When it comes to cleanliness in the cities, are dirty cities caused by inadequate budgets to keep the cities clean, sanitation workers who achieve less than expected, or people who litter?

Many consumers are concerned, even dismayed, over the length of time it takes to receive a letter via the postal service. Is it the government budget, inadequate administration and supervision, or the workers who are unproductive and don't care? Or is it the citizen who mails letters without a zip code? Whatever the combination of reasons, the delay and confusion reaches almost beyond the endurance of the average letter writer.

And so it is with automobiles. Are the defects found in automobiles caused by the company or by the employee? For example, if the door hinges break when a certain General Motors car is involved in accidents, then it is probably the hinge itself that is defective because of design, materials, or "cutting corners." Labor could have little to do with such a defect. The recall of potentially defective parts that could lead to unsafe driving conditions is also the fault of management, since it is responsible for engineering designs and plans.

However, there is also evidence that, owing to absenteeism or carelessness on the part of employees, bolts sometimes are not tightened or even put on at all. These defects may more clearly be assigned to labor. In any event, the consumer pays. Whether labor, management, or government is at fault, the consumer is inconvenienced, dissatisfied—even maimed.

In the service industry, which includes restaurants, airlines, and retail stores, service is quite poor. Sometimes it is totally absent or even insulting. The waiter who serves food cold or the chef who keeps frying eggs in the same old fat may be the cause of poor food and service; management may not be at fault. At the supermarket the impolite checkout clerk who overcharges the customer probably does not benefit from the extra charge in dollars and cents; however, he/she may be helping the manager recover from "excessive" pilferage in return for some extra time off. The loser, of course, is the consumer.

The point is that some consumer dissatisfaction is created by labor itself, despite the fact that when he/she leaves the job the worker becomes a consumer expressing dissatisfaction from the other side of the fence.

Labor and management could, jointly and separately, take steps to reduce some of the causes of consumer dissatisfaction by establishing who causes what and admitting that each must change if conditions are to improve.

BIBLIOGRAPHY

1. *Report of the Executive Council of the AFL-CIO,* Tenth Convention, Bal Harbour, Fl., 1973.
2. OLGA M. MADAR, Report delivered at the 24th Constitutional Convention, International Union, United Automobile, Aerospace and Agricultural Implement Workers of America, Los Angeles, 1974.

22

Business and consumer affairs

The word *business* suggests both a concrete and material thing and an abstraction. Business, whether it exists in the form of companies, groups, or individual entrepreneurs, comprises the seller-maker part of the buyer-seller-maker transaction. Through its actions and policies, it is involved in the antecedents as well as the consequences of every transaction, although it sometimes does not admit or recognize that it is. As a result, product servicing often has a greater impact on society than the use that was originally intended for the product. This means the product can affect the health and safety of nonusers as well as users. For example, pollution of air and water is becoming an increasingly serious problem for everyone, and some of this pollution comes from the manufacture and use of products such as automobiles and auto parts, which are not used by everyone.

X   Business has the choice of conducting its affairs legally and ethically or illegally and amorally. These choices are not openly considered when defenders of the "free enterprise" system overlook the responsibilities of business toward society.

x   To repeat a point made earlier, when business people suggest that they, too, are consumers, this is a partial truth. Whenever sellers or makers become buyers or users of products or services, they are consumers. But not everyone is a consumer all the time. This is especially applicable to people in their business roles. At such times the relationship between business and the consumer can vary from smooth to rough. Most of the time their goals are incongruent.

x   Business is its own spokesman. However, it should not be taken seriously when it presupposes that it knows what is best for customers, the country, and itself. This implies a kind of omnipotence that does not reflect reality. When business predicts that proposed changes will be bad for consumers, it may simply be resisting change and using the defense mechanism known as projection. On the other hand, it also may be telling an untruth. Business can be ethical, but it can also misrepresent, overextend, and deceive. It surely is not the sole purveyor of freedom in our society, nor the only standard-bearer of truth and ethics. Government, labor, and consumers are likely to have different views of the meaning of freedom.

x   When a consumer issue arises, such as whether gas stations should post their prices on signs large enough for passing motorists to see or whether utilities should use sources of energy that pollute the air or whether canned goods should be subject to date and nutrient labeling, one often finds that business presents arguments "for the good of the consumer"—that is, prices will rise if a particular law is passed. The question is whether this claim is propaganda or truth. The consumer had better decide on the appropriateness of solutions to consumer issues not only on the basis of arguments for or against the issue but also on the basis of who is stating the arguments and why. With incongruent goals, the other side must be expected to represent itself, regardless of who it claims to represent. Business should not be expected to represent the consumer.

The future of this country depends to a large degree on the attitude and behavior of the leaders of business. Business must recognize that consumer issues are here to stay and have to be solved. It has every right to earn a profit in return for its entrepreneurship. Labor, government, and consumers know this. However, the issue of profits is a result of goal incongruence and relates to how much profit, how it is made, and at whose expense.

x   Beyond the profit structure is the power structure. It would be well for business to recognize and admit the tremendous influence it wields. To a large degree it controls the destinies of all members of society. Business must recognize that its power influences the health and welfare of its employees and extends into the community in which it is located.

These influences extend beyond local communities. They cover the country. For example, the food and automotive industries directly affect the lives of all of us wherever we live. The disagreement as to whether bumpers can or should protect a car traveling either 2½ or 5 miles an hour from damage is pernicious. Arguing cost differences between the two bumpers is preposterous when one considers the other side of the cost picture— the cost of repairing the car or the injured human body.

A free society is a competitive one, but psychologists know a great deal about the dire consequences of unfair and ruthless competition. It leads to broken minds and broken bodies. It interferes with the development of the young and inflicts feelings of inadequacy on the grown. Finally, it leads to despair and feelings of uselessness in the aged.

Unfair competition leads to exploitation and fraud. In its ruthlessness it takes advantage not only of consumers but also of potential competitors. Fortunately, there seems to be an unwritten law preventing excessive power from stabilizing itself. This has been demonstrated many times and is probably one of the country's greatest assets. The excessive one-sided usurpation of power, be it by government or by business, results in an imbalance in which the powerful are eventually toppled.

The consumer movement is clearly an attempt to bring the existing imbalance of power into a more appropriate state of balance. Considering this, business' greatest need is to broaden its communicative scope and perspectives and, as a result, behave in a more mature fashion. It can achieve this change if it stops representing only itself—communicating primarily with its trade organizations, running conventions, and reading its own special interest magazines. This is carried to such an extreme that when it sees or hears national press or TV coverage it regards the message as unfair, biased, unrepresentative, and so on. It is difficult to imagine that a reasonable "free press" would be as antibusiness as some spokesmen claim.

Too often business regards its own market research, advertising, and product design as evidence that it knows what the consumer wants. This is self-serving and very often only part of the story. Market research and advertising tend to be narrow and provincial. They often miss the consumer needs of safety, health, and information.

Informed consumers agree that their rights related to "good" products and service should include safety, information, and choice. The consumer wants to be heard in the councils where decisions are made about product and service characteristics. The consumer also wants the right to redress when things go wrong.

Clearly, business must set up a system to enable it to *listen*.

Such listening posts should not be self-serving. Rather, what they hear should truly reflect what is going on. Business must set up direct channels of communication with consumers and consumer groups, and on an equal footing. The designation of a consumer representative within the corporate structure may not achieve the necessary results. In other words, the consumer, and business can and should relate in a better fashion. This can be achieved either by the opportunity to make meaningful inputs or by obtaining more information about outputs. Much dissatisfaction would be dispelled if only these two points were accomplished.

The point of this chapter is not really to determine what is good or bad about business. Its purpose is to report on the response of business to consumer issues.

To be sure, some issues and conflicts are caused by inadequate training and supervision of employees. As a result such employees overlook their role in a successful or unsuccessful transaction between the buyer and the seller of a product or service. What sanitation workers, nurses, checkout clerks, professors, tool makers, and bank vice presidents have in common is that they represent a business or institution directly or indirectly at the interface between the organization and the public.

The future success of many businesses will depend on their response to consumer pressure for better treatment and understanding. A most encouraging sign is that quite a few businesses are establishing new departments to handle consumer affairs. A study by Blum, Stewart, and Wheatley (1) attempts to trace the efforts and aspirations of those who were among the first to blaze the trail. The findings indicate that the new departments were organized to better coordinate the functions related to company-consumer interaction, as well as to establish new frames of reference and attitudes toward consumers. The personnel involved are highly motivated and enthusiastic. They are also realistic about the difficulties that confront them in attempting to solve consumer problems, especially from within the company. To improve their performance they suggest the need for sincere and active administrative support, as well as freedom to identify and empathize with the consumer point of view.

Consumer problems ranked as critical or highly important are reported in Table 22.1.

↯ If corporate departments of consumer affairs are to be successful, they should not merely attempt to treat symptoms. Rather, they should serve as agents for change. In addition, the new department should not report directly to any existing function such as marketing or public relations. It should have greater

TABLE 22.1   Consumer affairs problems ranked as critical or highly important, by industry type

Industry	Problem
Manufacturers of durable and semi-durable goods (automobiles, television sets, appliances, tires, etc.)	Product repair, production, and delivery
Food processors (cereals, dairy, products, bakery mixes, soft drinks, etc.)	Information flow to and from consumers, product formulation, and executive attitudes
Retailers (food, soft goods, petroleum)	Attitudes of executives and sales personnel, product performance, and information flow to consumers
Services (airlines, banks, insurance, federal government services)	Employee attitudes, service delays, and consumer expectations
Associations (apparel, pharmaceutical, financial, insurance, appliance)	Consumer knowledge and expectations, product design, and executive attitudes

SOURCE: M. L. Blum, J. B. Stewart, and E. W. Wheatley, "Consumer Affairs: Viability of the Corporate Response," *Journal of Marketing,* 38, 13–19, 1974.

scope in the gathering and interpretation of data and information, both good and bad, about all aspects of the business that are consumer related. A second and equally important function is to conduct meaningful research, which seems to be something they intend to do whenever they finish "putting out fires."

Since one of the reasons for undertaking this study was to identify fruitful areas of future research, the following are areas which the authors believe deserve systematic investigation.

First, why have the existing marketing departments of many large corporations (especially those purporting strong consumer orientation) failed to create a close and satisfying fit between consumer needs and corporate needs?

A second area for investigation might be the question, what is really meant by the managers of the consumer affairs departments when they say that one of their most critical problems is to change the attitudes of executives and other employees of the firm?

Third, must product repairs remain such a frequent subject of consumer dissatisfaction? How can the problems be reduced?

Last, the researcher might ask when, if ever, the often stated conclusion of consumer affairs executives, "we must educate the public," is a realistic objective. In how many subject areas? Which part of the public? At what cost? For what time period? To appraise the expected value of the approach, one should clearly know why such education does not now exist. (page 18)

They concluded that

The newly established departments of consumer affairs have been faced with day-to-day problems as well as those of fitting into a previously existing organization structure. In the short run, this situation has placed an emphasis on operations.

This response has typically consisted of performing a coordinating function among existing corporate departments and improving communication flows among corporate management, employees, dealers and consumers. In this way, the department heads believe they are favorably changing attitudes and generally increasing the level of consumer satisfaction with the company's product or service. The authors agree that this approach seems to be resulting in some forms of progress.

In the longer run, much more emphasis should be placed on research and innovation. New measures of consumer satisfaction must be developed. New methods of diagnosing the cause and nature of consumer dissatisfaction are needed. New clarifications are required to describe and sometimes change the amount of goal congruence between the corporation, its employees, and the consumer. (page 19)

In essence, and as Webster (2) points out,

Many companies have seemingly fallen into the trap of viewing consumerism in "us" versus "them" terms. They view consumerism as an attack on the company and the free enterprise system, rather than as a call for improved marketing performance and heightened business responsiveness to consumer needs. (page 96)

A psychologist might call this "we vs. them" attitude either paranoia or a paranoidal tendency. There is no doubt that more often than not business, government, labor, and consumers have incongruent goals. This should be recognized, but accusing the opposition of unamericanism is not the solution.

According to Aaker and Day (3), a new or expanded consumer affairs department should generally incorporate four related actions. One is to receive complaints and have the authority to resolve them, even if it is necessary to override other corporate departments. Another is to operate an information system to monitor consumer satisfaction as well as dissatisfaction with the company's products or services. Third, the department should represent consumer interests in policy-making sessions. And the fourth item is to contribute to corporate social objectives.

The question is whether corporations that establish consumer affairs departments really want an independent, consumer-oriented department instead of a mere facade. If the former, then they must create an environment in which such a department can achieve some degree of success. This new development must be strong enough for views to be exchanged on an equal footing with advertising, marketing, sales, production, service, and other departments or functions of business. Further, this exchange must be open and sincere; the new department must not be considered a maverick or a "customer lover."

Careful observation of many companies leads to the judgment that the emerging departments present a blurred image. Some are quite effective, some are not sure of their roles, and some either are deceiving themselves or have accepted a stylish name for something that formerly existed under a different name. In such instances the change of name is another exercise in futility.

In 1973 the Society of Consumer Affairs Professionals in Business (SOCAP) was formed. It includes people whose primary corporate assignment is consumer affairs. By 1975 the group had about 550 members. Even after attending some of the SOCAP meetings, the question of whether there is any value in establishing consumer affairs departments remains unanswered. On the basis of what is said at those meetings, especially when a speaker strays from the theme "what we want to hear is what we know and agree with," one would be forced to judge that there are few consumer advocates or sincere defenders in the corporate ranks. There are many whose point of view ranges from middle of the road to ultraconservative. The theme, expressed or unexpressed, seems to be that we have so many fires to extinguish that we can't get around to research or, for that matter, changing the views of management. It is rare to find a SOCAP member who really empathizes with the consumer. They seem to be merely carrying out existing policy. Some even marvel at their very existence.

What is odd is that new groups usually start off differently. Generally a major reason for the formation of new groups is to change or modify existing conditions. This group seems to be more concerned with organizing a professional society than with truly representing the consumer within the business structure. It remains to be seen whether creative solutions to consumer problems will result from the establishment of corporate consumer affairs departments.

A very different approach was offered by the now defunct

National Business Council for Consumer Affairs. This group, organized within the Department of Commerce, consisted of top executives of major corporations who had been appointed by then President Nixon. The problems and proposed solutions with which this group concerned itself are illustrated by the series of pamphlets prepared by its various subcouncils. It is difficult to know whether this council was business catering to government, government catering to business, or government exploiting a number of board chairman, executive officers, presidents, and vice presidents of corporations that would have no trouble making anyone's list of "who's who."

Four of the reports in the series are listed in Table 22.2. It should be noted that these reports vary considerably in length. It is difficult to establish whether the size variation is a function of perceived topic importance, writing style, or the seriousness of the issue. To get a better picture, each member of the four subcouncils was contacted by mail and asked the following questions:

1. What role did you personally play in contributing to the report?
2. Who actually wrote the report?
3. How would you rate the report?

The responses make for on interesting story. Based on 60 letters of inquiry, responses by either mail or phone reached a return rate of about 80 percent. Of those responding, almost three-quarters indicated that their activities included attending meetings, participating in the drafting of segments of the report, and other forms of involvement.

The letters of response were usually one or two pages in length. As might be expected, they reflected varying degrees of

TABLE 22.2

Title	No. of Pages	Date
1. "Violence and the Media"	2	August 1972
2. "Complaints and Remedies"	16	October 1972
3. "Financing the American Consumer: A business report on Consumer Credit"	20	November 1972
4. "Safety in the Market Place"	82	April 1973

SOURCE: Listing of four titles in National Business Council for Consumer Affairs.

satisfaction or dissatisfaction with the end product. The respondents were sincere, and a few were quite candid. Some referred to the recommendations as "old hat" and no longer appropriate. Others referred to the publications as excellent guidelines.

An analysis of the letters led to the conclusion that many participants felt such guidelines to be productive, but some seemed unhappy that there was no follow-up beyond the publications themselves. A few indicated that they had suggested specific recommendations and done some editing, but it is quite clear that the actual reports were written primarily by staff members within the Department of Commerce. A quote from one letter is revealing: "It did not take me long to sense the political implications . . . one of which demanded total loyalty and obedience. . . ."

What next? The ideal would be for business and consumer leaders to get together to draft guidelines, rules, and recommendations. This might be productive and informative for both sides. Progress might really be made if business and consumer groups worked together as peers rather than antagonists. This might actually lead to a smaller role for government.

It has been suggested that the liaison between government and business tends to be too close. The Department of Commerce pamphlets amount to virtual unity—except that the title page of each report states that "this report contains the results of studies by an Advisory Committee. It does not necessarily represent the policies or plans of the Department of Commerce or any other Federal Government Agency."

Violence and the Media (4) is all of two pages long. The following excerpt is illustrative:

> First, to encourage the development on an individual basis of specific policies and procedures by media, program producers, and all involved in the creation and delivery of media presentations, which will help eliminate gratuitous use of violence and provide standards for acceptable depiction of violence, when it has material relevance to the message to be conveyed.
>
> Second, to encourage advertisers and advertising agencies to establish individual policies designed to reduce further the use of violence as an attention-getting device in any and all contexts, whether it be an attempt to win attention for an advertisement or to win audience for a program.
>
> Third, to encourage intensive and careful research by academicians and appropriate agencies to determine more specifically the impact of depicted violence on the media's consumers, in the realization that further work is needed to identify clearly the nature and extent of the problem.

The report further states that

It is not our intent to imply that it is in the best interest of society for television programming to depict our community as being free of violence. Presentations by media are often necessarily a reflection of life as it was lived that day, and as such must mirror truthfully the good and the bad.

This amounts to nothing more than whitewash. Violence on sponsored programs does not portray life as it is lived today or any other day.

James P. Forkan (5), writing in *Advertising Age* (April 7, 1975), reports that more than 200 murders were committed on the three TV networks during prime time from January 1 through April 7, 1975. Forkan admits to unscientific sampling methods, since the survey was performed by him and his family; he also acknowledges that his study was, of necessity, incomplete. The question is whether 200 or more TV murders is a lot or a little and is to be condemned or praised.

Complaints and Remedies (6) makes the following recommendations:

RECOMMENDATION 1

The handling of consumer complaints should be swift, personalized, courteous, and as effectively managed as any other function of prime importance to the company, including increased personnel training in the handling of consumer communications, complaint follow-up, and appropriate involvement by senior management.

RECOMMENDATION 2

The money-back policy should be fully explored by companies not now offering it, and should be adopted wherever feasible as a means to resolve directly disputes with consumers.

RECOMMENDATION 3

Where refunds are not a practicable source of action, the feasibility of third-party complaint settlement procedures such as mediation and arbitration should be considered by sellers as an alternative form of redress. (page iv)

Financing the American Consumer (7) reflects more problems than the others—or else those who wrote it were more verbose. The report lists 8 recommendations and 13 codes of billing and collection practices. Recommendation 9, for example, states that "governmental agencies at all levels should avoid actions which unnecessarily erode consumer credit information systems." Code 11 states that "telephone calls should be placed between the hours of 8 a.m. and 8 p.m. unless other times are more convenient for the customer."

Safety in the Market Place (8) is by far the best of the four reports in the series. It recognizes that product safety involves manufacturers, retailers, voluntary standards organizations, product testing laboratories, and trade associations, as well as government and other organizations in a position to contribute to improved product safety. Recommendations are made regarding manufacturers (3), product safety standards (9), retailers (1), and public safety awareness (1).

The pamphlet includes the text of the consumer product safety act (Public Law 92-573, passed in 1972), which clearly states that it is "an act to protect consumers against unreasonable risk of injury from hazardous products." Essentially, it sponsors the setting of voluntary standards for product safety and would especially like to see an elevation in the authority and importance of the American National Standards Institute. It favors additional resources for this organization. Action on these recommendations would go a long way toward solving a perplexing problem. Most hearings on product safety, as well as other matters of interest to consumers, generally do not represent consumers adequately.

The report makes the following proposals:

> ANSI could pay for representatives who directly represent consumers on standards committees. ANSI's committees and other operations are open to public scrutiny at any time. However, there are few consumer advocates with the resources and the technical background required to participate in ANSI's work. As a result, consumer representatives are largely suspicious of the voluntary standards system. They, and other competent participants with non-commercial biases, should be on the inside, participating, rather than outside, criticizing. To accomplish this, ANSI could cover the expenses for qualified "consumerist engineers from universities, government agencies, consumer groups and other institutions in a position to broaden representation on standards committees. (page 43)

Business is replete with trade associations, which are primarily lobby groups for the promotion of special interests. They often publish trade journals, release news items to the mass media, and entertain. They are against most consumer issues on the general principle that the proposed solution (unless it is theirs) will increase the prices consumers must pay. Sometimes companies compete—meat trays made of plastic vs. those made of fiber, or soda in bottles vs. soda in cans—but these "fights" never get that rough.

In a very different category is the Better Business Bureau. There are about 140 bureaus located in the major cities of the

United States. Each has its own president, board of directors, and staff. Its membership consists of businesses in the area that support the organization. The separate bureaus are more or less autonomous, and they vary in effectiveness.

Two of the bureaus are intimately known to the author and deserve high ratings. They are the Greater Metropolitan New York and South Florida bureaus. The author has sat on the membership committee of the latter group and can confirm that not all businesses that apply are accepted. Moreover, businesses are dropped from membership if they do not conform to the standards of business ethics set by the bureau. The South Florida bureau handled almost 200,000 inquiries in 1974. About two-thirds were requests for information on particular companies and one-third were complaints. All of the complaints were investigated, and most of the investigations revealed discrepancies between expected and actual product performance. About 50 percent of the complaints were resolved to the apparent satisfaction of the consumer, which is a lot more consumer satisfaction than would exist without the bureau.

Better Business Bureaus are generally a good example of companies getting together to keep business honest. They believe this will result in better business. But too often business favors self-regulation, with the purpose being the prevention of actual regulation. Not so with a BBB. Its main contact is with consumers. For example, the South Florida BBB has about 3000 members, most of whom pay their dues, display the logo indicating membership, and conduct their businesses ethically. When they do not, or when there are misunderstandings, the complaint process, including compulsory arbitration, takes place. This is an example of working directly with consumers at the grass-roots level.

The various bureaus belong to a national body, the Council of Better Business Bureaus. Depending on business conditions and related fund raising, its budget may vary from $2 million to possibly $5–6 million a year. The scope, program, and duties of the Council are not as clear as they are in individual bureaus.

The Council has set up a National Advertising Division (NAD) to review advertising claims. In the CBBB *Overview* (9) the NAD reports that three national advertisers, Airborne Freight, American Telephone and Telegraph, and Menley and James Laboratories, voluntarily agreed to modify their advertising claims. In the case of Airborne, the misleading statement was against a competitor, Emory. AT&T had made an unclear pricing statement on one-minute long-distance calls, and in the case of

Contac, a Menley and James product, the NAD felt that the TV commercial could lead viewers to think certain ingredients in competitors' products were harmful or unnecessary. However, the NAD also investigated the following advertisers and found that they could substantiate their claims: Philco (Cold Guard refrigerators), Proctor & Gamble (Era laundry detergent), and Sterling Drugs (Body All deodorant). Thus, based on careful review, it appears that the NAD is attempting to do a sincere job in regulating advertising practices.

A large number of companies are now publishing information on "consumerism." The following quote does not come from an activist or even a professor—its source is *Context,* which is published by Du Pont(11).

> Of the vital issues facing business today few, if any rank higher than consumerism. Recent surveys indicate that consumerism is the nation's No. 1 business issue and that its problems are for business—not the public—to solve. Consumerism is potentially the most damaging problem business faces, and it is going to be around for a long time.
>
> One needn't look far for evidence to support these conclusions: today's news media are replete with stories about increasing consumer demands for safer and healthier products and for more truth about prices and values. In response to public pressure, more and more consumer protection bills are being dropped into legislative hoppers at all government levels: local, state and Federal.
>
> During the past 10 years, business became the target for consumer complaints and, in some cases, rightfully so. One result of this has been that the reputation of business—in spite of significant contributions during the decade—sank to an all-time low. While emotional rhetoric characterized much of consumerism's rise in the 1960s, business was tardy, at times, in responding to new consumer demands.

Context is moderately unbiased and indulges in a minimum of puffery about the virtues of Du Pont.

A company that has done a most outstanding job in preparing educational materials with taste and accuracy while keeping the company name in small print is J. C. Penney. For example, in the series "Insight into Consumerism" the issue of women and retail credit is presented in a most frank, candid, and impressive manner. The presentation includes different points of view as well as a rather comprehensive discussion of the problem women face in this area.

Forum is an educational publication of J. C. Penney. It is published semiannually and deserves favorable comment. Each issue is devoted to topics such as updating consumerism (12), creative decision making (13), quality of life, and youth's involvement. It presents all sides or aspects of the topic, and contributors are generally recognized as experts in their respective fields. The publication deserves attention, especially in comparison with some others, which pass on second-rate material to schools and colleges and only thinly veil their advertising or public relations aspects.

An area within the business sector that will be contributing increasingly to consumer dissatisfaction is the utilities. The local telephone, gas, and electric companies are government regulated, but so are the airlines. The difference between the two is that the utilities have no competition. Their profits are somehow related to their expenses.

The tie-in between utilities and government through special commissions on the state level leaves much to be desired. In the state of Florida, the Public Utility Commission issued a ruling that bars citizens from appearing before it without a lawyer. Now one does not need much psychological training to realize that "set" creates "perception"; obviously, the Florida Utility Commission cannot take the time to listen to citizens unless they have the funds to hire a lawyer.

As far as prices are concerned, we seem to have a demonstration that defies the law of gravity. In other words, what goes up stays up. For the average breadwinner it is hard to know which goes up faster, electric bills, repriced canned goods, or gasoline. At least that is the way it was in 1975.

An additional topic deserving of consideration as far as business and the consumer are concerned should be entitled "Shades of Gray." Business sometimes takes a stance that is legal despite the fact that such a position may not be basically either honest or truly representative of reality. One would hope that business would recognize that from a purely philosophical point of view legality, ethics, and honesty ought to be inseparable. Obviously, this is naive. Two instances of business acting legally will be reported. The question of ethics should be decided by the reader; the question of deception might also be pondered.

The first example refers to an organization called the Consumer Affairs Foundation, which is headed by the same person who runs the Boston Better Business Bureau. In correspondence with the then president of the Council of Better Business Bureaus, he wrote: "The Consumer Affairs Foundation is legally recognized as a nonprofit foundation." In other words, a Better

Business Bureau can apparently function in a dual capacity and as if it were honestly and truly a consumer affairs foundation.

In the South Florida BBB, organizations with two different names, either of which is misleading, are not only frowned upon but invariably denied membership. The Council should not promote a dual standard. Either the Boston Business Bureau and its "Consumer Foundation" should have separate offices and staffs, or the duality should be made clear. The point is that the Boston Better Business Bureau is not a consumer affairs foundation in the sense that it primarily represents consumers. One would hope that on moral grounds such misnomers would cease. The reason is that legally an organization has the right to exist and legally a person or a group of people can incorporate on a profit or nonprofit basis and call itself anything that is legal, even if it may not be ethical.

Another example of what is legal but can be misleading and confusing to consumers comes from Dade County, Florida. A commissioner proposed an ordinance that would ban pop tops and place a minimum 5¢ deposit on all beverage containers. A referendum of citizens rejected this proposal. The Center for Environmental and Urban Problems of Florida International University issued a report stating that "a key deceptive act by the organizational group of the Beverage Industry was to name their organization "Dade Consumer Information Committee'" (14). "In their endeavor to defeat the ordinance the Industry collected over $180,000. Of this amount $150,440 was collected in the name of Dade Consumer Information Committee." "Only 23 percent of the money donated to this committee came from Dade County sources. Out-of-state money accounted for nearly 74 percent of the total raised." These commercial messages, paid for by the Dade Consumer Information Committee (i.e., the beverage industry) and occasionally by Winn Dixie (a supermarket chain), generally carried the same type of deceptive message. Although initially taking a "scatter approach," the industry's campaign eventually settled on one major issue—cost. Its early advertising tried to "touch all the bases." It suggested that voters oppose the proposal for the following reasons:

1. The ordinance denies "freedom of choice."
2. The government is forcing recycling on the citizen.
3. Recycling wastes energy.
4. It wastes water.
5. There's a better way of handling litter.
6. Existing laws should be enforced.

The point at issue is that a business engaged in the seller-maker part of the buyer-seller-maker transaction is not a consumer. For business to use the word *consumer* in organizations that are not consumer oriented suggests the role of a "wolf in sheep's clothing," which leads to "you can fool some of the people some of the time."

Business must respond to the consumer movement by becoming an honest partner in transactions related to consumer affairs. When it does, then conflict will decrease and positive solutions acceptable to both sides will be attainable.

Probably the best way to end this chapter is to look for signs of change. The annual report of Federated Department Stores (15) may be just that. It indicates an attempt to be aware of people as consumers rather than just as customers, and to recognize the problems of society as they relate to business.

Readers with long memories may recall that bleak autumn afternoon in 1972 when newspapers headlined one of the most dramatic business stories of recent times. After months of inching toward what had once seemed an unattainable goal, the Dow-Jones average finally, on November 10, topped the 1,000 mark for the first time in history—thereby inspiring a good many prophets to herald the dawn of a bright new economic era.

What makes that day particularly memorable is that, less than two years later, the Dow again made front page news, this time for a different reason. On October 3, 1974—for the first time in almost twelve years—the average closed below 600. Now the commentators who, two years before, were dancing in the street, spoke somberly of the nation's troubled economic future.

I cite these figures not because they are new or surprising but because I want investors to know that their message has been received. A 400 point plunge in the Dow-Jones average is, I believe, your way of telling all of us in corporate management that you are apprehensive of the future. I understand your concern. And that is why this annual report—for the first time in Federated's history—carries not only the usual review of operations but this personal message from the chairman, a statement that, I hope, may give you both a new sense of tomorrow and a new understanding of the attitudes and beliefs, the dreams and convictions which will shape this company's future.

The single most important fact in America today, in my opinion, is not that we are suffering our sixth recession since 1945 but that the nation continues to be rocked by a series of social and cultural changes unprecedented in our history. Look, for instance, at this sampling of events of the last decade:

- An unpopular war deeply scarred the national character even as the moon landings gave us new reasons to be proud.

- After 200 years of deprivation, the black man rose up in righteous wrath and won at least a measure of the rights that are his due.

- During this same period, women intensified their demands for freedom and equality. Better educated, they found ready acceptance in the job market. Now more than 44 million women —up by 21 million since 1960—are employed. They are 38 percent of today's labor force—a figure that suggests changes as yet unrecorded may also be taking place in husband-wife relationships and in child-rearing practices as well.

- Regardless of whether or not all of us approve, there have been significant changes in attitude towards marriage. Now, fewer than 69 percent of American women are married and both marriage and birth rates are continuing to decline while divorce rates rise. Increasingly, singles and mingles are replacing the young marrieds of yesteryear as nonfamily households grow more rapidly than family households.

- A nation that had squandered its natural resources and ravaged its habitat for generations suddenly awoke to the fact that Mother Nature is not immortal either. Conservationists and environmentalists claimed our attention and thousands of hitherto heedless citizens clamored for air you can breathe, water you can drink, foods and drugs free of man-added contamination.

- Shortages came to the land of plenty: Beef. Paper. Sugar. Lines at the gas pump and bigger bills for heat and light. Amazingly, a people known world-wide for their conspicuous consumption found the will, if only temporarily, to turn down thermostats and rediscover both their feet and the buses, trolleys, trains, and carpools they had very largely ignored since World War II.

- Across the land respect for and confidence in even the most venerable institutions disappeared. Sacred cows by the dozen were slaughtered as Americans rose to challenge the authority of the "Establishment," be it of church, school, government or business. An index of their new disdain is a Harris poll taken late in 1974, which found that less than a third of us had confidence in religious leaders (32 percent), the executive branch of the Federal government (18 percent), the press (25 percent), business (15 percent), Congress (16 percent) and labor (18 percent).

As even that abbreviated list suggests, change in America has been both violent and rapid. It seems destined to continue. Not long ago I spent a weekend talking to some men and women students at a large eastern university. You wouldn't believe how different they are from their predecessors of even four years ago.

Gone is the sign-carrying militance of the sixties. Gone is the desire to sneer at materialism and flee to the commune. Gone is the blatant contempt for business. Instead, we have today, not a throwback to the structural beliefs of the fifties, but new and gentler revolutionaries who still want to change the world and are perfectly willing to do business with the Establishment as long as they need not pay it homage and as long as it pays them well enough to finance a way of life that will bring them joy and satisfaction, rather than the fur coat and country club they think their mom and dad sold out for. Make no mistake! Change will continue and may accelerate. The difference in generations is in style, not objective.

I have written at length about these matters—seemingly far distant from the world of merchandising—because, in reality, they are the essence of our business. The revolution of the last decade was recorded not alone by the newspapers and TV but at the counters of our retail stores as well. In fact, it could be argued that America's most sensitive social barometer is not its books or its movies; not its music, its campuses or its voting booths but the cash register that stands mute at the point of sale. And what that marvelously sensitive instrument has told us is that our customers have vastly different wants and needs than they've ever had before.

How are customers different? Perhaps the best way to give you a sense of what's happening is with a personal vignette. I started my retail career in the family store in Columbus, Ohio, more than 40 years ago. Back in those days, when customer research was virtually unknown, it was popular to talk about "typical" or "average" customers. We were even vain enough to imagine that there was a "Lazarus customer" and we thought we could describe her—an upper-middle-class housewife with a couple of well-scrubbed kids who thought coming downtown to shop at our store was one of life's great adventures. It was her practice to make a day of it—getting all dressed up for the occasion, having lunch "with the girls" and buying, in many cases, her clothing for a season, including, of course, the basic black dress and the serviceable suit. Sure, styles changed in those days, too, but the range of merchandise wanted by the customer was reasonably predictable even if the customer herself turned out to be less "typical" than the myth we had created.

Now step into 1975. Is there a new typical customer? No, that myth, I'm happy to say, has finally been laid to rest. Instead, we know that the revolution of the last decade has created a proliferation of life styles as millions of Americans —better educated, more mobile, seeking a new sense of individuality—decided to do their own thing. Walk down the aisles of our stores and you'll see for yourself. Yes, that affluent

Lazarus customer is still with us but look who's right behind her! A blue-jeaned school teacher; a computer technologist pushing a baby carriage on her day off; a personnel director on her lunch hour; a soon-to-be pediatrician in her med-school whites; a harried young couple anxiously shepherding three children up the escalator.

What this new diversity has done to retailing is to make us reconsider almost everything we once believed. Where once we catered to that typical customer, we now hope to be most things to most people—covering most taste levels, most price ranges and most kinds and varieties of merchandise. Now a woman is not only mate, mother and housewife but may also be a wage earner who needs, and can afford, both more and more kinds of clothing than her mother ever owned—jeans for housework and shopping, sportswear for the great outdoors, pants for the office, a special dress for that occasional great occasion.

Product proliferation has come to men's wear, too. There was a day, for example, when a shirt department could be stocked with eight to ten styles and in six neck sizes and four sleeve lengths. That works out to 192 items. But then came the explosion in men's fashion. Suddenly shirt styling demanded both solids and stripes in a wild profusion of cuts and colors. Today, that same shirt department carries a minimum of 864 items and the number is still going up.

Or look inside a home. With both partners working, living styles, often of necessity, have turned casual, broadening the range of furnishings required but with emphasis on simplicity and ease of care: loafing furniture for the family room, for example. Linens and dishwasher-proof china designed for barbecue or poolside entertaining. And remember the singles? Whole new shops in our stores now cater to their needs—bean bag sofas and plastic furniture created, not for permanence, but as an inexpensive stopgap answer to a transient way of life.

Storekeeping, too, has changed dramatically under the impact of these new customers. Sunday openings and later week-night hours have been tailored to the needs of working households. Charge and cash procedures have been simplified and automated to speed the handling of purchases by busy women. Sales clerks have been retrained to cope both with more sophisticated merchandise and more knowledgeable customers. Most important of all, these new customers have taught us to give almost as much emphasis to merchandise presentation as to the merchandise itself. Why is that important? For two reasons: because new branch locations put stores closer to customers, today's woman shops more frequently than her mother did, giving us new opportunities for impulse sales. And, since goods of every kind and description are readily available to all retailers, the successful merchant is the one whose product presentation whets the most customer appetites.

This, I can assure you, is no more than a taste of the change that has assailed us these last few years. Fortunately, I can report that, as our figures show, we have come through this time of trial in good shape. I believe there are three reasons why:

1. The department store, in my judgment, may well be retailing's most efficient customer-serving organism. Its basic strengths, its durability and adaptability have been demonstrated anew during this period of rapid change.

2. The men who formed Federated on the eve of the Great Depression were wise enough to conceive a form of organization that capitalized fully on the department store's natural advantages. They created, not a chain of stores, but a federation of largely autonomous local businesses. Each store retained its familiar local name, it familiar local character, its right to make its own day-by-day decisions. The genius of that method has never been more apparent than during these last turbulent years. While our form of organization was designed for department store use it has proved equally successful in our supermarket and mass merchandising divisions. Ralphs, for example, has far fewer stores than its competitors yet it attracts more customers than any other chain in Los Angeles. One of the reasons for this is that each store reflects its own neighborhood.

3. Perhaps most important of all, we have been blessed during this time of trial with as fine a supply of executive talent as this company has ever known. Many of today's executives joined us years ago and learned their trade in Federated's management development programs. Some chose us because our salary and benefit package is competitive with the best. Some because they wanted to work for a large and successful department store group. Some came because our form of organization puts decision-making authority as close to the customer as possible—which means that a man or woman fresh out of college can quickly take charge of a department, run the business as if it were his own, grow from there. And some, we like to think, came to us because this company has long insisted that both the corporation and its people devote some of their energies, not to profit-making, but to the public interest. That is why, wherever we operate, you will find us working on the problems that the community faces. It is why, for some thirty years, Federated has diligently sought not only to provide equal opportunity but to change the attitudes that are the real barrier to full minority employment. And it is

why today—whether the issue is inflation, consumerism, energy or the environment—you will find, I believe, that we are part of the solution, not the problem.

Now, what of the future? Are we confident? Yes, we are. And, I think, for very good reasons. One of those reasons is Vista. What is Vista? Well, about a year ago, during a meeting of our store principals, it became apparent that, no matter how well we may have coped with change up to then, the people who run our stores were understandably wary of the future and the even greater change it promises. Population growth is slowing. The explosive suburban expansion of the sixties is largely behind us. Life styles continue to proliferate as America learns to enjoy its new diversity. But what else may be ahead, we agree is not altogether clear. By mutual agreement, each division went home to conduct a bottoms-up review and analysis of its business: where it is now; where it would like to go; how it might get there; what it knows and what it needs to know. In-store task forces were formed and bright, young people joined top management in drawing a new road map to the future. Those 19 divisional plans are now being analyzed by men and women from division and corporate levels both for action and for the kind of exploratory research into unsolved problems that some require. For obvious reasons I can't reveal the money-making and business-building ideas that this process has turned up but I can tell you these things:

. . . This comprehensive Vista program is the most searching self-examination Federated has ever undergone;

. . . Vista will enable us to know our customers and to meet their new needs far better than we have ever known or been able to meet them before;

. . . Vista is worth the effort even if it produces nothing more than it has already produced—the enthusiastic response of people given the opportunity to participate in the shaping of their own futures.

Combined with this new enthusiasm we will continue to rely on our traditional management disciplines that are so important to our operation.

There are other reasons why we feel good about tomorrow. Geographically, we are already solidly entrenched in many of the right places for maximum growth: the sunshine belts of the west, southwest and southeast; the strong midwestern and border state markets; the metropolitan northeast corridor stretching from Boston to Connecticut, New York, New Jersey and Washington. Beyond that, I can report that we are presently studying every major U.S. trading area in which we are not represented with a view to answering three questions: Can we enter the market? Should we? If so, how should we go about it?

Federated will continue to program profitable expansion where we see opportunities. Obviously, the state of the economy will affect the pace of our expansion. Nonetheless, we are scheduled to build an average of about 1,900,000 square feet a year for the next three years, with the lion's share of this in department stores. We intend to maintain our financial standards and avoid profitless growth.

So how does it all add up? Last November, in an appearance before the New York Society of Security Analysts, we tried to put a dollar sign on the future. These are the numbers we came up with:

Our sales, now some $3 billion, will, we expect, increase to more than $5 billion from our existing divisions alone by 1979.

We anticipate that earnings will grow at a commensurate rate with Ralphs and Gold Circle making important contributions, but department stores providing approximately 85 percent of our 1979 profit dollars.

Unhappily, that projection is the one statement in this report that must be accompanied by an if. We will reach those goals if the present recession is short-lived—and the economy turns around, say, by late 1975. In any case, a more prolonged economic downturn would mean only that it might take us longer to hit those targets than we presently expect. Despite all the problems that our nation now faces, our faith in the essential soundness of the American economy is unshaken. We believe our country will continue to grow and prosper. And we believe we will continue to do those things that will permit Federated to share in that bright tomorrow.

BIBLIOGRAPHY

1. BLUM, M. L., J. B. STEWART, and E. W. WHEATLEY, "Consumer Affairs: Viability of the Corporate Response," *Journal of Marketing*, 38 (1974): 13–19.
2. WEBSTER, F. E., "Does Business Misunderstand Consumerism?" *Harvard Business Review*, 51 (1972): 41–45.
3. AAKER, D. A., and G. J. DAY, "Corporate Responses to Consumerism Pressures," *Harvard Business Review*, 50 (1972): 114–124.
4. U.S., Department of Commerce, National Business Council for Consumer Affairs, *Violence and the Media* (Washington, D.C.: GPO, 1972).
5. FORKAN, J. P., "Net TV Body Count: 200+ Murders in 1st Quarter," *Advertising Age*, April 7, 1975.
6. U.S., Department of Commerce, National Business Council for Consumer Affairs, *Complaints and Remedies* (Washington, D.C.: GPO, 1972).

7. U.S., Department of Commerce, National Business Council for Consumer Affairs, *Financing the American Consumer* (Washington, D.C.: GPO, 1972).

8. U.S., Department of Commerce, National Business Council for Consumer Affairs, *Safety in the Market Place* (Washington, D.C.: GPO, 1973).

9. Council of Better Business Bureaus, *Overview* (Washington, D.C., March 1974).

10. Good Housekeeping Institute, *What's Behind Good Housekeeping* (New York).

11. E. I. Du Pont de Nemours, *Context* (Wilmington, Del., 1973).

12. "Updating Consumerism," *Forum* (J. C. Penney), Fall-Winter 1972.

13. "Creative Decision Making," *Forum*, Fall-Winter 1973.

14. BRANDT, R. J., *Summary Report Dade County Bottle Ordinance* (Florida International University, Center for Environmental and Urban Problems, Miami 1975).

15. LAZARUS, R., *Federated Looks to Tomorrow* (Cincinnati: Federated Department Stores, 1975).

23

Advertising morality and social issues

Advertising is the leading exposer of the interests, intents, and motives of business. It represents the efforts of either the maker or the seller to communicate directly with the (potential) buyer and influence the consumer's attitude and behavior. Stated most simply and directly, advertising contrives to create favorable attitudes toward products or services so that it can influence the consumer to buy and use the advertised product or service.

Advertising is subjected to criticism not only because of what it does but also because of its very nature. It attracts the attention of the consumer more than many other activities of business.

By its very nature, advertising has high visibility, obvious effectiveness, and a strong influence on the economy in general. A company's advertising can directly affect the relative profitability of competing companies. However, that is only the tip of the iceberg. The role of advertising deserves thoughtful consideration.

$\times$ The influence of advertising on the consumer is immeasurable. For example, it can create product and service expectations beyond reality. But realistic or not, advertising directly or indirectly affects the lives of all of us. Among other things, advertising has a major influence on our health and safety. Just looking at the variety of products advertised, from laxatives to toys to automobiles to nonnutritious foods, can make one aware of the power and potential of advertising.

The influence of advertising on children is horrendous. The

youngest are often able to sing or recite commercials even before they learn nursery rhymes and, what is more, long before they know there is a difference between the two. Since it is known that children are most amenable to suggestion, the suggestive powers of advertising are often overly effective; the message is uncritically accepted by children of all ages.

Advertising causes dissension rather early in the family evolution, as when the child wants a toy, snack, or cereal advertised on TV and the parent, for various reasons, does not want the child to have it. In this type of situation parents do not always win. Quite a few report that they usually lose.

A further set of problems related to advertising includes the ones advertising itself creates because of its imperfections, as illustrated when it indulges in deception, exaggeration, and misrepresentation.

To consider advertising in relation to social issues and single it out from other aspects of business is unfair. Management makes the policy decisions and either "creates" or "buys" the advertising campaign, whether it is truthful, exaggerated, annoying, or what have you. Business must face up to the problems created by excesses in advertising and recognize that it has social and moral obligations in this connection.

There is no question but that retail selling influence is decreasing while advertising influence in product choice is increasing. This is so for many reasons. The growth of self-service retail outlets means, among other things, less need for selling on the part of salespeople. Self-service outlets run the gamut from food to clothing to health and beauty aids. Even those that still employ sales personnel have apparently downgraded their training to the point where the salesperson is generally uninformed about the product being sold. The result is that the maker's advertising and merchandise displays become the main source of in-store communication to the customer about the product's characteristics.

In this chapter we will recognize that the psychological influence of advertising is considerable but that the extent of that influence is, for all practical purposes, unknown. To be sure, many marketing, advertising, and psychological journals contain articles on this subject. But they either study rather narrow problems or, much too often, prove the effectiveness of a particular interest group. Incidentally, a large portion of the research on this subject seems to support the point of view of the research sponsor.

The primary purpose of this chapter is to raise questions that need answers. Unfortunately, it will not be able to answer them.

However, these questions are the essence of the controversy. If totally objective and independent research were conducted on a sufficient scale, cosponsored by a number of groups with different points of view, and if there were still another group to observe, audit, and evaluate the research, then some answers might be forthcoming. To date most research in this area tends to support the funding source.

The following are a few of the researchable and socially significant questions related to advertising: (1) What influence, if any, do advertisers have on the freedom of the media? (2) What effect does advertising have on the personal aspirations and satisfactions of the "lonely hearts," the underprivileged, and the handicaped? (3) What are the effects of advertising on children? (4) What influence does advertising have on the formation of attitudes, especially in the area of consumer affairs? (5) Does advertising stir up unwanted needs, or does it merely reveal unfulfilled needs that already exist? (6) What influence does advertising have in the area of social justice, especially as it relates to minority problems?

Advertising is intimately interwoven with the mass media. And because the media continually impinge on the sense modalities—audio (radio), visual (magazines and newspapers), or both (TV)—they have a profound effect on all of us. We look to the media for information and entertainment—and the media are supported by advertising which we pay attention to and are aware of in varying degrees.

Radio program format is likely to vary from one station to another. The music stations vary from rock to classical. In addition, radio provides news, weather, and talk shows. It is a personal type of listening and may be found in the bedroom, kitchen, living room, or family room, as well as car or beach.

Newspapers and magazines, of course, are visual. They, too, vary in format and style. They are read at the reader's pace and the reader's choice of time and place. Print has the advantage of greater permanence. Magazines use color to a greater extent and more effectively than newspapers. The advantage of color over black and white is that it presents a more realistic world of products.

Television has effective components of both audio and visual stimulation, and in any city there are likely to be stations representing the major networks. The format is not too different from network to network, though the programs are different.

Characteristic of all mass media is the fact that their income is obtained almost entirely from advertising. Since there is no doubt that all of these mass media are involved in opinion formation, the big question from the standpoint of consumer psychology is the degree to which the media are free to impart information objectively.

Politicians who regard themselves as having unfavorable coverage usually allege that the media are biased. However, a *free* press is one that cannot be controlled by government either. The balance of information provided by the media is such that one must never underestimate the importance of the media as a means of communication to consumers. Would the story of Watergate ever have unfolded were it not for the efforts of the mass media?

A problem of any form of communication, as reflected in the mass media as well as in advertising, is that the written or spoken word often is not as clear as it was intended to be. Even when the communicator intends to convey with utter clarity a specific message, the communication can often be interpreted differently by different people. This is so because the viewer or listener may differ in intelligence, attitudes, and motives or goals.

For an example of a message, its intent, and its various interpretations, one might refer to the statement that "all men are created equal." This has caused controversy not only among men but among some women, who resent the use of the word *men* and believe that women are left out.

The important thing for a consumer to recognize is that there is a need to be subjected to, even bombarded by, different points of view. Media, when reasonably free and uncontrolled by government as well as the advertisers who pay the bill, offer just that opportunity. And so the basic purpose of mass media should be to provide individuals with the opportunity to learn about different points of view. The consumer must *listen* to different points of view. Whether other views change individual attitudes or not seems not to be as basic as recognition of the need to understand what the other points of view are all about. It is in this setting that the question of freedom for the media is to be considered. Most media separate their advertising and business departments from their editorial and reporting functions. They do this to allow the latter to make free and unfettered statements that are uninfluenced by the advertiser and the point of view he represents. Is this idyllic or is it real?

Another controversial aspect of advertising is its effect on "lonely" or underprivileged people. People in all walks of life, whether they like it or not, live in specific environments and with certain life styles. Via TV and the other media, they all become aware of new and improved automobiles, television sets, watches, toys, food, instant credit, and so forth presented in prestigious settings unrelated to the conditions of most people's lives. Most of us do not live in huge colonial homes with semicircular driveways. Many families cannot buy every toy or snack advertised on TV. But the commercial impinges on the child and creates a want or a request to "buy me." Visit any supermarket and listen to a child asking for a certain snack or cereal and to what the parent answers. The parent is aware of the need to purchase nutritious food and is frustrated or embarrassed by the child's demands.

Further, most individuals live the way they do because there is not really much opportunity to change. When advertising suggests a new car, a new hair color, or a new toothpaste that will lead to romantic conquests never before realized, what is it *really* doing, and to whom? What happens to the very young, the aged, the poor, the ordinary person? To restate the question, does advertising promote discontent and dissatisfaction, or does it encourage people to go on to bigger and better things?

Probably the question most in need of an answer is the effect of advertising on children. A series of concerns relate to whether the advertising should be addressed to parents or whether the parents should be bypassed and the advertising aimed directly at children.

Parents are generally negative toward playthings that are battery operated, easily broken, or unsafe, and especially toward items that, in their view, push the child to grow up too fast. The Barbie doll, for example, is enormously popular with children. Many parents, however, are unhappy with the Barbie doll. They say they know no one with those "unreal" physical characteristics. On their own, most would not purchase the doll, but they concede that they are often forced to "give in" and buy a wide variety of toys because of the child's repeated pressure. Do we really need toys that cause early parent-child dissension?

To make matters worse, toys can be frustrating and deceptive. As part of a television commercial the child sees a toy as a glamorous thing, but the toy itself, removed from its "theatrical" setting, often turns out to be "no big deal." Thus advertising directly to children and using questionable techniques may be winning the battle and losing the war. In the long run more and more children must grow up with the memory that "those ads ripped me off."

Among the avant garde are the mothers and fathers who are opposed to all TV advertising—especially to children. Some will not buy any product advertised directly to children and insist not only that they are able to withstand the child's pressure but also that the child should learn sooner rather than later the realities of the world and some of the unrealities of advertising. In addition, there are children who don't think everything advertised on TV is "cool."

The two industries in greatest need of a reevaluation of their advertising policies with regard to children are the toy and dry cereal groups. A good exercise for the reader would be to go to a supermarket and compare the unit price of "children-advertised" dry cereals with that of other cereals.

Among some worthwhile studies in this area are those conducted by S. Ward. Ward has gathered some interesting data on the child's purchase influence attempts and the percent of parents who usually yield (1). Table 23.1 presents his findings. They strongly suggest that children do influence purchases of products advertised on TV, especially cereals, snack foods, candy, games, and toys. As children approach their teens, record albums and toothpaste enter their sphere of influence.

TABLE 23.1   Average frequency of children's purchase influence attempts and parental yielding

	Frequency of Child's Purchase Influence Attempts			Percent of Parents "Usually" Yielding to Purchase Influence Attempts		
		Age			Age	
	5–7	8–10	11–12	5–7	8–10	11–12
	Scale: 1 = often to 4 = never					
FOOD PRODUCTS						
Cereal	1.3	1.6	2.0	88%	91%	83
Snack foods	1.7	2.0	1.7	52	62	77
Candy	1.6	2.1	2.2	40	28	57
Food overall	1.8	2.1	2.1	52	54	59
PRODUCTS FOR CHILD'S USE						
Games, toys	1.2	1.6	2.2	57%	59%	46%
Record album	3.4	2.6	2.2	12	16	46
Overall	2.7	2.6	2.7	26	28	35
OTHER						
Toothpaste	2.3	2.3	2.6	36%	44%	40%
Aspirin	3.6	3.8	3.9	5	6	0
Laundry soap	3.7	3.8	3.7	2	0	3

SOURCE: S. Ward, *Effects of Television Advertising on Children.* Marketing Science Institute, Cambridge, Mass. 1972.

A controversy cannot exist without at least two sides. The more heated the controversy, the more emotional the arguments become and the more the facts are strained. A good example is offered by Ward (2). Table 23.2 clearly illustrates the self-reinforcement that opposing forces indulge in. It is easy to see that there is little room for mutual understanding. Once again we have parties talking at each other but doing very little listening.

The intensity of the battle has been increasing since the early 1970s. It centers on the amount of time devoted to commercials as well as their content. The conflict involves a number of different groups with somewhat different interests.

At the core of the controversy is the question, How many minutes of commercials should there be on any hour of televi-

TABLE 23.2   How businesses and consumerist groups view each other's positions on children and advertising

THE ISSUES:	Corporations Are Perceived as Believing:	Consumerist Groups Are Perceived as Believing:
Advertising's influence on children	There is nothing wrong with attempting to influence children to buy, or attempt to influence their parents to buy, advertised products.	Advertising to children is morally wrong.
	Children are rarely influenced by advertising anyhow.	Advertising exerts great influence on children, who lack sophistication to objectively evaluate commercial messages.
Advertising techniques	If advertising is not judged as misleading by government regulatory agencies, it may be broadcast.	Standards for evaluating advertising techniques are scaled to adult judgment; children cannot fairly evaluate commercial messages.
Ethics of advertising to children	Children are consumers: they represent an important market. Selling to children is necessary to maximize profits.	Advertising to children is inherently distasteful and unethical.
	Advertising to children supports the mass media.	

SOURCE: S. Ward, *Children and Promotion: New Consumer Battleground,* Marketing Science Institute, Cambridge, Mass. 1972.

sion and, further, should the exposure be the same for children as it is for adults? The networks have agreed to reduce total commercial time on children's prime time (Saturday and Sunday from 7 a.m. to 2 p.m.) from 16 minutes to 12 minutes per hour. However, consumer groups want this reduced to 6 minutes. (Consumer groups define a children's program as one aimed at the 2–11-year-old group for which 50 percent of the audience is in that age group.)

Since younger children sometimes cannot tell the difference between programs and commercials, the consumer groups want commercial breaks to be preceded by an announcement that a commercial follows. Even many adult programs state that "we pause for this message."

From the consumer point of view a major and necessary revision in the code would be severe limits on the advertising of sugared products on children's programs. This proposal has met with vociferous objections from the cereal manufacturers.

An unusual article on the subject appeared in *Advertising Age* (3). It is worth reproducing in its entirety because it is a complete account of how things go wrong when, on the one hand, business wants self-regulation and, on the other hand, it cannot or will not accomplish this goal. One also sees the role that consumer advocates play as well as, again and again, the role of governmental agencies. The article is all the more interesting because it was written by Stanley Cohen, a reporter who for many years has worked for *Advertising Age*, the acknowledged leading trade journal in the field of advertising. Score one for honest reporting!

HOW INDUSTRY LOST THE BALL
ON CHILDREN'S TV ADS

Washington, June 14—The creation of a powerful new self-regulatory unit to police tv ads to children has received less than general public acclaim, and Federal Trade Commission chairman Lewis Engman has declared that "the ball is now in the commission's court." The story of how the industry lost the initiative makes grim telling.

Children's tv ads have been a tender spot for many years, but a showdown was forced ten months ago when chairman Engman called for voluntary action on a new advertising code. Miscalculations, industry infighting and a reluctance to make tough decisions in the face of incessant attacks by consumerists followed, all combining into a classic case of how to boot away an opportunity to settle a situation through self-regulation.

With the government now considering nutritional advertising

rules, and more children's ad restrictions on the horizon, the story of what went wrong hopefully can provide some insight into how industry can avoid such disasters in the future. To get that story, ADVERTISING AGE has talked with many of the key personalities involved in the negotiations. What follows is a synthesis of these interviews defining the issues, narrating the course of events, and summing up the lessons as the industry participants see them.

There can be no doubt that the children's advertising unit of the National Advertising Division of the Council of Better Business Bureaus is off to a bad start. In announcing the industry self-regulation plan, leaders of the major associations were confident they were creating something capable of dealing with deceptions and unfairness. But ten months of acrimonious negotiations had poisoned the atmosphere. Consumerists and FTC leaders withheld endorsement and openly expressed skepticism.

In an admittedly temperamental situation, industry leaders persistently misread chairman Engman's intentions; evaded his challenge to make changes; kept the industry's major self-regulation unit, the National Advertising Review Board, on standby until the situation was almost out of hand; and ultimately unveiled a program anchored to Assn. of National Advertisers guidelines which were regarded as offensive and inadequate by both consumerists and FTC alike.

Consumerists who had been participating in the negotiations with the industry sat through a Council of Better Business Bureau news conference and then held their own rump session afterward to say they were "appalled." FTC chairman Lewis Engman has termed the NAD/NARB unit as "potentially a large step forward for compliance with existing rules," but he has said it shows the industry is not effective in making new rules, and he has announced a plan for FTC to set the pace on premiums and a number of other children's advertising issues.

Some in the industry, like Assn. of National Advertisers general counsel Gilbert Weil, claim this was inevitable from the start, "because the negotiations involved a fundamental clash in philosophies that put rational solution beyond reach." But others on the industry side who were unwilling to be identified by name said it really represents primarily a failure on the part of industry negotiators who responded emotionally, acted on bad information, and worked without understanding the political pragmatism in Washington.

Even now, before tempers have cooled, there are some who insist the NAD/NARB move will eventually be recognized as a responsible action on the part of the industry, which goes far toward providing an effective safeguard against ads which are unfair to children. Chairman Engman said his final judgment will have to wait until the program is operational, though he is not generally optimistic about its chances of responding on the tough issues. American Advertising Federation president Howard Bell calls it a "major accomplishment achieved in a short time," and American Assn. of Advertising Agencies' Chet LaRoche said, "Everybody got a helluva lot out of it. People got together, conducted a dialogue, and were able to define the issues."

Engman Angers Leaders

The course was stormy from the start. Industry leaders were perplexed and angry when Mr. Engman went before the young lawyers' section of the American Bar Assn. Aug. 4 to demand changes in children's tv. Many saw it as a political tactic, an effort to show that Mr. Engman, who had been a White House staffer, was going to be a tough FTC chairman.

Leaders of ad industry trade associations came away from an Aug. 10 meeting at FTC openly skeptical. On the other side of the table was a consumerist delegation noted for its hostility to advertising; Robert Choate, the man who became famous for blasting breakfast cereals; Peg Charren, whose Action for Children's Television was blistering the advertisers at the Federal Communications Commission and FTC; Warren Braren of Consumers Union, the man who quit the National Assn. of Broadcasters code authority and published documents from the NAB rules which implied that the industry pulled its punches in regulating cigaret ads; and others.

Consumerists claim they were there to begin negotiations toward a new children's advertising code, incorporating a number of changes spelled out in a working draft circulated by FTC's staff. ANA president Peter Allport, sounding a note which was heard frequently in future weeks, said he was there for "exploration," but not "negotiation."

From this shaky start, things got rapidly worse. Four subcommittees were created to look into such subjects as existing enforcement mechanisms, existing codes, methods of implementation and evaluation of past research on children. Weeks later, most of the subcommittees still had not met.

Consumerists Prepare Own Draft

Signs of trouble were evident by November. Complaining that the code-writing subcommittee had only met once, consumerists disclosed they were preparing their own draft. In mid-November, AAF's Mr. Bell protested to FTC that consumerists were bypassing the code-writing subcommittee.

FTC's director of consumer protection, Thomas Rosch, was not entirely sympathetic to Mr. Bell. He promised he wouldn't let the consumerists bypass the subcommittee, so he added Mr.

Choate to the membership, and made it clear to Mr. Bell that the subcommittee would end up working from Mr. Choate's draft unless the industry people came up with another.

Meanwhile, signs of discontent began to arise in industry ranks. Several major children's advertisers had hoped from the start NARB would move into the vacuum, but they learned that in September the National Advertising Review Council, NARB's "parent" organization, controlled by the same associations which were in the FTC negotiations, had told NARB to "wait and see."

By mid-January several big advertisers—M&M/Mars, General Mills, McDonald's Corp. and Coca-Cola were among the first— wrote NARB chairman Ted Etherington, proposing a major NARB role. NARB, however, was already making its first move. Kent Mitchell of General Foods had been designated to try to develop a policy for the steering committee. Chairman Etherington was conditioning other steering committee members for the likelihood that NARB would play an activist role.

The problem was inflamed, in part, by the nature of the issues. Food advertisers were nervous about changes which might regulate advertising of heavily sugared products—one of them told Mr. Etherington, "If this gets into sugar, our company will drop out of NARB, and I imagine others will do the same." Premiums were another insuperable obstacle. ANA's Mr. Weil held from the start that premiums were a non-negotiable issue.

Industry People Fear the Worst

Industry members got another jolt in late January when consumerists distributed their proposed code. The first sentence to catch their eye was a preamble that said they believe all advertising in or near tv programs designed for children should be discontinued. From that vantage point, industry people read only the worst into specific consumerist proposals, including bans on premium selling, host selling, and the promotion of heavily sugared foods.

By late January, the industry was groping for a new position. Advertisers who sought changes in the trade association positions urged ANA and NARB to come up with a plan providing for industry enforcement of flexible guidelines, including the NAB code and ANA guidelines, with consumerists serving in advisory committee capacities. A series of meetings followed, including rump sessions at AAF headquarters and special meetings of ANA members.

While the official record doesn't show it, there were informal contacts between individual industry leaders and consumerists, and it is known, for example, that Mr. Choate reviewed the problem with Mr. Etherington. By mid-March NARB announced it was working on a "high-priority" program to provide intensified review of national advertising to children.

But a March 21 meeting at FTC found the two sides badly polarized. Industry leaders objected point by point to the specific items in the consumerist code, but offered no alternative of their own. Industry representatives continued to insist no code was needed, and that in any event they were not in a position to commit anyone.

On rulings by Mr. Rosch, the assignment was suddenly modified. One of the knottiest problems—the advertising of heavily sugared foods—was removed from the discussions on the grounds that the commission is considering it as part of a trade regulation rule for food advertisers. Several other consumerist ideas related to the number and arrangement of commercials also disappeared from the agenda, as Mr. Rosch ruled they were FCC rather than FTC matters.

Choate Maps Counter-Offensive

Meanwhile, Mr. Choate had begun to develop a massive political counter-offensive, which industry strategists apparently failed to anticipate. He circulated information to strategically situated members of Congress about the numbers of commercials on tv, the use of special research techniques to test ads for child appeal, and other morsels likely to catch attention. At least five congressional subcommittees began pressuring FTC and FCC for progress reports, and a rash of special articles on children's tv appeared in major newspapers.

Behind the scenes, FTC's Mr. Rosch, who had worked sympathetically with industry people, became increasingly insistent that the industry have something specific for the May 20 meeting. Mr. Choate fired off a four-page letter to chairman Engman, complaining that negotiations were a "charade." Mr. Engman, in an appearance before the Senate Commerce Committee, seized the opportunity to say, "I am announcing for the first time that I am disappointed with lack of progress from the industry side."

Industry representatives were already working over final drafts of a plan to create a special children's unit in NAD, to maintain a continuing review of children's ads, to judge them for "fairness" from the standpoint of the child, and to create an advisory committee of experts to help the staff with the difficult cases.

As Mr. LaRoche tells it, the industry people thought they had something that would fit the bill. The review mechanism provided assurance that complaints would get expert handling. With the elimination of sugared foods and time standards issues, there seemed to be only a handful of specific items of disagreement—premiums, host selling, audio warnings, advertising of vitamins and dangerous products—and some of these could be considered as cases arose. While consumer activists would not have places on the advisory committee, neither would industry members. "Experience has proved you need independent, objective, rational people making the decisions," Mr. LaRoche contended.

At a May 6 meeting, William Tankersley of CBBB spelled out the details as it stood then: All accepted principles would be applied, but there would be no formal code. Only experts could serve on the advisory committee. As one insider recalls, he said, "We don't want the kind of confrontations we are having between Bob (Choate) and Seymour (Seymour Banks of Leo Burnett)."

But at a May 17 private presentation for chairman Engman the industry got a shock. He felt use of existing standards precluded progress on premiums and other issues that worry him. He termed the plan "inadequate."

At the May 20 meeting, Mr. Choate and others learned for the first time that ANA guidelines, including their preamble lavishly praising advertising to children, had been written into the plan. Irked by secrecy and irate over insertion of the ANA guidelines, consumerists were outraged.

At the meeting FTC's Mr. Rosch peppered the industry people with questions: Why the specific mention of ANA guidelines, and no reference to the NAB code? Was the industry trying to sneak through with a lesser standard? Mr. Choate snickered at the industry contention that consumerists would be allowed to "nominate" experts for the advisory group. "Considering our experience during the past 10 months," he commented, "a nomination by me would be a kiss of death."

Mr. Choate was in the back of the room while CBBB explained the plan to Washington newsmen. In the corridor afterward, he distributed a news release declaring, "They have proven once again that any significant action in this area will have to come from government." In a letter to chairman Engman he said, "The industry must now be considered to have its head in the sand."

According to the scenario, the recommendations of the code-writing subcommittee were eventually to be reviewed and endorsed by a larger "parent" group. But Mr. Rosch saw no purpose for more meetings. At AAF's meeting last week, chairman Engman gave his verdict: FTC will do its own thing on premiums, host selling and other issues. Was it preordained?

Bell Laudatory: Others Find Fault

AAF's Howard Bell believes the industry was "quite responsive." He says he never thought so much could be accomplished in 10 months. "I regret the rejection of our plan by consumerists," he noted. But other observers say there were mistakes all around, and that some of the most serious flaws were made by the industry negotiators.

Chairman Engman got off to a bad start, according to one observer who worked closely with industry negotiators, because he failed to fully research the situation or consult his fellow commissioners. FTC's staff "stacked the deck" by hand-picking the negotiators from both sides. "Perhaps the most serious error," this expert contends, "was vesting the industry role in the major trade associations, rather than the individual advertisers whose affairs were directly involved."

Consumerist publicity tactics puzzled and worried the industry negotiators, and on at least one occasion Mr. Choate lodged serious charges of bad faith which could not be substantiated. The preamble of the consumerist code confirmed the industry's worst fears.

On the other hand, this observer says, the industry managed to make the worst of a bad situation. Industry leaders failed to sense that chairman Engman was out on a limb, and that he needed a response which consumerists could accept. FTC pressured for a code, but industry leaders offered nothing more concrete than a promise of "continuing review."

Since ANA members put up most of the money, ANA tended to call the tune. "Codes stifle creativity, and they are easily evaded anyway," insists Peter Allport. "The only reason there is a reference to ANA's guidelines in the final plan is that we were pressured by Rosch and others."

ANA's antipathy to codes spilled over into one of the disputes that lingers from the negotiations' failure to commit NAD to apply the NAB code. Until the final draft, it looked as if NAD would agree to enforce all industry standards, including the NAB code. But specific mention of NAB disappeared after a final drafting session attended by Mr. Allport and Steve Campbell, former General Foods exec. and now CBBB vp in charge of NAD.

They admit they responded to pressure from the toy industry, which resents the NAB code. "Broadcasters write it and apply it, and advertisers have no input," the toy people told ANA. "Our organization should not enforce their code." Mr. Campbell admits to bias against the NAB code: "I fought it for four years at GF," he said. In any event, he stresses it applies to children's advertisers, whether NAD mentions it or not. "I would rather get a set of standards our industry will support than press for something the advertisers won't accept," he noted.

Industry Faltered: Tankersley

Mr. Tankersley, who formerly ran copy clearance for CBS, believes industry's efforts faltered on two major points: (1) Failure to offer at least one major concession which would leave consumerists and FTC with a feeling that something specific had changed, and (2) insertion of the ANA guidelines. He preferred no specific guidelines, but found consumerists and FTC unconvinced. If any were to be mentioned, he believes, then ANA guidelines alone would not do.

ANA initially assured industry negotiators the children's ad project wasn't going anywhere. But, alarmed over pressure for bans on premiums and heavily sugared foods, it opted for a policy on tough issues which resulted in raised eyebrows.

Departing from its historic opposition to FTC trade regulation rules, ANA told negotiators: "Let the commission do this by rulemaking." ANA argued this assured "due process" and full hearings; but consumerists and FTC staffers decided ANA's real goal was delay.

Mr. Weil, whose influence over ANA policy is widely recognized, contends that industry representatives were fearful of the "per se" solutions demanded by consumerists. "What's wrong with a premium which influences a child to get his parents to purchase a product if the child has not been misled about what to expect? What's wrong with the tv host doing the product sell if it's an honest spiel?" he asks.

"It is hard to find any substantial basis for what the consumerists were demanding other than that they are effective in selling products," Mr. Weil argues, noting, "So what was really involved was that advertising is effective, and we were starting from totally irreconcilable viewpoints."

Several observers from the industry camp stressed ANA's dominant role, and one—who is identified primarily with some of the interested advertisers—contends the industry's failures are due primarily to the shortcomings of its trade associations.

In addition to the ad industry associations, the industry position also encompassed a non-advertiser group—the NAB. Its observers attended the sessions, sternly denying that any concessions were warranted. And among the unresolved issues are those related to frequency and placement of commercials, which have become a separate dispute between consumerists, broadcasters and the FCC.

"Associations felt compelled to take safe positions to satisfy some of the conservative, and uninformed individuals who are influential in their operations," a source said. "The people making the decisions were unable to appreciate the realities of the Washington climate. In their innocence, they reacted emotionally, taking consumerist rhetoric literally. They were unable to sense that Peggy Charren was prepared to settle for far less than the code stated. The preamble was a throwaway, purely for public consumption."

Arrogance on All Sides

"Despite its flaws, the plan was a good one. But there was arrogance on all sides, and it gets less credit than it deserves. But the most inexcusable arrogance was on those who presented the industry plan. Their failure to include a role for consumerists or let anyone see it before the May 20 meeting was bound to assure it would not be acceptable to Mr. Choate, Ms. Charren and Mr. Braren."

"In summary," says this source, "the venture illustrates the ease with which consumers, regulators and businessmen can misunderstand each other. When politics and emotions get involved, it is easy for reasoned understanding and good will to get lost in the struggle."

Cohen has commented that "the goal is to find solutions to consumer information needs, rather than more work for lawyers." How true! In many respects this is not only the crux of the problem but a viable solution. When the opposing groups work as equals and government employees are trained to be objective and forthright, then progress can be made. Of course changes will have to be made. More important, those who do not initiate the proposed change will have to recognize that change is merely a movement away from the status quo. It practically never leads to doom and damnation, as is too often predicted, but then it never reaches the apex of the millenium either. Change is just a movement in one direction or another from the status quo. This leads to the question of whether the status quo should be defended. Is it best? And for whom?

To evaluate the problem of children's advertising codes and not refer to the parental role would be quite remiss. Parents who overindulge their children may well be avoiding parental responsibility rather than helping the child grow into adulthood. No one has ever been able to avoid frustration, disappointment, or dissatisfaction. Parents who hardly ever confront their children with reality may well be contributing more negatives than positives, more unhappiness than happiness. Training, learning, and development are as much a parental duty as the schools' responsibility. Parents *can* explain to a child why they will not buy certain cereals, snacks, or toys. For the future good of the child this may be more effective than just "caving in."

From undue influence on children let's move on to another effect of advertising. This occurs when the advertiser extends its role and attempts to influence people beyond the uses and characteristics of the product itself. One illustration should suffice. Warner and Swasey is a company that describes itself as concerned with "productivity equipment and systems in machine tools, textiles, and construction machinery." It advertised in *Forbes,* a financial magazine, in April 1974. A standard request for permission to reprint the ad was answered with, "Before returning your release form, we would like to have the textual material which will refer to the ad in question." The author believes such a request to be an unprecedented abridgement of academic freedom. Accordingly, the ad is not reproduced here, but the reader is invited to read it in any library or request a copy from the company.

The content of the ad may be described as follows. It refers to "do-it-now environmentalists" as "they." "They" stop off-shore drilling, stop building nuclear plants, delay the Alaska pipeline, and so forth. "We," by contrast, would rather listen to real environmental and technical experts instead of impractical "overnight theorists."

"They" are the unidentified "bad guys" who seem to have the power to stop anything. "We" are the "good guys." The question is, When is advertising merely propaganda? In terms of Berne's transactional analysis, is Warner and Swasey a parent, a child or an adult?

Another problem that does not have a clear solution relates to whether advertising creates unwanted needs or caters to existing unfulfilled needs. Those who raise the issue on an academic or even philosophical level are deserving of as much credit as those who concern themselves with whether the chicken or the egg came first. To date no clearcut evidence is available as to whether advertising creates needs or wants.

With advertising posing so many problems, it would seem that a priority or ordering system is needed. What is not needed is the creation of additional problems that are at best only symptomatic of a prejudgment or bias. For example, are two color TV sets in a family a result of affluence, an attempt to eliminate or reduce arguments, or the creation of a need to have two sets?

Probably advertising can successfully suggest a purchase to some of the people some of the time. Its ability to create a need in an individual when a prior predisposition does not exist is doubtful. On the other hand, advertising may sometimes result in poor purchase decisions. Ultimately, the consumer must develop defense mechanisms against the inequities of advertising. The consumer should also take a more personal role by not using products that are, in his judgment, offensively advertised while at the same time recognizing that others may not regard the same advertisement as offensive.

For example, what is regarded as pornographic or obscene is most often a matter of personal taste. Sometimes it takes the Supreme Court to decide, and then it often does not change one's personal taste but only makes it legal or illegal.

A chapter on problems related to advertising would be incomplete if it did not refer to the economics of advertising and its implications. Once again, only two examples will be offered. One is related to how much should be spent on advertising; the other is a much more comprehensive question, that is, whether advertising creates competition or monopoly.

The first question is treated most clearly by B. Lipstein (4), who discusses it quite fairly.

> The practice of budgeting on an advertising-to-sales ratio, as has been pointed out by Benjamin Lipstein of SSC&B, "places the advertising function in a perpetually defensive position," where it is subject to budget-trimming to help make short-term profits.
>
> "It is a posture that advertising will most likely retain," adds Mr. Lipstein, until such time as research comes up with the answer to the client's perennial question, "Am I getting my money's worth for my advertising dollars?"
>
> Nobody really knows how much money should be invested in advertising. And if advertising money is spent to increase sales and profits, as it certainly is, nobody really knows how much advertising contributes to those dual goals. "I know half my advertising is wasted—but I don't know which half," goes the plaintive old saw.
>
> Clarence Eldridge, former marketing boss of General Foods and later a management consultant, has said that two questions that plague advertisers are: "How can we make our advertising more effective? How much advertising is enough? Not only can't we predict how much advertising it is going to take to produce a given result, we can't tell, when the advertising is finished, just what has been accomplished." (page 22)

With reference to the question of whether advertising creates competition or monopoly, J. Backman (5) rather unequivocally takes the position that advertising is competitive and creates competition. His book reviews much data and includes the arguments of critics, but somehow it always favors advertising.

In the opinion of this writer, Backman's book is an example of many things published by professors who present only one side of a question. Business in general and advertising in particular would benefit greatly from less inbreeding, more awareness of their problems, and greater willingness to consider candid and objective solutions.

Advertising should stop playing the games of "tongue in cheek" and "ostrich." To be sure, the intelligent, experienced, and informed men and women in the advertising world know more about advertising than many FTC staffers. The problem is that they sometimes do not tell the whole story, and the FTC may easily become confused.

Progress and change will occur when advertising more openly recognizes its imperfections and tries to get rid of them. If advertising is ever to reach the desirable goal of providing information to mature adults, and if it is to become less prominent as a target of government and irritated consumers, then it would appear that it should concentrate on eliminating material that is deceptive, exaggerated, insulting, or irrational.

What all this adds up to is that advertising must incorporate a set of ethics that apply equally to "we" and "they." It should stop wasting its time postulating unclear standards that it does not intend to live up to. There is no question but that advertisements are sometimes misleading and convey false information. The weekly FTC reports reveal that quite a bit of this is done not only by the "fly by nights" but by the largest companies and advertising agencies. Credibility is a key to acceptance by the public. It should be obvious that the best game in town ought to be an honest one, but that is not so. Too many apparently blind defenders of advertising seem to see no evil and hear no evil.

Another game advertisers play is to exaggerate product differences that either do not exist or are marginal. The claim that a product gets clothes whiter than white or that an airline has the lowest fares is an exaggeration as well as a half-truth.

Continuing with advertising imperfections, reference should be made to ads that are just plain insulting to the intelligence of possibly even a moron. Conversations that are supposed to take place in the home, in the supermarket, or anywhere else just do not happen the way advertising depicts them. It is difficult to give examples because advertisers change theme, situation, and campaign quite fast. At the time of this writing, a TV commercial that can serve as an example is the one in which a man comes home, supposedly after a day's work, enters the kitchen, and yells, "I smell clean." His wife at first thinks he has gone berserk but then, after some sniffing and close contact, it is clear that she is stimulated by being able to smell that he is clean.

The list would not be complete without a mention of product demonstrations that create impressions that do not conform to reality. Campbell Soup has provided us with an example. The FTC complaint and order on this subject are reproduced here.

Pursuant to the provisions of the Federal Trade Commission Act, and by virtue of the authority vested in it by said Act, the Federal Trade Commission, having reason to believe that Campbell Soup Company, a corporation, and Batten, Barton, Durstine & Osborn, Inc., a corporation, hereinafter referred to as respondents, have violated the provisions of said Act, and it appearing to the Commission that a proceeding by it in respect thereof would be in the public interest, hereby issues its complaint stating its charges in that respect as follows:

Paragraph One: Respondent Campbell Soup Company is a corporation, organized, existing and doing business under and by virtue of the laws of the State of New Jersey, with its principal office and place of business located at 375 Memorial Avenue, in the City of Camden, State of New Jersey.

Respondent Batten, Barton, Durstine & Osborn, Inc., is a corporation, organized, existing and doing business under and by virtue of the laws of the State of New York, with its principal office and place of business located at 383 Madison Avenue, in the City of New York, State of New York.

Paragraph Two: Respondent Campbell Soup Company is now, and for some time last past has engaged in the sale and distribution of Campbell's canned soups.

Respondent Batten, Barton, Durstine & Osborn, Inc., is now and for some time last past has been, an advertising agency of Campbell Soup Company, and now prepares and places, and for some time last past has prepared and placed, for publication, advertising material, including but not limited to the advertising referred to herein, to promote the sale of the said canned soup and other products.

Paragraph Three: Respondent Campbell Soup Company causes said products, when sold, to be transported from its various places of business located in the State of New Jersey to purchasers thereof located in various other states of the United States and in the District of Columbia. Thus respondent maintains a course of trade in said products in commerce, as "commerce" is defined in the Federal Trade Commission Act. The volume of business in such commerce has been and is substantial.

Paragraph Four: Respondents, by means of advertisements which depict and have depicted a bowl or container of Campbell soup, apparently prepared in accordance with the dilution directions on the can, in a "ready-to-eat" situation, demonstrate the quantity or abundance of solid ingredients (garnish) present in a can of Campbell soup.

Paragraph Five: In truth and in fact, in many of the aforesaid advertisements, which purport to demonstrate or offer evidence of the quantity or abundance of solid ingredients (garnish) in a can of Campbell soup, respondents have placed, or caused to be placed in the aforesaid bowl or container a number of clear glass marbles which prevent the solid ingredients (garnish) from sinking to the bottom, thereby giving the soup the appearance of containing more solid ingredients (garnish) than it actually contains, which fact is not disclosed.

The aforesaid demonstration exaggerates, misrepresents, and is not evidence of, the quantity or abundance of solid ingredients in a can of Campbell soup; therefore, the aforesaid advertisements are false, misleading and deceptive.

Paragraph Six: In the course and conduct of its business as aforesaid, and at all times mentioned herein, respondent Campbell Soup Company has been, and is now, in substantial competition, in commerce, with other corporations in the sale of canned soup of the same general kind and nature as that sold by said respondent.

In the course and conduct of its business as aforesaid, and at all times mentioned herein, respondent Batten, Barton, Durstine & Osborn, Inc., has been, and is now, in substantial competition, in commerce, with corporations, firms and individuals in the advertising business who represent sellers of canned soup.

Paragraph Seven: The use by respondents of the aforesaid false, misleading and deceptive advertisements has had, and now has, the tendency and capacity to mislead members of the purchasing public as to the quantity of solid ingredients (garnish) in a can of Campbell soup and into the purchase of substantial quantities of Campbell soup by reason thereof.

Paragraph Eight: The aforesaid acts and practices of respondents, as herein alleged, were and are all to the prejudice and injury of the public and of respondents' competitors and constituted, and now constitute, unfair methods of competition and unfair and deceptive acts and practices in commerce in violation of Section 5 of the Federal Trade Commission Act.

Wherefore, the Premises Considered, the Federal Trade Commission on this 25th day of May, A.D. 1970, issues its complaint against said respondents.

ORDER

The Commission having considered the petition of SOUP, Inc., filed March 20, 1970, in which SOUP, Inc., moves for withdrawal of provisional acceptance of the consent agreement in this matter, for a hearing on the adequacy of the provisionally accepted consent agreement, for permission to intervene in this matter, and to be furnished at Commission expense with a copy of the transcript of oral argument heard February 5, 1970:

It Is Ordered that the motion of soup, Inc., to withdraw provisional acceptance of the proposed consent order be, and it hereby is, denied.

It Is Further Ordered that the attached consent agreement be, and it hereby is, finally accepted, and the Order to Cease and Desist contained therein issue.

It Is Further Ordered that the respondents herein shall, within sixty (60) days after service upon them of this order, file with the Commission a report in writing setting forth in detail the manner and form in which they have complied with this order.

It Is Further Ordered that the motions of soup, Inc. for a hearing, for further intervention in this matter, and for reconsideration of our February 24, 1970, decision be, and they hereby are, denied.

It Is Further Ordered that the motion of soup, Inc., for a copy at Commission expense of the transcript of oral argument in this matter heard February 5, 1970, be, and it hereby is, granted.

The opinion of the Commission accompanies this order.

Campbell Soup is willing to grant permission to reproduce in its entirety two news releases from March 24 and March 29, 1969, provided the exact context in which the releases are to be used is known to them in advance. Since the author regards this as an intrusion of academic freedom, only the F.T.C. material is presented.

The reason for including this material is quite simple. Too often one reads or hears about only one side of an issue. Knowing both sides of a controversy sometimes makes matters clearer.

The promotion of irrationality might be illustrated by the sex-toothpaste relationship. How using one brand of toothpaste rather than another will endow one with greater sexual prowess is hard to imagine. Nevertheless, the campaigns that relate sex and toothpaste are endless. If no one believes the campaign, why conduct it?

Where does all this lead? For one thing, business, through its self-imposed codes and self-regulation, tends eventually to encourage legislation that restricts advertisers from doing what they really know they should not be doing in the first place.

To illustrate, the following list presents proposed legislation for the 93rd Congress (6):

S.249   Low Tar and Nicotine Act. To amend the Federal Cigarette Labeling and Advertising Act to require the Federal Trade Commission to establish acceptable levels of tar and nicotine content of cigarettes. Moss —1/6/73—Commerce.

S.1165   Little Cigars Act of 1973. To amend the Federal Cigarette Labeling and Advertising Act of 1965, as amended, by the Public Health Cigarette Smoking Act of 1969, to define the term "little cigar" and for other purposes. Moss—3/12/73—Commerce.

> Reported 4/5/73 (93-103). Passed Senate, 4/10/73; reconsidered and passed again, with amendment, 4/30/73. Referred to House I&F Commerce, 5/1/73. Passed House, 9/10/73. Approved 9/21/73, P.L. 93-109.

S.1512   Truth in Advertising Act. To require the furnishing of documentation of claims concerning safety, performance, efficacy, characteristics, and comparative price of advertised products and services. Moss + 1—4/10/73—Commerce.

H.R.2282   Truth in Advertising Act. Provides that no advertisement can be disseminated if substantiating documentation is not available to the public. Makes advertisements in violation of provisions of this Act an unfair or deceptive act or practice. To be enforced by the FTC. Dingell + 1—1/18/73—I&F Commerce.

H.R.2744   National Institute of Advertising, Marketing, and Society Act. To establish within the FTC an Institute to study the impact of advertising and marketing techniques upon the consumer and society. Tiernan—1/23/73—I&F Commerce.

H.R.3827   A bill to amend the Federal Cigarette Labeling and Advertising Act to revise the warning statement required by that Act to be placed on cigarette packages. Lehman—2/6/73—I&F Commerce.

H.R.4521   A bill to amend the Communications Act of 1934 in order to prohibit the broadcasting of any advertising of alcoholic beverages. Hanna—2/21/73—I&F Commerce.

H.R.7319   A bill to amend the Federal Cigarette Labeling and Advertising Act to require cigarette packages to disclose the quantity of tar and nicotine contained in the cigarettes in the package. Lehman—4/30/73—I&F Commerce.

H.R.7483   Little Cigars Act of 1973. *Similar to S.1165.* MacDonald—5/3/73—I&F Commerce.

> Hearings held 5/22–24/73; reported 6/22/73 (93-323). Passed House, 9/10/73. Proceedings vacated. S.1165 passed in lieu, 9/10/73. Approved 9/21/73, P.L. 93-109. Similar bill: H.R.3828.

H.R.12576 A bill to amend the FTC Act with respect to misleading brand names. Rosenthal—2/5/74—I&F Commerce.

Incidentally, whereas 10 such bills are indexed under advertising, more than 500 bills are listed as consumer-related problems covering parctically every area of business life from advertising to warranties.

Not all of these bills will be passed in any one session of Congress, and many overlap. The point is that Congress is aware of consumer needs, but business and advertising continue to believe that lobbying can be as successful in the future as it has been in the past. Chances are, this assumption is false.

The secret arm of business is its lobbying activity; the open arm is its advertising. Consumers as individuals and groups are becoming more vocal and powerful. If it is true that money can be a source of power, it is also true that votes, when exercised for self-protection, can be an even greater source of power. The answer is for business and the consumer to work together more openly and with equal awareness that solutions are needed rather than continued controversy. While the battle continues, there is a growing drive to have businesses contribute a percentage of their advertising budgets to consumer groups, which, in turn, would evaluate the advertisements and grant some "truth in advertising" recognition. If this allocation amounted to only 0.5 percent of U.S. agencies billing, it would amount to more than 70 million dollars. What a windfall!

The problem is, which consumer group should do the evaluating? What would it do with the money? Once such questions are resolved, we may see the beginning of a better balance between the "haves" and the "have nots" than now exists, at least as far as advertising is concerned.

This issue of "revenue sharing" will become hilarious before it becomes serious. Consumers will argue that since they are the buyers they deserve a share of the action. The business community will insist that such nonsense will result in higher prices. It may even use advertising campaigns to inform consumers of the impending rise in prices, disregarding the possibility that the cost of such a campagn might also raise prices!

BIBLIOGRAPHY

1. WARD, S., "Effects of Television Advertising on Children," Remarks prepared for FTC hearings on modern advertising practices (Cambridge, Mass.: Marketing Science Institute, 1971).
2. WARD, S., *Children and Promotion: New Consumer Battleground* (Cambridge, Mass.: Marketing Science Institute, 1972).
3. COHEN, S. E., "How Industry Lost the Ball on Children's TV Ads," *Advertising Age*, January 17, 1974.
4. LIPSTEIN, B., "How Much Should You Advertise?" *Advertising Age*, November 21, 1973.
5. BACKMAN, J., *Advertising and Competition* (New York: New York University Press, 1967).
6. U.S., Department of Health, Education and Welfare, Office of Consumer Affairs, *Consumer Bills Introduced in the 93rd Congress* (Washington, D.C.: GPO, January, 1975).

24

The role of government in consumer affairs

Various institutions influence the role of the government in consumer affairs. It is probably true that business has the greatest influence. And it is probably also true that the government responds to that influence.

Business encourages the perception of democracy that prescribes that the government should not expand its responsibilities. It generally takes the stance that the government should not pass laws that would restrict its freedom. Accordingly, the fewer the laws that regulate business, the better. However, business is also in favor of laws that perpetuate and guarantee its freedom.

Second to appear on the scene is labor. It, too, is clearly in favor of the democratic system that preserves and extends its freedom. It favors the laws that business opposes, and vice versa.

More recently, the consumer movement and its leaders have started to exert pressure on the government to pass laws that extend its freedom and support the "consumer bill of rights"—to be informed, to choose, and so on. The consumer groups have, in a much less efficient way than business and labor, managed somehow to convey the great need for a reallocation of freedom, especially as it relates to the alleviation of problems confronting consumers.

The government is not a buyer, seller, or maker of products and services. It is the institution that passes and enforces laws calculated to protect some of the people most of the time. The addition of the consumer movement to the forces of labor and business results in greater awareness on the part of the government that consumer affairs are a matter of attempting to solve problems if not reduce conflicts.

Consumers' unhappiness, complaints, and dissatisfactions are becoming more readily heard by business as well as government. Consumers present the view that they need and deserve more justice and support than is afforded by present laws, especially in relation to health, safety, and the right to privacy.

Some people in government seem to be more aware that consumers need direct representation on an equal plane with farmers, labor, and business, which are represented by the Departments of Labor, Agriculture, and Commerce. Others do not see this need at all.

To unravel the story of the government's role in consumer affairs, one might begin with the President. Only a few Presidents have actively favored and supported the passage of federal laws to protect the consumer. Possibly the first was Theodore Roosevelt, with the Meat Inspection Act of 1906. A virtual hiatus followed, until Franklin D. Roosevelt's New Deal created a Consumers' Advisory Board headed by Mary Rumsey. After another interval, John F. Kennedy appointed a Consumer Advisory Council.

More important, Kennedy's message to Congress may truly be regarded as the "consumer bill of rights." The tragedy of his short term leaves many unanswered questions and unfulfilled promises.

It was for Lyndon B. Johnson to designate a President's Committee on Consumer Interests. He was also the first to appoint a special assistant to the President on consumer affairs, Esther Peterson. Without any precedent or guidelines, Peterson acted with vigor. However, her labor background and general stance rapidly aroused suspicion, even hostility, in various business quarters. In any event, there seemed to be a cause-and-effect relationship between her active support of a national boycott aimed at supermarkets and her replacement by TV personality Betty Furness. Apparently many people thought Furness would be "safer," but as it turned out she was quite active and effective. She enhanced the office and did a great deal to move the job into the permanence of bureaucracy.

When President Nixon came to office, he appointed Willie Mae Rogers as his part-time consultant on consumer affairs. This appointment turned out to be both unpopular and short-lived. Many consumerists felt that it downgraded an important job.

Others felt that there might well be a conflict of interest, since according to the White House, Rogers was to keep her job as director of the Good Housekeeping Institute. This raising of eyebrows resulted in an announcement that there was no official concern about a possible conflict of interest. However, a congressional committee pursued the matter, and Rogers withdrew her name. Nixon then (in 1969) appointed Virginia Knauer to the post.

An evaluation of the effectiveness of Knauer's role is exceedingly difficult. She is a moderate who usually demonstrates consumer identification only when the issues are safe. She does not seem to have enthusiastic support from any source. But she has held her post for a long time with very few attacks. She provides a lesson in how to get along in Washington. The formula may well be to do something but never do it too strongly or too clearly. By developing this syndrome to perfection, one can be identified as representing the consumer while not creating enemies.

Probably her measure of success is that she has what it takes to be in two consecutive administrations where lip service rather than ardent support is the political maneuver that keeps consumer issues and affairs on the "Washington back burner."

Knauer has also served as director of the Office of Consumer Affairs of the Department of Health, Education and Welfare. In both roles her major responsibility has been to act as the government's spokesperson in matters of interest to consumers and to compile information about such matters.

One such effort resulted in the *Guide to Federal Consumer Services,* published in 1971, which lists about 90 federal agencies and bureaus involved in consumer services starting with agriculture and ending with veterans administration.

Another compilation is *State Consumer Actions '73,* a synopsis of more than 300 consumer-related laws passed at the state and local levels. In the foreword, Knauer writes that the government intends "to seek out, encourage and support those additional measures necessary to better assure the public an honest and informative market place."

Still another publication is the *Directory of State, County and City Government Consumer Offices.* It reports that as of March 1974 all 50 states had at least one state consumer office. There were also offices in the District of Columbia, Puerto Rico, and the Virgin Islands. Twenty-nine states had more than one such office with coordinate or separate responsibilities. A total of 93 such offices existed at that time on the state level. There were also 80 counties and 44 cities reporting consumer offices.

Most state offices are attached to the state attorney general's office and enforce fair trade practices in their respective states. On the county and city levels the person in charge is likely to have the title of director of consumer protection (or consumer enforcement).

A value of the publication is that it lists the names and addresses of each of the approximately 225 people in charge of consumer affairs on the local level. Such a listing makes it possible for individuals and groups to contact an informed person who might be helpful in furnishing information or solving a consumer problem.

In addition to the concern of the executive branch of the government with respect to consumer issues, the various legislative bodies as well as the regulatory and enforcement agencies are increasingly active on behalf of the consumer.

In many ways the issue of whether there should be a single federal agency to represent the consumer or whether the existing mosaic should remain in effect hinges on whether one believes that centralization leads to power and effectiveness as well as a more uniform policy. The issue can be better understood by looking at the position taken by business. It strongly opposes a centralized agency, much more than it opposes existing agencies. The question is, Why is business against a single agency to handle consumer affairs? Could the designated head really become a czar?

The system that currently exists consists mainly of the major regulatory agencies, including the Federal Trade Commission (FTC), the Food and Drug Administration (FDA), the General Services Administration (GSA), the Federal Energy Administration (FEA), and the new Consumer Product Safety Commission.

The FTC publishes a weekly news summary (1) in which its "actions" against possible violators of the law are reported. A review of eight issues (December 27, 1974, to February 14, 1975) is illustrative of the FTC's involvement with business practices. Its three main activities are hearings on proposed trade regulation rules, complaints, and consent agreements.

The editor's note indicates the framework within which the FTC works.

EDITOR'S NOTE

The following applies to all complaints and proposed complaints in this issue:

THE FEDERAL TRADE COMMISSION ISSUES A COMPLAINT WHEN IT HAS "REASON TO BELIEVE" THAT THE LAW HAS BEEN VIOLATED. SUCH ACTION DOES NOT IMPLY ADJUDICATION OF THE MATTERS ALLEGED.

To avoid repetition, the following language applies to all consent agreements mentioned in this issue:

A CONSENT AGREEMENT IS FOR SETTLEMENT PURPOSES ONLY AND DOES NOT CONSTITUTE AN ADMISSION BY RESPONDENTS THAT THEY HAVE VIOLATED THE LAW. WHEN ISSUED BY THE COMMISSION ON A FINAL BASIS, A CONSENT ORDER CARRIES THE FORCE OF LAW WITH RESPECT TO FUTURE ACTIONS. A VIOLATION OF SUCH AN ORDER MAY RESULT IN A CIVIL PENALTY UP TO $10,000 PER VIOLATION BEING IMPOSED UPON A RESPONDENT.

Areas in which hearings have been scheduled include flammability of plastics, advertising disclosure, automobile fuel economy claims, and food advertising.

Among the consent agreements reached during the same period were the following: Warranty practices in mobile homes (Skyline plus three other major manufacturers); unfair selling practices; a ban on false claims for skin preparations; truth in lending; false and unsubstantiated claims for pet foods (General Foods); and bringing lawsuits in distant or inconvenient courts (Montgomery Ward).

The complaints included deceptive debt collection forms and misrepresentation; illegal price fixing (Rubbermaid); unfair and deceptive recruiting, selling, and collection practices (Encyclopedia Britannica); mispresentation by an employment agency (Gateway Overseas Services); false uniqueness claims for air conditioners (Fedders); and unavailability of advertised items (A&P).

The problem is that most complaints and consent agreements take a very long time to reach a decision. By that time, however, the original problem may no longer exist.

The companies named here are not necessarily different from their competitors. The names have been included to suggest that big as well as small companies are violators or alleged violators of good business practice, if not of the law itself.

The other side of the coin is best represented by the FDA. Four laws passed by Congress authorize the majority of its activities (2):

The Federal Food, Drug and Cosmetic Act requires that foods be safe and wholesome, that drugs be safe and effective, and that cosmetics and medical devices be safe. All these products must be properly labeled.

The Fair Packaging and Labeling Act requires that labeling be honest and informative, so that shoppers may easily determine the best value.

The Radiation Control for Health and Safety Act protects consumers from unnecessary exposure to radiation from x-ray machines and consumer products such as microwave ovens and color TVs.

The Public Health Service Act establishes FDA's authority over vaccines, serums and other biological products. It also is the basis for FDA's programs on milk sanitation, shellfish sanitation, restaurant operations and interstate travel facilities.

The FDA disseminates literature in which it takes positions on various foods, additives, drugs, and appliances as they relate to consumer health. For example, it accepts meat tenderizers prepared from papaya. This additive is destroyed by cooking or by the gastric juices in the body. With reference to MSG (monosodium glutamate), in 1969 baby food manufacturers discontinued use of the substance. It can still be used without a label declaration in mayonnaise and salad dressings, but it must be included on the label if it is present in canned vegetables and tuna fish. The FDA also took action to ban the Relaxacizer, an electrical gadget for waistline reducing and, among many other things, has issued standards for packaged nuts.

An interesting paper by Jacoby and Small (3) compares the FTC and FDA approaches to deceptive and misleading advertising. The two agencies have very different approaches. The FTC relies on three types of evidence of deceptive advertising as substitutes for consumer data. They are the "initiative approach," dictionary definitions, and "experts." The FDA counterpart is *misleading* advertising. It establishes who and how many are being misled by distinguishing ads that are either "false and/or unfairly balanced" from those that are truthful and fairly balanced. The decision as to whether an advertisement is deceptive or not is settled in the courts, usually without empirical data of any validity. The decision related to misleading advertising seems to be more readily established in accordance with valid scientific methods.

As Jacoby and Small astutely conclude,

There were two primary objectives in preparing this manuscript. First, we wished to contrast the manner in which the Federal Trade Commission and the Food and Drug Administration approached the subject of deceptive and/or misleading advertising. The respective approaches are different in several important respects. Hopefully, attention to these differences will stimulate clarification and refinement of the basic issues which underlie deceptive and/or misleading advertising. In our opinion, the approach which the FDA is considering adopting focuses more directly on the central issues involved, is more rigorous in a scientific empirical sense, and is subject to less varying interpretation. Without such an objective, systematic approach to the evaluation of advertisements, judgments regarding the acceptability or unacceptability of advertisements will remain open to legitimate criticism by a variety of concerned groups.

Our second objective in describing the FDA's Bureau of Drugs' current thinking and intended empirical approach vis-á-vis misleading advertising was to lay it bare and open it up for discussion and constructive criticism. While we believe it represents a good start, we also believe it can be substantially improved upon. For example, a variety of approaches for developing a valid and equitable criterion level (of n%) are being considered and the independently generated input of others on this issue would be particularly helpful. Accordingly, and inasmuch as policy and practice in this domain will no doubt affect us all, we conclude with an invitation to interested others from all segments of the consumer research community to consider and contribute to the resolution of the very important issues underlying deceptive and/or misleading advertising. (**page 20**)

The GSA also has a consumer product information center. It publishes one-pagers with titles like *What Happened to Mushrooms, Investing in Gold, Headaches, Your Child's Emotional Health, Your Right to Credit, Microwave Ovens,* and *Car Care and Service.* These are primarily announcements of government pamphlets for sale or available free from Consumer Information, Pueblo, Colorado 81009. The center also publishes a quarterly index of selected federal publications of interest to consumers.

The FEA is a relative newcomer to consumer affairs. In response to the Middle East oil embargo, it was assigned Project Independence. The project intended to evaluate the nation's energy problems and develop a national energy policy. The project report is a tome almost two inches thick containing contributions from over 500 professionals. It was started in March 1974 and with a November publication date might well have set a record for speediness in government projects.

The report indicates that energy demand has been growing at a 4–5 percent rate per year. It also reports that the United States' self-sufficiency in energy ended in 1950 and that coal production is at 1940 levels, crude oil production has been declining since 1970, and natural gas consumption exceeds new discoveries since 1968. Further, it indicates that the effects of the embargo were a $10–20 billion drop in gross national product and an additional 500,000 unemployed. Various strategies are discussed and numerous figures and statistics are presented. In fact the publication contains an overdose of statistics, economics, and technology. Amazingly, it omits, avoids, or simply does not recognize the needs and attitudes of ordinary consumers heating their homes, operating various appliances, and driving their cars.

From a "national emergency" point of view the project considered such things as the 20 mpg automobile, increased use of mass transit, and via subsidies to encourage more efficient use of energy. It made a thorough study of energy sources and alternatives. However, it completely overlooked a basic reality. Failure to understand or motivate citizens invites resistance and might well make the achievement of energy independence impossible.

The government must recognize that it is dealing continually with a better informed and more sophisticated public. The WIN buttons proposed by President Ford never got off the ground —and for good reason. Consumer cooperation is needed if Project Independence is to be achieved—and that is what consumer psychology is all about. The FEA seems to be too technically oriented and appears to overlook consumers' needs and goals and the conditions necessary to gain their respect and cooperation.

The manufacture and sale of products that impair the health and safety of users is obviously a consumer issue. The question as to whether unsafe and unhealthy products are sold knowingly is quite academic to a person who has been injured by such a product. The solution is to prevent the manufacture of such products. Obviously, products that threaten consumer health and safety go beyond food and drugs; they include an assortment of flammable materials, electrical products, toys, bicycles, and aerosols, to name just a few.

In May 1973, after untold misery, injury, and death, the Consumer Product Safety Commission was established by an act of Congress. The Commission's goal is to substantially reduce injuries associated with consumer products covered by four acts previously administered by other federal agencies: the Flammable Fabrics Act, the Hazardous Substances Act, the Poison Prevention Packaging Act, and the Refrigerator Door Safety Act. This sets an interesting precedent, at least as far as consumer affairs are concerned. It reallocates enforcement and assigns it to a new agency that places consumer safety in primary focus. It follows that more centralization of consumer affairs would result in greater efficiency by regulating and enforcing the acts and having more authority to "do something."

Further, this act has teeth in it. Knowing violators of the act can bring penalties up to $500,000 as well as jail terms. The act also provides that the commission must conduct research and set standards.

Consumers should pay attention to this new agency. If it gets into the hands of do nothing bureaucrats, then we will have more of the same. If it establishes a close liaison with the special interests of business and lobbyists, then again, we will have more of the same. If it makes provisions for independent research and investigation and sets up an equitable hearing system in which consumers are given equal time, then something new and wonderful may be on the way. The ultimate gain could be products that will not harm the health and safety of consumers.

The commission's fact sheets are well done. Three are reproduced here to illustrate their value.

FACT SHEET

U.S. CONSUMER PRODUCT SAFETY COMMISSION
WASHINGTON, D.C. 20207

NO. 33: AEROSOLS

The U.S. Consumer Product Safety Commission estimates that each year nearly 5,000 people receive emergency room treatment for injuries associated with aerosols. These pressurized cans are used by consumers to dispense pesticides, paints, hairsprays, medications, and many other household products. There were over two billion aerosol cans manufactured in the U.S. last year, and almost all of us use aerosols.

- Wilma discarded an empty can of insect repellant into a waste-paper fire. The can exploded and a piece of flying metal pierced her jugular vein. Wilma died fifteen minutes later.
- Eight-year-old Jimmy used a hammer and nail to puncture an old can of spray paint. The can exploded hurling pieces of metal into his face and upper chest, cutting him severely.
- Laurie was smoking while she used an aerosol can of hairspray. Her cigarette ignited the spray and she received severe burns which permanently disfigured her face.
- Mr. Carr was spray painting a bookcase in his basement. There was no ventilation, and the fumes accumulated to such a level that he became dizzy and collapsed. When his wife found him, he was dead.
- Six-year-old Ken found a can of insect spray and accidentally sprayed it into his face. He was seriously burned by the chemical.

These illustrations represent the following accident patterns associated with aerosols:

1. *Explosions caused by high temperature*—Throwing an aerosol can into a fire or storing it near a radiator or in the sun could cause an explosion.
2. *Explosions caused by puncturing*—Even if you think the can is "empty," there can be enough pressure to cause an explosion if it is punctured.
3. *Flammability of contents or propellants*—Some propellants, such as propane, are highly flammable, and many of the "usable contents" are also flammable. Some sprays will burn like a blowtorch when ignited by matches or other flame sources.
4. *Toxicity of contents or propellants*—The propellants (such as vinyl chloride) can be toxic if used in unventilated rooms and inhaled in quantity. Some people who "sniffed" aerosols have suffered dizziness, lack of coordination, nausea, headache, or blurred vision. Others died. Aerosol sprays can also cause heart trouble, skin problems, respiratory problems, and have been linked to cancer.

5. *Chemical burns*—These are often caused by children who misdirect the spray.

The U.S. Consumer Product Safety Commission offers the following suggestions for the safe use, storage, and disposal of aerosols:

1. *Use*
   - Read instructions and warning statements carefully *before* using.
   - Have plenty of ventilation when you spray indoors because of the toxicity of the contents and propellants.
   - Don't ·smoke while spraying because many aerosols are flammable.
   - Don't use sprays near heating appliances, gas stoves, or other flame or heat sources.
   - Keep your body well covered and wash exposed areas after spraying. This is especially important with insecticide sprays.
   - Stop work at the first sign of dizziness, nausea, headache, blurred vision, or skin irritation. Seek fresh air immediately, and call a doctor if the symptoms persist or are severe.
   - Don't use aerosols around food because the spray can contaminate the food.
2. *Storage*
   - Keep the container in a cool location; some aerosols can explode at 120°F. or higher.
   - Do not expose to direct sunlight, radiators, stoves, or other sources of heat. Don't leave aerosols in your car where inside temperatures can reach high levels on hot days.
   - Keep out of the reach of children.
3. *Disposal*
   - Dispose of aerosols with other non-burnable trash.
   - Do not puncture the container. There are some devices on the market which purport to be safe mechanisms for puncturing aerosol cans, but the procedures for using them are rather complicated and can be dangerous if not carefully followed.
   - Do not throw "empty" aerosols in incinerators or trash compactors. They still contain propellants which can build up pressure and cause the can to explode.

Teach children about the hazards associated with aerosols—explosions, flammability, and toxicity.

NO. 41: PLASTICS

Plastics are widely used today in upholstered furniture stuffings, rug pads, mattress cores, wall insulation and paneling, and in the interiors of cars, planes and mobile homes. Plastics are easier to mold than traditional materials, such as wood, glass and metal, but they tend to release more heat and smoke when they burn. Some plastics release deadly fumes during fires.

> The entire downstairs of the Wilson home was destroyed before the fire could be extinguished. The family was found dead in the bedrooms upstairs where they had been overcome by poisonous gases and smoke released by burning foam furniture and the foam pad under the rug. The flames never reached them.

Fire hazards associated with certain plastics include:

1. *Rapid flame spread.* Once ignited, some plastic materials burn rapidly and can spread flame to nearby materials.
2. *Extreme heat.* Some plastics generate high temperatures quickly when they are ignited.
3. *Large amounts of dense smoke.* Burning plastic materials produce thick, black smoke limiting visibility and making it difficult for victims to get out or for firefighters to get in.
4. *Toxic gases.* When burned, plastics produce carbon monoxide, and some produce toxic gases such as hydrogen cyanide and hydrogen chloride. In most cases, people die from the smoke and carbon monoxide gas before the flames reach them.

There are both fibrous and non-fibrous plastics. The fibrous plastics include polyesters, nylons, and other fibers used in plastics. (The hazards associated with fabrics are described in Fact Sheet No. 17 on Flammable Fabrics.) The non-fibrous plastics include polyurethane foam, polystyrene, and polyvinyl chloride, and others. The polyurethane foam is often flexible and is used in upholstered furniture and mattresses. It can also be applied as a spray to walls and ceilings, and some restaurants have experienced tragic fires when their foam-covered walls have ignited and spread fire very quickly. Polystyrene can be made in a rigid form which looks remarkably like wood, and it is often used for wall paneling, countertops, and furniture. Polyvinyl chloride can also be rigid, and it is used in many applications, such as plastic plumbing installations. There are many other types of plastics as well.

The Federal response to the fire hazards of plastics has been made by several agencies:

- National Highway Traffic Safety Administration—NHTSA has responsibility for the flammability of materials used in vehicles such as automobiles and buses, and standards have been set for these materials.
- Federal Aviation Administration—FAA has responsibility for the flammability of interior furnishings in airplanes, and standards have been set.
- Federal Trade Commission—FTC has accused 26 plastics manufacturers of misrepresenting the serious fire hazards associated with plastics by labeling many plastics as "self-extinguishing" or "non-burning." This FTC complaint will require the plastics industry and testing laboratories to develop new flammability tests and accompanying labels.

The U.S. Consumer Product Safety Commission has responsibility for the flammability of interior furnishings in homes, and a standard is being developed for upholstered furniture. Flammability standards have already been established for rugs and mattresses.

Some controversy exists over the flammability of plastics. Some point out that plastics will form a char which resists further burning and insulates to retard further heat generation. Others say that once ignited most plastics will burn rapidly and produce highly toxic gases and smoke. Research is presently being conducted by industry laboratories and by the National Bureau of Standards to provide more detailed information relating to the dangers of burning plastics.

Chemical flame retardants have been developed and can be applied to plastics during the manufacturing process. These may become more widely used in order for plastics to meet new Federal safety standards. However, there is no effective "home treatment" which consumers can use to make plastics less flammable.

The U.S. Consumer Product Safety Commission offers the following suggestions for consumers to reduce potential hazards associated with plastics:

- Be aware that all plastics—even the polystyrene cups which are used for coffee—will burn if the ignition source is hot enough. A match or hot electric coil could ignite plastic.
- Some plastics can produce gases which can kill you.
- Consider the use of other less flammable materials instead of plastics whenever possible.
- Put a smoke detector (which can be purchased in some department stores for about $50) outside your bedroom door or at the top of the stairwell to provide early warning if a fire does occur.

FACT SHEET

U.S. CONSUMER PRODUCT SAFETY COMMISSION
WASHINGTON, D.C. 20207

NO. 47: TOYS

Skates, tricycles, toy trucks, cars, non-flying airplanes, boats, toy wagons, and balls are among children's favorite playthings. But last year, according to U.S. Consumer Product Safety Commission estimates, approximately 150,000 people received hospital emergency room treatment for injuries associated with toys.

Falls are the most frequent type of accident, but many serious injuries result from children swallowing small parts or placing tiny toys in noses and ears, from exploding gas-powered toys, from flammable products, and from sharp edges.

1. *Banned Toys*

The Commission has authority under the Federal Hazardous Substances Act as amended to ban hazardous toys and other children's products from sale. Since 1970, more than 1500 items, mostly toys, have been banned. The banning regulations provide that toys having the following characteristics are banned hazardous substances:

- toy rattles containing rigid wires, sharp points, or loose small objects that could become exposed and cause cuts, punctures, or other injuries.
- any toy with noisemaking parts that could be removed by a child and swallowed or inhaled.
- any doll, stuffed animal or similar toy having parts that could become exposed and cause cuts, punctures, or other similar injuries.
- lawn darts and other sharp pointed items intended for outdoor use that could cause puncture wounds, unless they have included appropriate cautionary language, adequate directions, and warnings for safe use and are not sold by toy stores or stores dealing primarily in toys and other children's articles.
- caps intended for use with toy guns or toy guns that cause noise above a certain level.
- "baby bouncers" and similar articles that support very young children while sitting, walking, or bouncing, which could cause injury to the child such as pinching, cutting, or bruising.
- toys known as clacker balls which could break off or fracture and thereby cause injury.

On September 3, 1973, a safety regulation for electrically operated toys went into effect. The regulation specifies maximum temperatures for these toys and requires reliable electrical construction. Electrical toys now must bear warning labels that state they are not recommended for children under a certain age. In the case of toys that contain a heating element, the manufacturer may not indicate that the toy is recommended for children under eight.

Currently, the Commission is developing new regulations that will provide more comprehensive safety standards for all toys and offer special protection for young children under the age of eight.

2. *Compliance with the Law*

Manufacturers, distributors, and retailers have legal responsibility for making sure that they do not sell dangerous toys. CPSC inspectors, working out of the Commission's 14 area offices, regularly conduct surveys of factories, warehouses, and retail outlets to insure compliance with the law. The Commission also receives the cooperation of the Customs Bureau to check imports for possible hazards.

Consumers also assist the Commission to canvass the marketplace for dangerous toys. Consumer Deputies, volunteers from clubs, retirees, and university students, visit toy stores across the country in an attempt to identify banned toys and have them removed from shelves. The Deputies are trained by Commission staff. Serving in an unofficial status, they ask the store manager to remove suspect toys from sale and to check the supplier to find out whether the toy is banned. Most store managers are happy to cooperate, but sometimes it is necessary to schedule a follow-up visit by an official CPSC inspector.

3. *Toys, Toys, Toys*

Each year, 5,000 new toys enter the marketplace. This holiday season will find over 150,000 different kinds of toys for sale in an estimated one million retail outlets.

Despite the efforts of toy manufacturers, retailers, CPSC inspectors, Consumer Deputies, and other Federal, state, and local government agencies, it is impossible to examine every toy.

But it is possible for parents, relatives, and older sisters and brothers to check every new toy they buy and every old toy around the house for possible hazards.

The Commission has the following suggestions for toy safety:

- Buy toys that suit the skills and abilities of the child. Avoid toys that are too complex for young children.
- Look for labels that give age recommendations or safety information such as "Not Recommended for Children Under Three" or "Non-Toxic" on toys likely to end up in little mouths.
- Watch out for toys that have sharp edges, small parts, or sharp

points. Avoid toys that produce extremely loud noises that can damage hearing and propelled objects that can injure eyes.
- Explain to the child how to use toys properly and safely.
- Always try to supervise young children while they play.
- Insist that children put their toys away so they do not get broken and so that no one else trips or falls on them.
- Examine toys periodically. Repair broken toys and discard toys that cannot be fixed.

Remember: Protect your child from serious toy-related injuries. THINK TOY SAFETY.

The role of government in consumer affairs is increasing because business' volunteerism has no teeth and is very often a delaying tactic. Volunteerism is a form of cooperation that depends on the benevolence of the particular company or businessman toward the consumer. Under ideal conditions volunteerism is an excellent solution. Under real conditions, however, its effectiveness is unpredictable.

As government on all levels becomes more and more active, its role is evolving in piecemeal fashion, without a master plan. For the present, government disseminates lots of information without measuring its effectiveness. It passes laws as a result of judgments made after hearings in which the adversaries present their arguments, mainly without the benefit of research data. It then attempts to enforce those laws, so there is more delay as the adversaries go through the legal process. Finally, legal resolutions are reached, usually when the problem no longer exists and has been replaced with a new consumer issue.

The government's involvement in consumer affairs will be no panacea. Just as the consumer is no match for business, neither is government when it comes to experience in handling (and evading) consumer issues.

The consumer must realize that the government's entry into consumer affairs offers a possibility of help but no guarantee of solutions. *The consumer must do things on his/her own.*

As for the government, it should be concerned about two factors that can produce failure. It will fail if it overlooks the great need to develop a more comprehensive system of two-way communication between consumers and bureaucrats, who somehow forget that they represent consumers as well as business. It will also fail if provisions are not made to balance the relative powers and freedoms of business and consumers. Business and its lobbyists have the money to go to Washington and be heard. Some are there all the time with that one purpose in mind. Consumers are disadvantaged insofar as they generally are not as well organized and most of their representatives do not have the money to get to Washington. The Product Safety Commission and other governmental units involved in consumer affairs must recognize that fair hearings need fair representation on all sides. Maybe funds to pay consumers to attend hearings should be provided by the government the way it provides funds to establish bureaus and agencies and pay the employees involved in consumer affairs. After all, how can they deal equitably with consumer affairs if the parties involved are not represented equally?

BIBLIOGRAPHY

1. Federal Trade Commission, *Federal Trade Commission News Summary* (Washington, D.C.) March 14, 1975.
2. U.S. Department of Health, Education and Welfare, No. 1021 (Washington, D.C.: GPO).
3. JACOBY, J., and C. B. SMALL, "Deceptive and Misleading Advertising. The Contrasting Approaches of the F.T.C. and F.D.A.," Purdue Papers in Consumer Psychology, Paper No. 146 (Lafayette, Indiana: Purdue University, 1975).

IS THERE
A BETTER WAY ?

Incongruency of goals, disparity of freedom, the imperfections in the marketplace and the intensification of conflict promoted by adversaries is what we are all about.

Business, consumers, government, and labor must change if their interactions are to become effective. Continual provincial interests prevent understanding that can lead to better life styles.

All parties should start to work together as peers if our society is to achieve a more efficient, honest, and productive marketplace. If this is achieved, then more attention will be devoted to problem solving as well as alleviating many mutual distrusts.

25

Utopia,
next stop

Ever since Sir Thomas More wrote *Utopia* in the early 1500s, the quest for utopia has been regarded as both a beautiful vision and an impracticable scheme. Some religions believe perfection is attainable only in heaven, but it is a pleasant pastime to strive for it on earth.

This chapter dreams about utopia in terms of consumer affairs. The substance of the dream is the application of consumer psychology, not only to better understand the origin of consumer issues but also to help resolve them.

Psychology and psychotherapy are merely tools. It is the responsibility of the individual to recognize the need for change and to carry it out.

A salient characteristic of this book is that it is critical. By this we mean it makes judgments. Books can simply record the findings of others and select those that are noncontroversial, or they can attempt to stimulate thought. If it does so, and if this results in greater willingness to accept change on the part of individuals or possibly some institutions, then the title of this chapter may be appropriate.

Some of the points of view expressed, by themselves, will not achieve utopia, but they might remove a blemish here and an imperfection there if some action results. To arrive in utopia it will be necessary to overcome inertia, start moving in a planned and predictable direction, and while enroute change the switching systems that take us over the same old pathways.

The adversary system rules the roost of consumer affairs. This system may or may not solve problems, but it always engenders conflicts and controversy. The proposed application of psychological knowledge would reduce or eliminate conflicts by encouraging people to listen to what others have to say and thus gain greater insight into them as well as into oneself. A fundamental step is to recognize the phenomenon of change and to learn to cope with it rather than resisting or fighting it.

The reallocation of freedom would produce greater equity. Free enterprise must surely mean that a transaction should be equally "free" for the consumer and the businessman. This concept cannot be fiction or fancy; it must be real. The consumer surge toward a greater share of freedom is recent, but it is comparable to the earlier labor movement and to the self-allotted freedom of the employer. In other words, consumers have the same rights to be informed, to choose, and to be heard that business does. However, in practice these rights are usually abridged.

This of course leads to the view that honesty and sincerity on the part of both business and the consumer should not be merely a goal; they should be part of any aspect of human relations (remember, this chapter is about utopia).

The fact that all four groups involved in consumer affairs—business, consumers, government, and labor—have incongruent goals must be recognized. Even in utopia incongruent goals will probably occur. However, the awareness that such incongruence exists can lead to better relations.

One of the better ways to reach utopia is to recognize that research is a vehicle for gathering data under potentially the most objective conditions. But some people and institutions are strongly opposed to research. It would appear that quite a few prefer the imperfections of the present; they would be bored and restricted by the perfection of utopia. They will do their best to turn research into a missile to be used in the controversies of consumer affairs.

Since few people have ever been to utopia, there is little experience to draw upon. This may be quite an asset. Experience can prepare one better for yesterday than for tomorrow, but tomorrow is where utopia may be.

Consumer research must emerge as a specialized field. It must define its purpose as gathering data to help solve consumer issues. Solving complaints is just the "putting out the fire" stage. Complaint handling may or may not be too little, but it surely is too late.

A host of issues define the parameters of consumer research;

they include, first and foremost, health and safety. The arguments, legal and otherwise, as to whether a product is safe to use and is not damaging to health are confusing. But if truth is essential in any area of consumer affairs, this is it. Surely ethics and honesty must predominate when health and safety are concerned. Everyone is fallible, not excluding those who conduct research, but some researchers seem to plan their research so as to obtain the desired conclusions. There is probably a need for research to develop standards so that legitimate research can be differentiated from biased or dishonest research.

The second echelon of consumer research is product performance research. This is done by Consumers Union, but more is needed.

Research on consumer issues should take place before hopeless factionalism prevents the possibility of different sides working together in search of the truth. If the issues are to be resolved, then research must focus on unit pricing and its effects, along with TV advertising to children and nutritional labeling, among many other problems. Consumer research must also deal with the special problems of special consumers such as the young, the old, and ghetto dwellers.

At the core of consumer psychology is, of course, the consumer. The "consumer bill of rights" will be operative only if the consumer insists on it. The consumer in a buyer-seller-maker transaction is disadvantaged. The sooner this is learned, the better. And by *learning* we mean modification of behavior. The consumer must learn to unset the traps, build defenses, and avoid being manipulated. He/she must learn to avoid the "consumer's illusion."

What consumers need most is greater power and more effective action. What they need least is powerlessness and protectionism. To be blunt, the consumer must become an adult in the world of consumer affairs and not stay in the childhood stage of dependency and overprotection.

Consumers need stronger local and national organizations with professionally trained leaders. Someday universities will have schools of consumer affairs just as they now have schools of business, engineering, and law. A body of knowledge is emerging worthy of a college curriculum.

To accomplish these goals, new sources of revenue must be tapped. A share of business belongs to consumers. The working out of the details will take some doing.

Business must also change. Less lip service and, in some quarters, less double dealing will help. The stated goals of business groups are quite noble. The problem seems to be that some business representatives neither read nor remember them. Business must understand that the customer is a *peer*. When consumers are treated as equals, transactions can go forward with greater equity.

The government is burdened with an ever-expanding bureaucracy. Its mountains of paper work, its legal circumlocutions, and its lack of internal communication add to the confusion.

Bureaucrats live and operate within an economic system of profit and loss but are unaffected by the system. Their salaries are guaranteed, as are their increments and tenure. They flourish in good or bad economic times and never suffer the consequences of loss—or, for that matter, the pleasure of profit. For these and many other reasons, they do not have to rush into risk taking or decision making. They take their time; in fact some have learned that problems appear to go away if they postpone the decision-making process long enough. Many bureaucrats have brought procrastination to the level of an art form. They seem to be unconcerned that others, including business and consumers, are held up when decisions are not made within a reasonable length of time.

Labor has not really taken consumer affairs to heart as a top priority. Labor demands protective legislation while trying to avoid any inference that some consumer issues are caused by its own actions.

So many of the pathways to utopia are blocked. And now we get to the proposed last stop on the way to utopia. Ultimately, consumer and business groups will have to work together as equals and bypass the government. Direct communication between consumer and business groups as *equals* will make a third party (i.e., the government) unnecessary.

How will consumer groups become equal to business? Business must sooner or later recognize that the effort to fight change is costly. It gnaws away at the profit structure. If business gave only a small percentage of those funds to competent consumer groups, there would be less money wasted on fighting and more spent on constructing a utopia in which issues that directly involve both the consumer and business can be solved equitably.

Index